Also by John Eisenberg

The Longest Shot: Lil E. Tee
and the Kentucky Derby

Cotton Bowl Days

Growing Up with Dallas
and the Cowboys
in the 1960s

JOHN EISENBERG

SIMON & SCHUSTER

SIMON & SCHUSTER
Rockefeller Center
1230 Avenue of the Americas
New York, NY 10020

SIMON & SCHUSTER and colophon are registered trademarks
of Simon & Schuster, Inc.

Designed by Deirdre C. Amthor

Manufactured in the United States of America

10   9   8   7   6   5   4   3   2   1

Library of Congress Cataloging-in-Publication Data

Eisenberg, John, 1956–
    Cotton Bowl days : growing up with Dallas and the Cowboys
in the 1960s / John Eisenberg.
        p.   cm.
    Includes index.
    1. Dallas Cowboys (Football team)—History.   2. Eisenberg, John, 1956–   .
3. Football fans—Texas—Biography.   I. Title.
    GV956.D3E57   1997
    796.332'64'097642812—dc21   97-15083
                                                                      CIP

    ISBN 0-684-83120-1

PHOTO CREDITS

1, 4: Dallas Cowboys
2, 6: Dallas Cowboys Weekly
3, 11: Eisenberg family
5: AP/Wide World Photos
7, 8: Dallas Cowboys/Bob Lilly
9, 13, 14, 15: NFL Photos
10: Gittings
12: From the collections of the Dallas Historical Society

To my parents,
with love and gratitude

Acknowledgments

This is a book about memories. Some are mine, and some are those of former Cowboy players, coaches, and fans. A list of those interviewed: Herb Adderley, Doug Alexander, George Andrie, Jack Anthony, Jim Boeke, Gil Brandt, Ron Chapman, Art Donovan, Robert Draper, Leonard Epstein, Mike Gaechter, Walt Garrison, Cornell Green, Adlene Harrison, Calvin Hill, E. J. Holub, Sam Huff, Don Hullett, Lee Roy Jordan, Vernell King, Tom Landry, Eddie LeBaron, Bob Lilly, Tony Liscio, Bill Livingston, Warren Livingston, Frank Luksa, Dave Manders, Don McIlhenny, Bill Mercer, Johnny Minx, Ralph Neely, Pettis Norman, Dick Nolan, Don Perkins, Jethro Pugh, A. K. Quesenberry, Mel Renfro, Bob Ryan, Steve Sabol, Tex Schramm, Harry Sebel, Billy Jack Smith, Allen Stone, Hank Stram, Inestor Surrells Jr., Milton Tobian, Jerry Tubbs, Jack Wertheimer Jr., and Wes Wise. My thanks to all for their time and their memories.

A number of people were of particular help along the way. Jack Gibbons and Molly Dunham, my editors at the *Baltimore Sun,* were gracious in giving me the time I needed to write. Leonard Epstein served as an unofficial sounding board and copy editor, and also provided essential research materials. Jean and Seymour Eisenberg read versions of the manuscript and offered advice and support. Scott Waxman, my agent, got the project off the ground and provided sustained encouragement. Jeff

Neuman, my editor at Simon & Schuster, knew where I was going from the beginning and helped me get there. The Dallas Cowboys' publicity department made available their incredible clip files, as well as photographs and phone numbers. The people at the Dallas Public Library provided a tape of an interview with my grandfather from years ago, as well as other research materials. My thanks to all of them, and to everyone else who offered support and encouragement. But thanks most of all to Mary Wynne, Anna, and Wick, for their love, patience, and understanding. I couldn't do it without them.

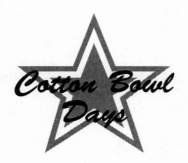

Cotton Bowl
Days

Chapter One

When I was a boy in Dallas in the 1960s, Cowboy games at the Cotton
Bowl were a family affair. My grandfather, Louis Tobian, owned 10 season
tickets and lorded over them with patriarchal sway. The regular Sunday afternoon crew included me, my father, my Uncle Milton, my cousin Louis,
my grandfather, and such semiregulars as my mother, my sister, my grandmother, my aunt Carolyn, my great-uncle Isadore, his wife Bayla, my aunt
Minnie, my cousins Laurie and Susan, my cousin Jack, his wife Bee, his
son Jack Jr., and various other relatives, politicians, rabbis, friends, and
strays. We all drove to the games together, crammed into a long yellow station wagon with wood paneling on the sides. My great-uncle Bill, the oil
wildcatter, rarely came because when he did he would sit there coaching
the team and calling plays before the ball was snapped, and my grandfather couldn't stand to listen to him.

I was the youngest, the baby of the entire family. My father, Seymour
Eisenberg, a doctor who was then the chief of medicine at the Dallas Veterans Administration Hospital, began taking me to the games soon after
the Cowboys joined the National Football League as a pitiful expansion
team in 1960. I was four years old that autumn, barely old enough to count
the downs. My father thought he was getting away with one, mixing his

weekend parental chores with the conviviality of a football game, but within several years I was there by choice.

When I was six, in the midst of my apprenticeship as a fan, I rose from my place on the Cotton Bowl's wooden benches as the quarterback, Don Meredith, held onto the ball too long and was tackled while attempting to pass. "Just throw the son of a bitch, Meredith!" I hollered. In the ensuing silence, my father quickly explained that my sister, five years older, had taught me that language. Right.

When I was eight and vacationing at my other grandmother's house in Winston-Salem, North Carolina, my father helped me fall asleep one restless night by suggesting that I play out an imaginary Cowboy game in my mind; he knew that would comfort me in an unfamiliar bed. "Send Perkins up the middle on first down," he said, smiling from the foot of the bed. He always joked about the predictability of Cowboy coach Tom Landry's play-calling on first down, complaining that it never strayed from a simple run up the middle by the fullback, Don Perkins. (He was not alone in his criticism. Perkins ran so often on first down that fans chanted, "Hey, diddle diddle/Perkins up the middle.")

When I was ten, the Cowboys outgrew the failings of their infancy and became a championship contender. I followed them with the single-minded zeal of young love. I knew the uniform numbers, heights, and weights of every player, and all of their relevant statistics. I knew the years and rounds in which they had been selected in the college draft. I knew the final scores and salient details of every game the Cowboys had played for as long as I could remember.

My grandfather, whom we called Pop, was amazed and amused by his grandson, the walking Cowboy encyclopedia. When he gathered the family for dinners at Arthur's, a steak house where his portrait hung, or at the Egyptian Lounge, a vaguely dangerous place on Mockingbird Lane where we sat in the dark smoky club room and occasionally saw a Cowboy player eating spaghetti after a game, Pop would steer me around the room to his friends at other tables and, wearing a wry smile, pepper me with questions. What was the score at Pittsburgh in '63? Who was number 77? Where did Bob Lilly go to college? I never let him down.

Most of the players were average in the early days and largely unknown outside Dallas, but in my parochialism I saw them bathed in the bright lights of stardom. There was Amos Marsh, the talented but mistake-prone fullback. ("They gave him his plane ticket out of town and he fumbled it," my father said.) There was Eddie LeBaron, the Cowboys' first quarterback, a little widget who taught Meredith the ropes. There was Sonny Gibbs, a six-foot-seven quarterback from Texas Christian University who proved far better as a conversation piece than a player. There was Colin Ridgway, an Australian punter who was going to revolutionize the game but instead kicked balls straight up in the air.

The team's first stars were Perkins, a tough little fullback who made All-Pro in '62; Jerry Tubbs, a heady linebacker from Oklahoma; Frank Clarke, the team's first big-play threat; and Meredith, Dallas's first pro sports superstar, a charismatic East Texan who carried on a love-hate relationship with the city.

The Cowboys were not losers for long. During the early '60s they shrewdly accumulated a group of players who melded into a playoff contender, and rose to the NFL's top tier, surpassing more established franchises in New York, Chicago, Detroit, Philadelphia, and Washington. These players began the Cowboys' run of success that continued for two decades.

There was Bob Hayes, the "World's Fastest Human," winner of the gold medal in the 100-meter dash at the '64 Olympics, transformed magically by the Cowboys into an end running the fastest pass routes ever witnessed. There was Bob Lilly, the quintessential Cowboy, a small-town Texan who became a Hall of Fame defensive tackle. There was Mel Renfro, a Hall of Fame cornerback who tantalized with his quickness. There was Lee Roy Jordan, the mean middle linebacker, of whom assistant coach Ernie Stautner once said, "If he was as big as Butkus, he'd be illegal." There was Dan Reeves, the drawling halfback with a rare feel for the game.

These were the heroes of my youth. Just as young fans in New York were raised in the thrall of Jackie Robinson's Dodgers and Mickey Mantle's Yankees, and those in Baltimore fell for Johnny Unitas and the Colts after they beat the Giants in "The Greatest Game Ever Played" in '58, those of us who grew up in Dallas in the '60s lay claim to the Cowboys as secular religious figures. Meredith, Renfro, and Perkins were my Mantle, Robinson, and Unitas.

On the Sundays when the Cowboys played at the Cotton Bowl, my father and Uncle Milton collected me and my cousin Louis from Sunday school at Temple Emanu-El on Northwest Highway (the last hour seemed to last a hundred minutes), and drove across town to Lakewood and my grandparents' two-story brick house on Swiss Avenue, a graceful, old-money street with a grassy island running down the middle. On cold days I raced upstairs, took off my Sunday clothes, and changed into the winter clothes my mother had sent along. On warm days I took off my Sunday school tie, stuffed it into a pocket, and went to the game in a dress shirt and slacks. Then it was back downstairs to the rambling kitchen at the back of the house, where everyone gobbled down a sandwich or a bowl of soup, banged out the screen door and found a seat in the overcrowded car.

My father usually drove, with Pop sitting next to him in the front passenger seat, ordering him when to turn left and right. Pop had the route all mapped out. Avoiding the main streams of traffic, we negotiated the back roads of East Dallas to Fair Park, motoring slowly through sad neighborhoods of small wood-framed houses with cluttered front yards and sagging porches. Louis and I sat in the third seat, facing backwards, giggling and giddy with anticipation and oblivious to the lower-middle class sea we parted as we drove along.

Over the years our route was burnished into my memory along with the Cowboy players' numbers and statistics: down Swiss to Beacon Street, left onto Lindsley Avenue, right onto Parry Avenue. Parry took us to the state fairgrounds, where we made a devilish U-turn in traffic for which my father summoned his courage all week, and glided to the entrance of a parking lot next to a railroad yard just outside Fair Park's north entrance. We paid a dollar to park on the gravel by a fence and began the long walk through the fairgrounds to the Cotton Bowl. We went past the Women's Building, past the Automobile Building, past the peanut and popcorn hawkers, and stopped to buy a game program for 50 cents from a stout, dark-haired man who stood on the same grassy spot every week. The late morning was cast in a slanting light, the anticipation in the air almost palpable. The crowd was casually dressed and mostly male, wearing cotton shirts and slacks. My father often stopped and visited with friends; many of the fans knew each other, as if they lived in the same small town.

Once we reached the Cotton Bowl, we walked around the outside of the stadium until we reached Gate 2, the front gate, where we climbed the steps and handed over our tickets. (My father would not let me hold mine until I was older and "more responsible.") After crossing through the cool darkness of the concrete concourse, we went up a small incline and burst into the light and color of the stadium bowl. The big moment of my week was at hand.

We usually arrived when the teams were warming up on the field, or even earlier, while the players were still getting taped in the locker rooms and only a few thousand fans were in their seats. Pop liked getting there early. He was in his seventies by then, walking with a cane and neither seeing nor hearing well, and he loathed the long walk from the parking lot to the stadium. We arrived early to give him time to get to his seat without feeling rushed.

To pass the time before kickoff I leafed through the program, staring at the black-and-white photographs of the players' faces, or I asked my father for 50 cents and went downstairs to buy a soda. I savored the anticipation in the air, the quiet lull before the high drama of the game. The Cotton Bowl was a colorless, outdated concrete stadium, but it seemed as glamorous to me as a floodlit Broadway theater. It had no luxury suites, few bathrooms, little leg room, and no amenities other than small electric scoreboards in the end zones—but to me it was the ultimate setting for a game, a monolith that seemed to stretch from the earth to the sky. I had never seen a place so big, or so grand.

A stadium had existed on the site since 1921, when the city built what was then called the Fair Park Bowl, a 15,000-seat stadium made of wood that was first decried as a white elephant until football proved popular enough to fill the seats. The original stadium was torn down in 1930 and replaced with a 45,000-seat concrete structure called Fair Park Stadium, which was renamed the Cotton Bowl in 1937. Upper decks were added in the late '40s, in response to the soaring popularity of Doak Walker, a Heisman Trophy winner who played for Southern Methodist University. The capacity rose to 75,347, making it one of the country's largest stadiums.

Our seats were in the lower deck on the "home" side, behind the Cowboy bench. We had a straight line of 10 seats on row 45 in section seven, perpendicular to the 20-yard line closest to the tunnel from which the players emerged. The seats were just spaces marked off on wooden benches with no backrests. The seat numbers were painted in black stencil on the wood, and the paint was badly faded, as if it were the original coat from

1930. Splinters were commonplace; a seat cushion was the height of modern technology.

Pop had purchased a bond to help finance the upper decks in the '40s, and he still had friends in high places. He carefully selected our seats with two strategies in mind: He would not have to navigate many steps because the entrance to the section was right by our row, and we would not get wet in the rain because we were just underneath the upper deck. Pop always sat in the aisle seat, rested his hands on his cane, and planted the cane in front of him, effectively blocking the end of the row. Woe unto any person with a full bladder or an empty stomach who had to scoot by him to get to the aisle. Pop took it as an affront to have to move once he was installed; only grudgingly, and most unenthusiastically, would he raise his cane, stand up, and let anyone pass. My father always suggested that I take care of my business before kickoff. A boy who sat farther down the row came squeezing past us several times a game; Louis and I giggled quietly as Pop grew more and more exasperated.

The calm before the game gradually built to the emotional peak of the introductions of the starting lineups, a moment of glory and high ceremony that I always found compelling. Each player ran onto the field alone, to resounding cheers reserved solely for him. It was the moment when I was most envious of the players, the moment I always envisioned when I pictured myself in a Cowboy uniform (which I often did). I studied the players intently and knew their different styles of running onto the field: Lilly slowly and ominously, Jordan rapidly and almost angrily, Meredith with the easygoing gait of a country-music star. The imaginary games I played in my backyard could never begin without a re-enactment of this ritual.

After the opening kickoff came the game, three hours of exultation and despair, shouts and groans. The grownups around me set a relatively dignified example, cheering at the right times, rarely booing, almost never cursing. (Except for an occasional "Throw the son of a bitch!") My father was not given to wild applause or cheers, just fervent hopes he maintained with restrained passion. Uncle Milton occasionally exploded in a loud cheer. Pop brought a radio and an earplug and listened to the play-by-play broadcast on KLIF. He demanded perfection and fumed over the inevitable mistakes.

We never stayed until the final gun, even if the outcome was undecided.

The long walk back to the car loomed, and Pop did not want to get stuck in traffic. Our customary departure time was the middle of the fourth quarter. The family joke was that we arrived at eleven o'clock and left at two for a game that kicked off at one, which was all right with Pop because we had stayed three hours, the length of a game. We never told Pop the joke.

We piled into the car and listened in prayerful silence to the final minutes of the game on the radio. Hurriedly, under Pop's purposeful gaze, my father wheeled the station wagon out of the narrow parking lot and onto the side roads that took us back to Pop's house. We never got stuck in traffic; Pop would not have stood for it. Back at his house, the rest of the family dispersed, Pop sighed and went upstairs to watch the late game on television, and I said my good-byes and rode home with my father, Uncle Milton, and Louis, who lived next door. We listened to the postgame show and reflected on the game. I headed for the backyard as soon as we made it home, my imagination stoked and ready for a re-enactment.

Our familial game-day routine did not extend to the Sundays when the Cowboys played out of town. We operated as separately on those days as we did collectively on "home" Sundays. My aunts, uncles, and cousins watched on television in their homes; I watched with my parents, in our den. At halftime my father and I would make a run to Red Bryan's smokehouse and pick up barbecue sandwiches to take home and eat in front of the game. (Red's was not as tasty as Sonny Bryan's, the legendary barbecue dive where Nobel Prize winners lunched, but Sonny's was not open on Sundays.) When we didn't make it home in time, we sat amid the lush barbecue fumes and listened to Bill Mercer's play-by-play on the car radio.

There was rarely anyone else watching with us on those afternoons. My father, a gentle man with a wry sense of humor, was not given to making demands or proclamations as the head of the household, but he was particular about his Cowboy games: He did not want to watch at a friend's house, or over brunch or cocktails, and he really did not want anyone watching with us at home. He was not antisocial, he just took the games seriously and wanted to concentrate, and he knew he could not pay attention as closely as he wanted if the game was part of a social occasion. On the few days when he was forced to watch in the company of others, he went grumbling and felt out of place.

Our focus on "away" Sundays was so sharp that we were offended if friends had the gall to call during a game. Cowboy games were not the time for gossip or serious conversation; a call was not welcomed in those three hours. Those who did call were scorned when the receiver was back on the hook. What planet did they live on? There were several regular offenders, including one of my mother's best friends, and another woman who always seemed to call just as the most important game of the year was beginning. They were oblivious to the importance of the Cowboys. We were incredulous.

My attachment to the team was pure in that it revolved around the games, the players, and the Cotton Bowl experience, not the shrill hype so prevalent today. Pro football was simpler then, in the days before Orwellian passing schemes and mass situational substitutions on every play, and the fan's experience was simpler, too. Cable television and sports talk radio were not yet around to take every conceivable notion and nuance and drive them into the backs of your eyeballs. Interest was still driven by wins and losses, not by salaries, uniform colors, personalities, commodities, and advertising campaigns. Unlike today, you could not buy everything from a toilet seat to a credit card with your team's logo on it. I had no Cowboy jackets, T-shirts, or sweaters in my drawers, no Cowboy posters on my walls, no Cowboy pens or pencils or helmet telephones on my desk. I had no highlight videos, no computer games, no signed limited-edition jerseys. That was 21st century stuff.

The symbols of my support were prehistoric. I had a blue wool hat with a little white tassel on top and a Cowboy emblem on the front, which I wore in cold weather. I had a pair of Cowboy pajamas that shrunk in the wash and failed to last. I had a small Cowboy figurine with an oversized bobbing head. I had an incomplete set of Cowboy bubble-game cards, which I collected on bicycle trips to the 7-Eleven and stashed in the empty Cuesta-Rey cigar boxes Pop gave me; I always seemed to get Don Bishop, a fine but obscure cornerback, instead of Don Meredith. I had a collection of game programs. Pop gave me a ball autographed by the '65 team, which, I was told, was not for use in the backyard. My friend Leonard won a free autographed ball that year by collecting a set of Coca-Cola bottle caps with the players' pictures printed on the inside. He tilted the odds in his favor by sticking his hand up the soda machine at the bowling alley and pulling out dozens of discarded caps.

A lot more was left to a boy's imagination in those days. I spent hours alone in my backyard playing out imaginary games, running around and falling and spewing a breathless play-by-play in imitation of the TV and radio announcers. As I went along I filled in the score-by-quarters page from the previous Sunday's Cowboy program. Sometimes I came inside and typed up a newspaperlike account of "my" game.

Football was my obsession; I turned everything into a game. When my parents gave me a set of Lego blocks, I pieced together teams of football players instead of battleships and castles, marked off a field on my play table, and staged thunderous games. Given construction paper for art projects, I made up my own set of football cards and invented a game using pennies as balls. When I got a little older I took up Strat-O-Matic football, a board game utilizing cards, dice, and NFL statistics to simulate play. For me, this was the perfect vehicle for surviving the seemingly endless week between real Cowboy games—a fantasy world into which I could disappear. It became my fiefdom. I spent hours alone in my room, behind closed doors, playing out regular season schedules and playoffs, and keeping elaborate statistical charts.

I had school friends with whom I talked and gossiped about the team in that breathless way that kids do, reviewing the games on Monday mornings and arguing the various debates of the day. (Usually whether Meredith was or was not a bum.) But most of my friends didn't have tickets to the games, and none seemed to know as much, or care as much, as I did. My Cowboy fraternity was my family, not my friends.

The Cowboys were hardly a box-office hit in their early years. They drew an average of 22,647 fans a game in their first three seasons. College football was more popular; the '40s and '50s had been a golden era for the college game in Dallas, and the noise from those days still resonated in the early '60s. The SMU Mustangs, Pop's first love as a fan, had sold out the Cotton Bowl in the '40s and early '50s, and continued to draw well. Texas and Oklahoma played their annual border war every October at the Cotton Bowl, during the State Fair, attracting a sellout crowd, national television cameras, and thousands of partying students. The Cotton Bowl Classic was one of the four major bowls played on New Year's Day, matching the Southwest Conference champion—usually Texas, Rice, or TCU—against another top team from around the country. Doak Walker, Rice's Dicky Maegle, and Syracuse's Jim Brown were among the stars who turned the game into a major event.

Pop had not attended high school or college, but he was a serious college football fan. His interest dated to the '30s, when SMU introduced big-time sports to Dallas with nationally ranked football teams. He saw it as his duty as a citizen to cheer for the home team and support home events. He was an SMU season ticket holder, and he bought blocks of tickets to the Cotton Bowl and the Texas-Oklahoma game every year. He even kept an eye on the Highland Park Scots, the local high school power, who were popular around town and drew large crowds on Friday nights.

Against the backdrop of such interest in the college and high school games, it was fair to wonder if the pro game would ever plant roots and grow in Dallas. The nightmarish example of the Dallas Texans, an NFL team that came to town in 1952 and left the same year, certainly suggested that the city was not fertile soil for pro football.

The Texans' franchise came from New York, where, as a team called the Yanks, it had lived in the shadow of the more popular Giants and compiled a 1–9–2 record in '51. The league office, noting the big college crowds and general swell of football interest in Dallas, bought the franchise and awarded it to a group of Dallas businessmen led by a 31-year-old textiles executive named Giles Miller. The price was $300,000, with two-thirds covering the cost of breaking the Yanks' lease in New York. The franchise itself was valued at $100,000.

The arrival of pro football in Texas was at first viewed with optimism by the national press. The Texas economy was booming in the wake of World War II, creating a perception that success came effortlessly deep in the heart of Texas. *New York Times* columnist Arthur Daley pointed out that putting a team in Texas, where "they grow money," should help the NFL. A columnist for the *Los Angeles Herald* went so far as to make up a poem:

Oh, give me a home where the millionaires roam
And three-hundred grand is just hay;
Where seldom's allowed a discouraging crowd
And the Cotton Bowl's jammed every day.

After considering naming the team the Texas Rangers, Miller and the owners settled on Dallas Texans. A hot issue was the presence of three black players on the roster. The Southwest Conference was not integrated, and the idea of paying to watch blacks play football sat uneasily in many fans' minds. Within days of the announcement that the team was coming, a *Dallas Morning News* columnist reported a rumor that the Texans were "going to trade the three Negro players for one outstanding performer." In the same column, an unidentified team owner denied the rumor with this comment: "Chances are that all three of the colored boys will be with the club next fall."

The Texans came to town minus quarterback George Ratterman, whose contract stipulated that he would not have to follow the franchise if it left New York. (He wound up in Cleveland.) The remaining players, including stars Buddy Young and George Taliaferro, both of whom were black, and future Hall of Famers Artie Donovan and Gino Marchetti, reported to training camp in Kerrville, in the sweltering hill country outside Austin.

"It was awful," Donovan said. "It was so hot that the ants stayed in the ant hills. There were these huge rattlesnakes in the tall grass by the field. If the ball went into the grass, no one wanted to go in and get it because they got bit by the snakes. We sent in the equipment manager, a guy named Willie Garcia. He managed a Mexican restaurant in Dallas for one of the owners, so they made him our equipment manager. He was a one-legged guy with a wooden leg, so we figured he had a 50 percent better chance of not getting bit by the snakes."

The coach was a former Notre Dame quarterback named Jim Phelan. "He was one of the greatest men I ever met," Donovan said, "but he didn't know a thing about football. At practice we used to bat the ball back and forth over the goalposts like we were playing volleyball."

When the players broke camp in September and came to Dallas to open the season, the owners asked them to wear Cowboy hats and boots at a press conference. "We said, 'What do we want to wear this shit for?'" Donovan said. "A couple of guys wouldn't put the stuff on."

The Texans' first game, on Sept. 28, 1952, was a 24–6 loss to the Giants at the Cotton Bowl. The crowd, which included Pop and my father, was announced as 17,500. The next weekend, only 15,000 came to watch the 49ers and star runner Hugh McElhenny pound the Texans, 37–14. Giles Miller and the other owners lacked the resources and expertise to market the team. Their crowds looked even more paltry when the Texas-Oklahoma game played to the usual sellout in October. SMU averaged more than 37,000 fans a game that year. The presence of black players did not help the team's popularity; the Cotton Bowl was still segregated, with black fans herded into the corners of the end zone sections. It quickly became clear that Dallas was not ready for a pro football team, particularly one that lost every week.

By November there was talk that the Texans would fold. The Dallas Citizens Council refused the owners' request for a $250,000 loan. "They made a big fuss about coming out to save the franchise when we played the Rams, but it rained and no fans showed up," Donovan said. Miller and his group gave up and turned the franchise back over to the league with five games left in the season. The players practiced in Hershey, Pennsylvania, and played their remaining games on the road. The last practice in Dallas was on November 13th, after which the goal posts and blocking sleds were put in storage. The players left Dallas and never returned.

The Texans' only hurrah came in a Thanksgiving Day game in Akron, Ohio, against the Bears. Three thousand fans were in the stands on a dank afternoon. The crowd was so sparse that Phelan jokingly told the players they would go into the stands and personally greet every fan instead of going through the usual announced introductions on the field. The Texans then went out and surprised the Bears, 27–23, for their only win in 12 games.

The franchise relocated to Baltimore, where it was renamed the Colts and immediately sold 15,000 season tickets. The Colts were winning championships and playing to sellout crowds at Memorial Stadium by the end of the decade. "The town went ape and we became heroes for life in Baltimore," Donovan said. "Dallas never knew we came and went. They saw us as carpetbaggers."

That Dallas would have two professional teams just eight years later seems profoundly foolish, but such was the case. Not only did the Cowboys arrive in '60, costing owner Clint Murchison all of $600,000, but a team in the fledgling American Football League also began playing that year. Owned by Lamar Hunt, the son of oilman H. L. Hunt, the AFL team was called the Texans and also played at the Cotton Bowl.

Competing for fans with each other as well as with college and high school teams, the Cowboys and Texans attempted to build followings. They gave away tickets, resorted to promotional shenanigans, and insulted each other, all to no avail. Each team drew few fans. There just were not enough in Dallas to support two pro teams.

Hunt gave up after three years and moved the franchise to Kansas City despite winning the AFL championship in '62. Even though the Cowboys had Dallas to themselves after that, they still struggled to capture the city's fancy. They had a losing record in each of their first five seasons, a slow developmental curve that tested the fans' patience. Their average crowd was just 32,671 in '63 and '64, well below the league average of 44,524. There was little traffic to fight before games, no long lines at the concession stands, no big crowds squashing you into your seat.

Dallas was still a frontier outpost as a pro sports town. There was no major league baseball in North Texas until the Rangers moved to Arlington in 1972, and the National Basketball Association would not expand to Dallas until 1980. Television coverage of teams in other cities was limited in the '60s, so you supported what you had at home. The big summer diversion was a Texas League baseball team that played at Burnett Field in South Dallas. Later on, there was another Texas League team, the Dallas-Fort Worth Spurs, who played at Turnpike Stadium in Arlington. A minor league hockey team, the Blackhawks, played at the State Fair Coliseum to small crowds of displaced hockey nuts. The Chaparrals, of the American Basketball Association, came to town dribbling red, white, and blue basketballs in '66.

On summer nights I stashed a radio under my pillow and listened to Gordon McLendon, one of the pioneers of Dallas radio, fake "live" play-by-play broadcasts of the Spurs' games; he sat in a studio, read batter-by-batter results off a wire ticker and reported them as if he had just seen them. I also followed the Chaparrals, who had such players as Cincy Powell and Cliff Hagan, and played at SMU's Moody Coliseum, where a courtside bleacher seat cost two dollars. SMU's basketball teams, led by Denny Holman, Carroll Hoosier, and Charlie Beasley, often filled Moody for important Southwest Conference games, to which I dragged my father as often as possible.

Had I been born earlier, I surely would have become a college football fan and prayed in the temple that Doak Walker built; as it was, I knew the names and uniform numbers of many college players, and our family still trundled off faithfully to the SMU games, the Texas-Oklahoma games, and the Cotton Bowl games. But college football was a fading light in Dallas when I came of age as a sports fan. The Cowboys began to shine; they won division titles and played to big, roaring crowds in their final years at the Cotton Bowl, before moving to Texas Stadium in '71. Cheering for them often was a heartache, the result of a succession of playoff defeats, but they were a young, thrilling team, and it was impossible not to fall under their spell. The city stopped when they played.

These were the nascent days of a team that would become known as America's Team in the late '70s. Many fans are barely aware that the Cowboys even existed before Roger Staubach, the daring Hall of Fame quarterback who perpetrated so many comeback victories. They did exist B.S.—Before Staubach—in a charismatic incarnation, rougher around the edges, more humble, more human. They were not America's Team in those days. But they were Dallas's team.

A fan's support is never more intense than in the early years, before the mind is cluttered with thoughts of sex, cars, music, and the complexities of adulthood. Many fans find other teams to cheer for as they grow up—at college, or in a city to which they move—but there is always room for just one team in their heart, the team that causes them to cheer and cry long after they've supposedly outgrown such childishness. Often, it's the team that mattered to them years ago, above all else.

I turned 40 years old in 1996, living in a brick rowhouse in Baltimore with my wife and our eight-year-old daughter and five-year-old son. I still cheer for the Cowboys. I did not lose the urge during four years at the University of Pennsylvania in the late '70s, nor have I lost it in the last 18 years, in which I have earned a living as a sportswriter, first as a reporter for the *Dallas Times Herald,* where I covered high school sports, SMU football, and the Dallas Mavericks from 1979–84, and then as a feature writer and columnist for the *Baltimore Sun* beginning in 1984.

I still separate my autumn Sundays into two categories: Cowboy wins and Cowboy losses. My fealty is a reflex after all these years, an immutable habit. The bond that I developed as a child in the Cotton Bowl days is strong. The Cowboys have inevitably dropped among my priorities as I've taken on a career, marriage, and parenthood, and had much of my passion for sports quashed as a professional observer, but they are still my team. Even as they've become too arrogant and lawless for my tastes in the

'90s, I still blot out their blemishes and cheer for them on Sundays. They contributed half of the 12 players suspended for drug use by the NFL in a 12-month period beginning late in 1995, and one of their former players, linebacker Robert Jones, said in '96 that he was all but ostracized in Dallas because he was a family man and not a womanizer. It is not a pretty picture. But I still cheer for the Cowboys, even if I no longer admire them. Judging them and rooting for them are separate concerns.

Admitting such a lifelong love is, for me, tantamount to confessing a sin. The first commandment of my profession is "no cheering in the press box." Dick Young, the New York sportswriter, coined that phrase as a rebuke to his brethren who allowed partisanship to cloud their powers of observation. On one of my first assignments for the *Times Herald,* a University of Oklahoma football game in 1979, the press box announcer barked that anyone who cheered for the Sooners would "get thrown down the elevator shaft." I knew then that I would have to cheer privately for the Cowboys.

My concern was eased when I discovered that I was not alone in press boxes around the country, that other sportswriters also tended to have favorite teams they cheered for when no one else was looking. I have worked with lifelong supporters of the Los Angeles Dodgers and the New York Giants, just to name two. I suspect that most people in my profession harbor such a secret.

It also helped that I took a job in Baltimore at age 27 instead of remaining in Dallas. Covering a team up close tends to extinguish any allegiances; the forced, confrontational marriage that exists today between athletes and the press surely would have diminished my cheers, perhaps even extinguished them. I have no doubt that it's easier for me to root for the Cowboys from a distance, disconnected from the suffocating hype and seemingly endless stream of off-field controversies.

Shortly after I became a columnist at the *Sun* in 1987, I wrote that I had grown up cheering for the Cowboys. The Cowboys were in Washington to play the Redskins, and it was a slow news day. A wiseacre editor put this headline on the column: Mama, Don't Let Columnist Grow Up to Like Cowboys. Very funny. A friend left this message on my answering machine: "I can't believe you did that."

Since Baltimore did not have an NFL team between the Colts' departure for Indianapolis in 1984 and the coming of the Ravens, transplanted from Cleveland, in 1996, I have rarely crossed paths with the Cowboys. I have managed to raise a veil of neutrality on the few occasions I have written about them, and I even criticized them after a playoff loss to Detroit in 1992. I can separate my professional duties from my loyalty to the cause. But it is just a pose.

The notion that my allegiance might wane with age was forever refuted in 1994, when the Cowboys played the Bills in Super Bowl XXVIII. I'm often assigned to cover the Super Bowl, but I was home that year because of an upcoming trip to the Winter Olympics, so I watched the game on television. The Cowboys were heavily favored, but they played sloppily and trailed at halftime. If they lost it would be embarrassing, a major up-set, and the possibility bothered me more than I was willing to admit. My heart hammered and my mind raced, distracted, as I hurriedly read bed-time stories to my children before the second half began. I was a wreck. I had learned long ago not to take their games as seriously as I had when I was a boy, and yet here I was, years later, discovering that that devotion was still intact. I was so relieved when the Cowboys rallied to win that I called my father in Dallas. "That was exhausting," I said. I knew he would relate.

Living away from Dallas has also readjusted the lens through which I see the Cowboys and their fans. I have come to understand how fortunate I was to land in the constituency of a winner. Cowboy fans have had it easy. The New York Giants went 23 years without making the playoffs, yet they seldom failed to sell out a game. Same with the Philadelphia Eagles, who went 18 years without making the playoffs. I was introduced to this constancy as a freshman at Penn in 1975, when I finagled a seat to the Cowboys–Eagles game at Veterans Stadium and sat among longtime Eagle fans who popped open beers every quarter and relieved themselves in their empty cups. When Roger Staubach threw a touchdown pass out of the shotgun offense and I ventured a meek cheer, one fan told me to "shove the shotgun up your ass." I would have, gladly, if I had had a shotgun.

Cowboy fans would not have remained so loyal to a loser. Staubach once said that "Cowboy fans love you, win or tie." Attendance fell sharply when the team declined in the late '80s after two decades of success. The average crowd for a home game at Texas Stadium dropped 23 percent in a span of four years, from 58,726 in '86 to 45,486 in '89, the year of the holocaust in which Jerry Jones took over, fired Landry, and started from scratch with a team that won one of 16 games.

I was home for the Christmas holidays that year and went to the last game of the season with my father. It was a sunny day, but bitterly cold. The water pipes at the stadium froze and the bathrooms were closed, forcing fans to use spot-a-pots. The crowd was announced at 41,265, but was clearly smaller. The Packers won easily. The Cowboys had come full circle, back to the early Cotton Bowl days: they were losing in front of small crowds, their popularity an iffy proposition.

My father and I were there because we would have it no other way. He was a Giants-style fan, willing to endure the bad days, and I had that bond that had formed when I was a boy in the Cotton Bowl days. I am astonished at what I still remember, at the frozen moments that come tumbling out of the musty vaults of my memory, as clear as the day they went in. I remember the game the Cowboys lost to the Steelers in '62, because an offensive lineman was found guilty of holding in the end zone on a 99-yard touchdown pass, the penalty wiping out the score and awarding the Steelers a safety that provided the difference in the game. (After that season, the NFL reduced the penalty for holding in the end zone from points to yardage.) I remember seeing Jim Brown make two of his best runs at the Cotton Bowl: In '63, he crashed into a pile of players and disappeared, but kept churning, popped out, and ran 70 yards for a touchdown; and in '65, he broke five tackles on a five-yard touchdown run around left end. (Meredith said later it was the greatest run he ever saw.)

I remember the dramatic play in '66 in which Bob Hayes, sealing his legend in his second pro season, caught a short pass over the middle against the Giants and sprinted all the way down the middle of the field, pursued by his former college teammate at Florida A&M, Clarence Childs, a defensive back who was almost as fast as Hayes, but not quite. Sportswriters labeled the play, "The Chase."

I remember the championship games against the Packers, the nightmarish playoff losses to the Browns, all the highs and lows of the exhilarating but frustrating decade in which the Cowboys rose to prominence but also became known as "Next Year's Champions." I remember playing an imaginary game in my backyard in which Sonny Gibbs played quarterback for the Cowboys. I remember sitting in class one Monday morning in fourth grade, wondering if I had the patience to make it to the next Sunday, when the Cowboys would play again and life would be worth living. And whenever I am walking down the street and smell a cigar, I remember my grandfather sitting in the aisle seat, his hands resting on his cane, an earplug planted in his ear, quietly rooting like hell for the home team.

Chapter Two

When I attempted to recall what I knew about the Texans, the American Football League team that played in Dallas in the early '60s, my memory bank returned a shiny white blank. I had no idea that their uniform colors were red and white, or that their helmets were old-school treasures with a map of Texas outlined on the side. I remembered none of their games and few of their players' names. I was still in kindergarten when they moved to Kansas City in '63, but their inability to register with me was not just a function of my youth; the reason I draw a blank on the Texans is that Pop took stock of them and the Cowboys when both teams came to town, and, summoning the full powers of his patriarchal authority, refused to endorse the Texans as worthy of our family's support. That was that. They became invisible in our family.

Pop had many unwritten rules governing his rooting interests—which, in turn, governed our rooting interests. He cheered first for Dallas, then Texas, then the United States. He cheered for SMU against the rest of the Southwest Conference, and the Southwest Conference against the rest of the world. He cheered for Republicans in presidential elections, except when a Texan, Lyndon Johnson, ran as a Democrat in '64. He cheered for the National League in the World Series because of the Houston Astros, who brought major league baseball to Texas as the Colt .45s in '62, but he

switched his allegiance to the American League when the Rangers moved
to North Texas in '72. He always cheered for someone; he could not watch
a game without an "us" and a "them," and always had a reason underlying
his support. Some of his reasons were more oblique than others: He
cheered for the Cincinnati Reds against the Boston Red Sox in the '75
World Series because the state of Massachusetts prohibited offshore oil
drilling, a position he saw as hurting Texas business.

As a Dallas team, the Texans figured to warrant his support. Instead,
they were ignored. Why? They belonged to an upstart league, a brash and
rebellious confederacy that rose up to take on the NFL establishment.
Pop was an establishment man; he believed in stable, traditional ventures.
Choosing between the Cowboys and Texans was easy for him: The Cowboys would bring to Dallas such traditional powers as the Chicago Bears
and the New York Giants, while the Texans would play tacky newcomers
such as the Los Angeles Chargers and Denver Broncos. To Pop, the Texans
were just a junior varsity.

Oh, his disdain was relatively mild: He read about the Texans in the
sports pages of the local papers, and he cheered for them, as we all did
when they played the Oilers in the '62 AFL championship game. My
cousin, Jack Wertheimer, Jr., managed to attend several Texan games without getting drummed out of the family. Still, Jack took his girlfriends to
see the Texans; Cowboy games were a higher cause, reserved for family.

The '62 AFL championship game provided me with my only Texan
memory, a droplet lost in the tidal wave of my Cowboy recollections. I
spent the day playing at a friend's house, with the game showing on a
black-and-white TV set in the den. We used it as background noise while
we played. The guerrilla wars of GI Joe, our heroic Army figure, were far
more important.

I was stunned to learn, years later, that the Texans and Cowboys had
shared Dallas equally, that Pop's mandate had blacked out of my memory
a team that was every bit as popular around town and considered every bit
as newsworthy as my beloved Cowboys. The teams were alike in many
ways. They shared headline space in the newspapers. They had similar-
sized followings. They had wealthy owners. They had rookie head coaches
with much to prove. (The Texans' coach was Hank Stram, then an obscure
assistant from the University of Miami.) The Cowboys had Meredith and
LeBaron at quarterback; the Texans had Cotton Davidson and Len Daw-

son. The Cowboys had Don Perkins running the ball; the Texans had a slashing star from North Texas State named Abner Haynes. The Cowboys had Bob Lilly anchoring their defensive line; the Texans had E. J. Holub. As important as Meredith, Perkins, and Lilly were in my house, Dawson, Haynes, and Holub were in others. That the Texans did not exist in my world meant only that my world was incomplete.

The Texans actually staked a claim to Dallas before the Cowboys. Lamar Hunt had tried and failed for several years to buy an NFL team and move it to town. After he was offered only 20 percent of the failing Chicago Cardinals, who moved to St. Louis, he became frustrated and met with NFL commissioner Bert Bell to encourage expansion. Bell told him that Bears owner George Halas, chairman of the NFL's expansion committee, believed Houston and Buffalo would get new teams before Dallas. Hunt, a third-string receiver in his college days at SMU, was tired of not getting to play; in a radical move that forever changed pro football, he decided to start a new league. He banded together owners in seven other cities, including Houston and Buffalo, and announced the birth of the AFL on April 27, 1959. The league office would be in Dallas. Hunt's team would be called the Texans.

"Three weeks after our announcement, Halas held a press conference in Houston to say that he was recommending that the NFL expand to Dallas and Houston," Hunt said. "They hadn't shown serious interest in expanding before our announcement. It was apparent they had identified the strong points of the AFL and were trying to cut the legs out from under us."

Clint Murchison, Jr., was soon identified as the probable owner of the NFL's new Dallas franchise. The son of a flamboyant entrepreneur who had built a fortune in the '20s and '30s investing in real estate, construction, railroads, and oil, Murchison had a master's degree in mathematics from the Massachusetts Institute of Technology, and oversaw his family's wide variety of business holdings, which included an oil company, a publishing house, and a company that manufactured BB guns. He, too, had tried and failed to buy several existing NFL teams and move them to Dallas in the '50s.

On Halas's advice, Murchison hired Tex Schramm as the franchise's general manager. Schramm had served as the Rams' general manager until '57, then moved to CBS-TV as an assistant director of sports programming. A tip from Wellington Mara, owner of the New York Giants, led

Schramm and Murchison to hire Tom Landry as their head coach. Landry was a native Texan who had been an assistant coach with the Giants and lived in Dallas in the offseason.

The franchise was approved on January 28, 1960, at the owners' meetings in Miami Beach. Murchison and his partner, Bedford Wynne, paid $600,000. Hunt said later he "didn't think there was any doubt" that the Texans' arrival in '59 hastened the NFL's decision to expand to Dallas. In a speech at the Oak Cliff Exchange Club in March of '60, Hunt said the NFL was coming to Dallas because "it feels it can collapse our league if it can cut off the founding city."

A faction of old-guard NFL owners wanted the new franchise to begin playing in '61. George Preston Marshall, owner of the Redskins, led the faction, but Murchison secured Marshall's support with a wicked trick: He secretly bought the rights to the Redskins' fight song. "Marshall's pride and joy was that Redskin band," Schramm said. "Clint told him, 'No franchise in 1960, no fight song.' Miraculously, all of a sudden, we were starting in 1960. We needed that. We told them, 'Hey, we're going to have competition (in Dallas) and we need to start at the same time.'"

Improbably, just eight years after the Texans' disaster of '52, Dallas had two professional football teams. Hunt predicted the city would not support both, and suggested the Cowboys would have to leave because the Texans were determined to stay. Murchison responded that Dallas would just have two teams if Hunt was staying, because the Cowboys were also staying. The war of Dallas had begun.

As badly as the NFL wanted the Cowboys to carry its flag and crush the Texans, its fathers were not overly eager to fortify the Cowboys for the fight. Since the franchise was not approved until two months after the NFL's college draft, the Cowboys had to play their first season without drafted players. This weakness, a result of the NFL's decision to rush into Dallas to try to squash the AFL, haunted the Cowboys throughout their early years. Schramm and Landry were forced to trade future draft choices just to field a legitimate team in '60. Long before their first game, they traded choices in the first, fifth, sixth, and tenth rounds in the '61 draft, and in the third, fourth, fifth, seventh, ninth, and twelfth rounds in the '62 draft, receiving immediate help in return. The first choice in '61 went to the Redskins for Eddie LeBaron, an undersized but deft veteran quarterback.

"Not having a draft that first year was a huge setback," Landry said.

"We always seemed behind after that. It was crazy for a new team to give away its first draft pick, but we had to get a team on the field."

The Cowboys needed to get players from somewhere. Schramm wanted to begin signing collegians in '59, before the owners approved the franchise, but interim NFL commissioner Austin Gunsel refused to provide a copy of the standard contract. The franchise did not exist, Gunsel said, until the owners voted. Schramm improvised. He wrangled a copy of the contract, duplicated it, and sent his talent scout, Gil Brandt, on a secretive search for bodies. Brandt had done personnel work for Schramm in Los Angeles and lately earned a living as a baby photographer; aggressive and resourceful, he started on the East Coast and swept across the country collecting talent. Eighty players signed with the Cowboys before the franchise was approved. The first to sign, according to Brandt, was Jack Crouthamel, a Syracuse lineman. Schramm was appalled that Crouthamel's contract included an $8,000 signing bonus.

The Cowboys opened offices in an unpartitioned corner of the lobby of the Texas Auto Club building on Central Expressway. While he negotiated contracts on the phone, Schramm sat across from travelers mapping out vacations. He and Landry shared an office. The franchise that would one day be known as America's Team was off to a humble start.

The league was not entirely bereft of concern for the Cowboys. When Schramm cleverly signed Meredith to a personal-services contract with Murchison after the '59 season, securing his services without a draft pick, Halas conspired with Schramm to make sure Meredith played for the Cowboys. Halas's Bears drafted Meredith in the third round and traded him to the Cowboys for a third-round pick the next year.

Next came the expansion draft, expected to provide the core of the new team. The other 12 franchises were allowed to protect 25 of their 36 players, leaving little for the Cowboys. "We had a lot of guys on the way down," said Jerry Tubbs, a linebacker drafted off the 49ers' roster who would spend 28 years with the Cowboys as a player and coach.

The best of the expansion draftees were Don Heinrich, a backup quarterback from the Giants; L. G. Dupre, a halfback from the Colts; Don McIlhenny, a running back from the Packers who had played at SMU; Tubbs, who chose to play for the Cowboys instead of teach school; Bob Fry, an offensive tackle from the Rams; and Frank Clarke, an end from the Browns who became one of the Cowboys' best receivers. That was not nearly enough for the foundation of a quality team. "The Cowboys started with a bunch of 'never weres' and 'never will bes,'" said Dick Nolan, a cornerback for the Giants who joined the Cowboys as an assistant coach in '62.

As the Cowboys and Texans stocked their rosters before the season, football fans in Dallas decided which team to support. There was no law against supporting both, but few did. The war split the city down the middle. The Cowboys appealed to the country clubbers, the establishment, the patrician elite; they had the support of the Salesmanship Club, a businessmen's charity organization that sponsored an exhibition game at the Cotton Bowl. The Texans attracted the young, the disenfranchised, and the hip. Even though Hunt's family was among the wealthiest in the country, his team was the underdog.

"The Texans came first, and we were pretty excited about them," said Ron Chapman, then a disc jockey on KLIF. "When Murchison brought an NFL team to town, a lot of people got bent out of shape that this new upstart team had come along to take away the glory from the Texans. My first reaction was, 'Hey, don't mess things up with this Cowboys team. We like the Texans.'"

The teams convened their training camps in July. The Texans went to Roswell, New Mexico. The Cowboys met in Forest Grove, Oregon, on the campus of Pacific University. An incredible 193 players tried out. "It was like a Greyhound bus station," LeBaron said. "I threw passes to guys I had never seen before and never saw again."

The Giants' Frank Gifford had made headlines at a promotional appearance in Dallas several months earlier by predicting that the Cowboys would finish above .500 in their first season. He was just showing loyalty to Landry, his friend from the Giants, but it was apparent long before the end of training camp that Gifford had grossly overestimated Landry's team. "I knew we were going to be lousy," Landry said. "We had a bunch of castoffs. It was tough going."

Landry and Meredith began forming their complicated relationship in Forest Grove. They shared a Texas heritage—Landry was from Mission, Meredith from Mount Vernon—but that was all they shared. It was as if the football gods had played an ironic trick and thrown together two personalities as different as sunlight and darkness. Their marriage would always be uneasy.

Landry was 36 years old and a head coach for the first time at any level. He had already lived a full life. As a teenager he flew B-17 missions over occupied European territory in World War II as part of the Eighth Air Force. After his discharge, he returned to the University of Texas and played on teams that won the Sugar Bowl and Orange Bowl in the late '40s. After one season with the New York Yankees football team, he joined the Giants in '50 as a defensive back, part of coach Steve Owen's famed umbrella pass defense. He became a player-coach in '54 and retired from playing a year later to become a full-time assistant to head coach Jim Lee Howell.

He was renowned as a football intellectual long before he came to the Cowboys. As a player-coach with the Giants he pioneered the 4-3 alignment utilizing four linemen and three linebackers. It quickly became a standard in pro football, replacing the "Suicide 7" five-man front.

"We used two variations, the 'inside 4-3' and 'outside 4-3,'" said Dick Nolan, who played in the Giants' secondary for seven seasons beginning in '54. "On the 'inside,' the tackles jammed the center and (middle linebacker) Sam Huff filled a hole off the (offensive) guard. On the 'outside,' the tackles stepped out and shouldered the guards, and Huff filled the middle."

Howell put Landry in charge of the Giants' defense when Landry retired from playing after the '55 season. The Giants won the Eastern Conference and played in the NFL championship game three times in the late '50s, thanks largely to Landry's defense. He spent hours studying films and organizing detailed game plans. "He probably knew formations and sets better than anyone in the league," Nolan said. "He knew Jim Brown better than Jim Brown knew himself."

Serious, detached, almost professorial, Landry was good at his job. After the Giants shut out the Browns to win a playoff game for the Eastern Conference championship in '58, the Browns' Lou Groza said, "Only one man could have done this to us: Tom Landry." Jim Lee Howell said after that game that Landry "was the best coach in football," a comment that would follow Landry for years.

Howell knew how to pick assistants; Vince Lombardi was his assistant in charge of the offense for five seasons beginning in '54. Lombardi and Landry composed what had to be the greatest staff of assistants in pro football history. It was apparent even then that both were of rare coaching stock. "All I have to do is pump up the balls," Howell joked.

Howell retired after the '59 season, and Giants owner Wellington Mara offered the job to Landry. It was an attractive job, but Landry was being courted by Bud Adams, owner of the AFL's Houston Oilers, and Landry wanted to coach in his home state. Mara, alarmed at the prospect of losing such a bright coach to the AFL, told Schramm that Landry was interested in coaching in Texas. The tip paid off; Landry jumped at the chance to remain in the NFL and become the Cowboys' coach.

"I was thinking about quitting coaching altogether and going into business," Landry said. "When Clint and Tex called, I told my wife, 'Well, we might as well take a shot.' The thing was, I wasn't so sure that the Cowboys were going to last more than a couple of years in Dallas. I lived here, and Dallas was a city that didn't turn out unless you won. If you didn't win (the fans) said, 'We'll go do something else.' And I knew we wouldn't win for awhile as an expansion team. But it came down to figuring, 'Why not just take a shot?'"

Jim Lee Howell congratulated the Cowboys on the hire, but warned, "Tom is a warm person, but not so much with his players. Sometimes he gets impatient with them and doesn't pat them on the back. He expects them to go out there and do their jobs. He's so much smarter than most of them. He's like (Browns coach) Paul Brown, a perfectionist."

Meredith was as whimsical as Landry was dry, as lighthearted as Landry was serious. When reporters asked why his nickname was "Dandy Don," Meredith replied, "Because I am." He walked around training camp humming songs and snapping his fingers, and spent hours bouncing golf balls off the floor in his dorm room. Landry viewed football as a somber endeavor, but Meredith saw it as a game. He had signed a five-year contract worth a staggering $25,000 a year, but he was such an appealing character that his teammates were not jealous.

"Everyone loved Don immediately," said Wes Wise, who was the sports anchor at Dallas's ABC affiliate in '60 and later served five years as the city's mayor in the '70s. "I was out at the training camp in Oregon that year, and he was very charismatic even then. He got the rookies to stand up and sing their alma maters at dinner, and organized other singing games and events. You couldn't help but like him."

Landry attempted to fashion his ungainly collection of players into a team, but the task was almost impossible. Many veterans saw the Cowboys as a low-stress venture. "The camp was an awfully laid-back deal," Don

McIlhenny said. "Not as a result of what Tom did, but I think a lot of the guys there, myself included, had sort of a laid-back attitude. Sort of casual. It didn't seem nearly as uptight as other training camps I had been to, probably because not much was expected of us. That's probably why we delivered the way we did."

They drew an estimated 40,000 fans to their first exhibition game at the Cotton Bowl, a 14–10 loss to the Colts in the Salesmanship Club game. Four days later, they scored their only victory in six exhibition games, beating Landry's old team, the Giants, 14–10, on a makeshift field laid over a baseball diamond at Fairgrounds Stadium in Louisville, Kentucky.

On the last weekend of September, both teams played their first regular-season home games. On a humid Saturday evening, the Cowboys lost to the Pittsburgh Steelers, 35–28, before a crowd estimated at 30,000. On the first play in franchise history, there was confusion in the backfield and LeBaron was thrown for a loss. The Cowboys took a 14–0 lead, but quarterback Bobby Layne led the Steelers from behind with touchdown passes covering 28, 48, 65, and 70 yards. The next day, the Texans drew an estimated 42,000 fans to their 17–0 victory over the Los Angeles Chargers. The *Morning News* reported that the paid attendance to both games was not known.

The Texans tried everything to get fans out to their games. They put certificates good for free tickets in balloons set loose over the city. They gave away tickets in packages of corn chips. They gave away tickets to drivers who had their windshields washed at Sinclair gas stations. They signed up 18,000 kids to their youth organization, the Huddle Club; for a dollar, a Huddle Clubber got a membership card that got him into games for free. To tap the corporate community, Hunt hired 30 attractive young women to drive around town in convertibles selling tickets. The girl who sold the most got to keep her car. "And then the girl who kept the car also got to keep Lamar," Stram said; Hunt married the contest winner.

The Texans also scheduled game-day promotions to entice fans. One day, Hunt and Ron Chapman competed in a punt, pass, and kick contest before the opening kickoff. An "exploding scoreboard" turned out to be a line of Army mortars buried in the picnic grounds outside the stadium. (Gary Cartwright, a sportswriter for the *Morning News,* wrote that the mortars failed to inspire either team but almost made South Dallas surrender.) There was Friend of the Boy Day, and Barber Day, at which barbers wearing white jackets were admitted free. "I think we had 100 or 110 barbers and maybe a few dental assistants," Hunt said. "We tried a lot of things. We were starting from scratch and trying to build an allegiance. We succeeded in drawing more people than the Cowboys, but the revenue was minimal."

The Cowboys were not quite as casual with their tickets, but they also resorted to stunts and special promotions to lure fans. An adult who purchased an unreserved end-zone seat for three dollars could bring in five children for free. An appearance at one game by Roy Rogers and Dale Evans, who drove around the field in a convertible at halftime, was a disaster; kids tossed programs, paper cups, and ice cubes at the movie stars. Rogers stood up in the back seat of the car and shouted angrily at the fans. Police hauled 65 youngsters to jail for a lecture.

"We got people in there (free) but not nearly to the extent that (Hunt) did," Schramm said. "We concentrated on building a team and did not go into the marketing and giving tickets away, whereas he flooded the market with free tickets and bowling day and what have you. We had to establish ourselves with a little bit more integrity, because we were the National Football League."

The Texans had an 8–6 record in their inaugural season and generated a crowd-pleasing average of 26 points a game. They announced an average per-game attendance of 24,500 fans, though fewer than half of them had paid. The AFL struggled to draw fans in its first season, but it was a high-scoring, exciting league. "It was a little bit second-rate, but it was entertaining and people enjoyed going," said Allen Stone, then a high-school student in Casa Linda, now a broadcasting executive in Dallas.

"I was a big Texan fan, and so were all of my friends," said Walt Garrison, a future Cowboy fullback who, in those days, was in high school in Lewisville. "We didn't go to any Cowboy games. The Texans had Abner Haynes, who was a local guy, and they had a winning team even though they played in the AFL. Dallas fans don't care what league you play in as long as you win."

The Cowboys did not win in their first season. They played 12 games, lost 11, and tied one. Their collection of castoffs was no match for the rest of the NFL. The Browns beat them, 48–7. The Colts beat them, 45–7. Lombardi's Packers beat them, 41–7. For the fans, the highlight of the Browns game occurred when the Cowboys finally scored after allowing 48 points: The horse that galloped around the Cotton Bowl after touchdowns smashed into an ambulance at the end of the stadium. The Cowboys were indeed a low comedy act in their first season. Wearing white pants, dark blue jerseys with stars on the shoulders, and white helmets with blue stars on the side, the Cowboys were as undignified as they were incompetent. "We tried something different with the uniforms, but it didn't work," Schramm said.

Attendance shrank as the season progressed. The Cowboys drew 16,000 fans for the Rams and just 10,000 for the 49ers on a drizzly afternoon in November. The few fans that came that day, including Pop and my father, sat underneath the upper deck to stay dry, giving the stadium a deserted appearance. As the Cowboys waited in the tunnel to run onto the field before the game, Meredith looked up at the empty stands and said, "Well, we finally did it. We scared everyone off."

For the season, the Cowboys announced an average per-game attendance of 21,417 fans. That was lower than the Texans' average by some 3,000 per game, although both totals included freebies, and were thus useless as barometers of hard support. Still, the parity in the stands made it clear that the lordly NFL had a fight on its hands.

"You went to the games to see the other teams, not the Cowboys," Allen Stone said. "You went to see Johnny Unitas and the Colts, Jimmy Brown and the Browns, Frank Gifford and Kyle Rote and the Giants. It was exciting that they were coming to Dallas for the first time. People cheered for them as much as they did for the Cowboys, if not more. There'd be applause when Jim Brown broke off a run."

The Cowboy players were aware of their unpopularity. "I think the fans were a lot keener on the Texans early on," said Don McIlhenny, who was second on the team in rushing, with 321 yards, in that first season. "The Texans really hustled after fans. Lamar really tried to work it. Clint didn't. I will always remember the time Don Heinrich and I went out to the State Fair as members of the Cowboys to sign autographs. A booth was set up and people came by. I had started a few games. Everyone knew Heinrich from his days with the Giants. But we had more people taunt us than ask us for autographs. They didn't want our autograph, they just wanted to say something nasty to us about the Texans being better. It was a miserable experience. The people didn't poke sticks at us, but almost. It was like being in a cage or something. Most of the people in that building were Texans fans. I see these (Cowboy) players now and people think they walk in the clouds, but there was a time when a Dallas Cowboy was an object of scorn."

The two teams never played a game, but their rivalry was bitter. Murchison and Hunt were personal friends, as were Landry and Stram, but the fight for fans and players was vicious. Both teams drafted Meredith, Lilly, and E. J. Holub. During the '60 season there was a rumor in the papers about the Cowboys moving to Minneapolis; NFL commissioner Pete Rozelle suggested that Hunt had planted the rumor to sabotage the Cowboys. Hunt, hardly denying the charge, admitted he had heard the rumor from two sources. "Ridiculous," said Bedford Wynne, the Cowboys' co-owner.

After the season Hunt further rankled the Cowboys by suggesting that the teams play an exhibition game for charity the next season. It was an ingenious proposition: Hunt knew the Cowboys could not accept the challenge—they had everything to lose—yet they would look like killjoys for turning down a game the fans wanted.

If the teams had played, Landry said years later, the Texans might well have won. "Oh, I think so," Landry said. "They surely would have had a chance. I suspect that they were the better team. They never had a chance to prove it, but they were assembling some pretty good personnel that wound up giving the Packers a pretty good game in the first Super Bowl (in '67), and we had castoffs."

Wes Wise notes, "I'm surprised to hear Tom admit that. I suspect he's right, the Texans probably did have a better team at first. But admitting that would have raised a ruckus back then."

Indeed, in those days the Cowboys claimed not even to notice the Texans. The Cowboys said they were concerned only with building their team, not with how many fans they or the Texans drew. They said they would need five years to build a quality team starting from scratch; the implication was that they would begin to draw more fans when they won games in the established NFL. They conducted themselves with, Wise said, "not arrogance so much as a certain superiority."

The Texans hated it. "We rooted for the Cowboys to lose," Hank Stram said. "We wore our hearts on our sleeves. It was an emotional matter for us, a cause, because we were in this new league. We had thought we were in good shape starting a team in Dallas, and then all of a sudden, out of the clear blue sky, the Cowboys came to town. It just didn't seem fair, and that feeling pervaded our team. Everyone played with strong purpose, to try to be the team that survived."

The Cowboys fretted about the Texans more than they admitted, of course. More than once, Wise said, Schramm called to complain about a sportscast that Schramm felt had given more attention to the Texans. Hunt also complained about media coverage; he was so displeased with newspaper coverage of one promotional stunt that he threatened to buy advertising space and tell the story himself. Both sides were touchy, emotional, and defensive.

"It was fun, but a bitter fight," Hunt said. "Both teams were brand new and struggling. The Cowboys were selling a product where they weren't going to win, and we were selling a product where no one knew the names of the teams or players. It was very frustrating. Just a bad situation."

One player symbolized the war—a defensive back named Jim Harris. He had played quarterback at Oklahoma in the '50s and defensive back for two years in the NFL, with the Eagles and Rams, before retiring after the '58 season to enter the oil business in Dallas.

"I told the Rams I wouldn't come back (in '59) for less than $10,000, and Pete Rozelle (then the Rams' general manager) offered me $9,500," said Harris, now an oil business executive. "It was fine. That was what you did in those days, played a couple of years and went on to something else. Pro football wasn't a big deal."

Harris was working in Dallas when the AFL sprouted up and the Texans came to town, and he changed his mind about playing after Hunt offered him a $13,000 contract. The Cowboys, desperate for proven players, saw that Harris was in Dallas and obtained his NFL rights from the Rams. When Harris tried to play for the Texans, the Cowboys went to court and obtained an injunction preventing him from playing. They claimed Harris was their property because his NFL contract included an option year that had never been exercised. "They were trying to break the AFL by having the AFL contracts voided," Harris said.

Landry, Rozelle, Schramm, and Hunt testified in a protracted court case. The Texans won a decision freeing Harris to play the second half of the '60 season for them, but the Cowboys pressed on and got the injunction reinstated before the '61 season. The Texans, weary of the fight, finally just let the Cowboys have him. Harris played the '61 season for the Cowboys.

"I got razzed for having come from the AFL," he said. "It was tough going. Landry worked everyone extremely hard and they didn't have a lot of good players. I hurt my ankle, and Landry and I argued a little. It was a 'my way or the highway' deal with him. He was in his second year and he hadn't won a game in '60. We fought all the way through. After the season I went in and told him I was quitting. I could make $8,000 (in the oil business) without taking all that crap."

Today, Harris lives in Louisiana and owns an oil and gas exploration company. His brief pro football career is best summed up in a trivia question: Who was the only player to suit up on both sides of Dallas's pro football war?

"I wanted to play for the Texans, I really did," he said. "I liked Lamar. The Texans were kind of the favorites in town because the Cowboys were trying to knock the AFL out. But the best thing that ever happened to me was having to play for the Cowboys. The NFL was a tougher league and I quit. Had I stayed with the Texans, I probably would have gone on to Kansas City, had a football career, and never become a geologist. And this business has been far more fruitful than football."

By the time Landry came to Dallas, the 4-3 defensive alignment he had pioneered with the Giants was the standard in pro football. That meant he now had to come up with ways to beat his own creation.

The 4-3 was revolutionary in that it asked players not to chase the ball and let their instincts guide them, but to read "keys" in the developing play and react accordingly. "You did what you were supposed to do, not what you wanted to do," longtime Cowboy defensive end George Andrie said. Landry decided that deception was the best way to attack a defense built on recognition and instant decisionmaking. Trickery, Landry figured, would cause the defenders to hesitate while making their reads and wind up out of position.

Thus was born a second Landry creation that would revolutionize football: the wide-open offense. The Cowboys entered the NFL playing the antithesis of straightforward, old-fashioned offensive football. They used a multitude of alignments and shifts, and put backs in motion before the snap. The linemen went through contortions before setting; they put their hands on their knees, paused, then stood straight up before lowering into a three-point stance. Landry called his creation the "multiple-set offense." The Cowboys used it to try to trick their opponents instead of physically beating them, to outsmart them instead of out-muscling them.

"The only way to beat the 4-3, as I saw it, was to keep the defense off-balance so it wouldn't be able to react to what you were doing," Landry said. "Plus, we didn't have a lot of (good) personnel in the beginning and we were very small, so we weren't going to go out and beat people physically. We had to try to fool people."

Paul Brown was football's resident innovator, but he had a dominant runner in Jim Brown, and thus no need for a fancy offense. "All he had to do was give the ball to Jim Brown and get everyone out of the way," Dick Nolan said. "No one else was using the multiple-set schemes when Landry started it."

Ironically, the Texans were the only other team in pro football using a multitude of alignments and shifts. "Stram got to doing it, too, but he just copied it from Tom," Dick Nolan said.

"The whole concept was to confuse the other team from the moment you broke the huddle and went to the line of scrimmage," said Pettis Norman, who played nine years for the Cowboys as a tight end. "It was completely innovative. You could see (defensive) players looking around kind of confused at what was going on. In fact, people laughed at us. Players laughed at us. They thought we were kind of sissies. Fans would talk about 'that sissy stuff.' They thought it was funny."

Sam Huff, who had played for Landry in New York, said, "I thought they were crazy. They wore themselves out running on and off the field and all over the place before the snap."

It soon became clear why Landry had felt the need to acquire LeBaron: The complicated offense required an experienced quarterback. Meredith was the team's future quarterback, but he was fresh from college and not ready to govern Landry's calculated madness. LeBaron, though small at five-foot-seven, was quick-footed, adept at handling the ball, and smart.

"I don't know whether they traded for me solely on that pretext,"

LeBaron said, "but it was a complicated system. A difficult system. Initially we did it well, but there were problems as we went along. We kept changing things week by week. The playbook itself wasn't so difficult, but we did make a lot of changes as time went on."

LeBaron threw 25 interceptions during the '60 season, a total that would stand as the franchise record for 20 years. He had little support. The entire stable of backs produced just 1,049 rushing yards and six touchdowns running behind a miserable line. LeBaron's favorite receivers were Jim Doran, the first Cowboy to go to the Pro Bowl, and Billy Howton, a veteran who had played seven seasons with the Packers and one with the Browns. It was not nearly enough. The Cowboys lost to the Eagles and Cardinals by two points, the Lions by nine, the Bears by 10, and the Redskins and 49ers by 12. After they tied the Giants in New York late in the season, they flew home and were met at Love Field by two fans holding up signs of encouragement.

"I talked to Tom at one point," LeBaron said. "I said, 'You know, if we simplify the offense a little bit we might win some of these games.' Tom said, 'That may be right, but we're putting in an offense and defense that ultimately will beat the Browns and Giants. That's who we have to beat to win the championship. Beating some of the lesser teams now is not the important thing.' He knew where he was going. After we chatted, I said, 'Fine.'"

The Cowboys were a laboratory experiment in helmets and cleats as Landry tried to uncover what worked against a 4-3. Much of the experimentation was done in practice at Burnett Field, the city's minor-league baseball park, set in the shadows of downtown. That was the Cowboys' practice facility for their first two seasons, and it was hardly lavish. (The Texans, representing the supposedly fly-by-night AFL, worked out at a clean, modern facility on Central Expressway.) The Cowboys' locker room was drafty and dirty. Their trainers worked out of a ladies' rest room with pink walls. At night, rats came out and chewed on the players' helmet linings and shoulder pads. The players learned to hang their gear over water pipes to keep the rats away. The shower drains often clogged; as much as a foot of water would gather.

"One day it was so cold in the locker room that some guys lit a fire in a barrel," Don McIlhenny said. "They went out to practice, and all of a sudden all this smoke came billowing out from inside. It looked like the stadium was on fire, which wouldn't have surprised anyone, but it was just a bunch of tape and trash that had been in the barrel."

The practice field was set in the outfield, on bumpy terrain, next to billboards advertising funeral parlors, ice cream shops, and insurance companies. The field, set on the Trinity River flood plain, was reduced to mush after a rain.

"One day it was so wet we couldn't practice," McIlhenny said, "so we all got on a bus to go somewhere to practice. Well, we drove around town looking for a place and wound up at Grauwyler Park, on Harry Hines Boulevard. Tom and Tex got out and walked around and looked at the grass and said it was all right, so we got out and practiced. There wasn't a soul around. No one stopped or noticed. This was the Dallas Cowboys. No one cared. If you did it today there'd be 10,000 people, cars, helicopters, the press. . . ."

Pro football was just different then. It was still a part-time vocation; many players worked second jobs in the morning before reporting for practice and meetings after lunch. "You didn't work that hard," said Lilly, who joined the Cowboys as a rookie in '61. "Meetings and practice took about five hours, which left you time to do other things. You made about as much money as you'd make doing anything else."

Jim Harris said, "You look back and realize how inadequate things were. My shoulders and everyone's shoulders were killing them in '61 because the Cowboys, to save money, did not have cantilevered shoulder pads. Flat pads were cheaper. Everyone had sore shoulders because the Cowboys had second-rate pads. But that was part of it in those days."

The Cowboys' first season was so dismal that they sold 300 fewer season tickets for their games in '61. The opener of their second season, played before 23,500 fans at the Cotton Bowl, resulted in their first regular-season victory. The Cowboys trailed the Steelers late in the fourth quarter, 24–17, but they scored a touchdown and got the ball back when Tubbs intercepted a pass. A long pass from LeBaron to Howton set up a 27-yard field goal by Allen Green at the final gun.

"My friends and I ran right out of the stadium whooping and hollering like we had won the World Series," said Doug Alexander, then a teenage fan from North Dallas, now an accountant. "After we calmed down in the parking lot we said, 'What are we doing out here? Why'd we do that?'"

Two wins in three weeks against the league's newest expansion team, the Minnesota Vikings, gave the Cowboys a 3–1 record. A crowd of 41,500 came out to watch them play the Giants at the Cotton Bowl. The Cowboys trailed by only a touchdown late in the third quarter, but the Giants' Erich Barnes intercepted a pass and returned it 101 yards for a touchdown, and the Giants went on to win, 31–10.

When the teams played again in Yankee Stadium two weeks later, the Cowboys scored an upset, 17–16, before 60,000 fans. With a 4–3 record and half the season to go, the Cowboys were giddy with big ideas, but only 20,500 fans came out to their next home game and the Cowboys lost to the Cardinals. They went sharply downhill from there, finishing with five losses and a tie for a 4–9–1 record. Their average attendance rose slightly from the year before, to 24,571 fans a game, but there still were far more empty seats than fans.

"We sat in the upper deck," Doug Alexander said, "and we were just about the only people up there. There'd be three of us, two or three cops, maybe five people at one end and five people at the other. Twenty people, total, in the entire upper deck."

Still, the '61 season was an improvement on many fronts from the pitiable '60 season. Four victories was better than none. Attendance did not drop so precipitously late in the season. Several star players emerged. Don Perkins, who had sat out the '60 season with a broken foot, rushed for 876 yards and was named the NFL's Rookie of the Year. Howton caught 56 passes, and Frank Clarke emerged as a deep receiving threat, averaging 22 yards on 41 catches. Lilly, though inconsistent in his rookie season as a defensive end, had the look of a budding star. Meredith, playing substantially for the first time, passed for 1,116 yards and nine touchdowns.

The Texans were the ones who experienced decline and disappointment in '61, the result of a six-game losing streak in midseason. They finished with a 6–8 record, playing in front of sparse crowds. Their average attendance dropped almost 7,000 fans per game from the year before. They were no longer a sporting curio so much as just plain weird.

"One time Stram coached a game from on top of a tower on the sidelines," E. J. Holub said. "This was the AFL, so anything went. He used the tower in practice and liked it so much he decided to use it in the game. He told the equipment manager to hook the thing up and take it down to the

Cotton Bowl. Well, the guy hooked it up to his trunk and was driving down Central Expressway and forgot that it was sitting back there up in the air, and he hit a bridge and cratered the thing. He had to get a welder to weld it back together right there on the spot. When Stram got on top of the tower at the game, the people sitting behind him on the 50-yard line started yelling at him and throwing stuff because they couldn't see. But he stayed up there. The players had to push the tower around when he wanted to move."

The truth was that neither the Texans nor the Cowboys were winning the war. Hunt's prediction was becoming a reality: Dallas was not big enough to support two teams. Their combined attendance suggested that one team could succeed, but it was too much to expect a city of 600,000 residents to support two. Even Los Angeles could not support two, as the Chargers learned in one season before moving to San Diego. Only New York and Dallas had teams in both leagues after that.

The small crowds did little to disprove the notion that Dallas simply was not a pro football town. Houston Oilers executive John Breen joked that the Texans and Cowboys should play a winner-take-all preseason game, with the winner getting to leave Dallas. Staying there, Breen implied, was a death sentence.

Yet even as both teams floundered, Dallas was beginning to experience the power of the marriage of football and television, a marriage that, like Hunt's decision to start a new league, would forever change the sport. The Cowboys' road games were broadcast on Channel 4, the local CBS affiliate. The Texans' road games were on Channel 8, the ABC affiliate. The broadcasts amounted to three-hour advertisements for the teams and players.

"Even though our crowds were small, there was tremendous interest in both teams engendered by TV," Hunt said. "My experience was that people knew the players' names and numbers, but they learned them from watching the games on TV, not from coming out to the stadium. People liked to stay at home and watch rather than go."

The rest of the country was beginning to experience the same phenomenon. The AFL had a contract with ABC to broadcast some regular season games nationally instead of just in local markets, an idea that the NFL scorned at first but quickly copied. (Rozelle signed the NFL's first network

TV contract in '62.) At the AFL owners meetings after the '61 season, Oilers owner Bud Adams said that his quarterback, George Blanda, formerly of the Chicago Bears, was more popular now in Chicago than when he played there because of national TV broadcasts.

At those meetings, Hunt reiterated his belief that Dallas could not support two teams. He also reaffirmed that the Texans were not moving. Three months later, a federal judge rejected Hunt's $10 million antitrust lawsuit against the NFL, ruling that the NFL had not conspired to put the AFL out of business. The lawsuit had stipulated that the Cowboys would have to leave Dallas if Hunt won the case. More than ever, it appeared that the Cowboys, true to Murchison's word, were staying put.

The Cowboys were so desperate for fans that they held weekly luncheons at which fans could ask Landry questions. Though not thrilled with the arrangement, Landry was unfailingly polite. "He would answer any stupid, foolish question from anyone," said Bill Mercer, a radio announcer who became the Cowboys' play-by-play voice in '66.

He was not as amiable with his players. "In those first years, boy, Tom was hard to handle," Tubbs said. "He was kind of like my high school coach. He wouldn't say much about the good things you did; that was what you were supposed to do. But when you looked at game films and he went over your mistakes, that was tough. He wouldn't yell, but he would stand there and make comments that cut right through you. Players would just sit in there and sweat."

LeBaron had a different view. He and Landry were peers who had played against each other; LeBaron was almost another assistant coach. "We would occasionally go out socially in the offseason," LeBaron said. "He was difficult in the early days, but he was under a lot of pressure. We were competing with Texas and SMU. He was a brilliant thinker who demanded a lot of his players and himself, too. As time went on he probably changed a little, but he couldn't understand people who weren't dedicated to playing and winning, and in the early days we had some guys who weren't dedicated."

Despite their obvious limitations, the Cowboys suddenly turned Landry's offensive vision into a reality in '62. They scored more points than every other NFL team except the champion Packers, averaging 28 per game. LeBaron and Meredith often alternated downs, shuttling back and forth from the sidelines with plays Landry called. Perkins rushed for 945 yards, Amos Marsh for 802. Howton caught 49 passes and Clarke caught 47. Landry's shifts, hitches, and feints covered up a weak offensive line.

Their win–loss record barely improved to 5–8–1 because the defense allowed 402 points, setting a franchise record that still stands. The secondary was so weak that Dick Nolan, who had retired from the Giants to join Landry's staff, had to put his uniform back on. "I was pretty beat up and committed to starting coaching, but Tom came to me and said, 'Hey, how would you like to play again?'" Nolan recalled. "I said, 'When do you want me?' He said, 'Tomorrow.' That was the first game of the season. I played all year."

The starting cornerbacks were a rookie, Mike Gaechter, a track star from the University of Oregon, and a veteran, Don Bishop. The pass defense allowed almost 100 more yards per game than it had allowed in '61. "We had a terrible time," Nolan said. "Poor Gaechter would try to play a zone and just take off after people. He just didn't have the instincts yet."

Still, the season was nothing if not interesting. Marsh scored on a 71-yard run, an 85-yard pass, and a 101-yard kickoff return. Gaechter returned an interception 100 yards. Clarks caught 10 passes for 241 yards against the Redskins. Meredith and LeBaron each threw 15 touchdown passes. "At least we had a team going, finally," LeBaron said. "You could see Tom was going to make this team good."

They had a 4–3–1 record in early November when they played the Giants at the Cotton Bowl before more than 45,000 fans. "There was even a traffic jam," wrote Bud Shrake, a sportswriter for the *Times Herald*. But the Giants won easily, 41–10, and LeBaron suffered a leg injury, ending the quarterback shuttle. Meredith did not fare as well running the offense alone. Repeating their pattern from the year before, the Cowboys slumped down the stretch, winning one of their last six games.

The city remained largely uninterested. The Cowboys' average attendance declined almost 3,000 fans a game from the year before. A November game against the Bears drew just 12,692 fans. "I had moved to Dallas from Chicago in '62, and I got season tickets because I had been indoctrinated to the NFL by the Bears and Cardinals," said Harry Sebel, a stockbroker. "The scene at the Cotton Bowl was sad. They would announce 10,000 fans, but there weren't 10,000 people within a square mile of the stadium."

Disc jockey Ron Chapman said, "There was lingering resentment toward pro football in general. It was perceived as trying to steal the thunder from the college rivalries, which still meant something. Plus, the games were on Sundays, and, dammit, you weren't supposed to do anything else on Sunday except go to church. Tom Landry helped with that; if it was OK for Tom to do it, it must be OK."

The Texans fared no better. They announced an average of 400 more fans per game than the Cowboys—"Texans By A Field Goal" reported the *Morning News*—but their totals, as always, were padded by free tickets and concealed a miserable bottom line.

"There was this ongoing debate in all of our minds as to which team was going to survive," Pettis Norman said. "Because both of us were doing kind of pitiful. Both of us had more people in uniform than in the stands at most games. The first game I played for the Cowboys was an exhibition game in Cleveland, part of a doubleheader with 83,000 people in the stands. To come home and play before 5,000 or 6,000, that was a tremendous letdown. It made you wonder how long we could survive. It was always in the papers, always a question of who outdrew whom. In fact, neither of us were drawing. There was always a question in my mind as to whether either one of us would be around for very long."

The Texans drew just 13,557 fans for a game against the Raiders in late November, and just 18,384 for their last home game of the regular season. Their crowds were particularly disappointing because the team, led by Dawson and Haynes, won the AFL's Western Division title with an 11–3 record. When the *Times Herald*'s sportswriters devilishly selected an All-City pro team after the season, they picked 13 Cowboys and nine Texans, a breakdown that infuriated the Cowboys.

On December 23rd at Jeppeson Stadium in Houston, the Texans played the Oilers for the AFL championship. It was a defining moment for the new league. An overflow crowd of 37,981 filled the stands, but, more importantly, an estimated 56 million viewers watched on national television. They saw a game that was every bit as dramatic as the NFL's famous Colts–Giants championship game in '58. The Texans led 17–0 at halftime, but the Oilers rallied with 10 points in the fourth quarter to force overtime.

Near the end of the first overtime period the Texans' Bill Hull intercepted a pass and returned it to midfield. Jack Spikes caught a pass from Dawson for 10 yards and ran for 19 more to put the Texans in scoring range. Tommy Brooker kicked a 25-yard field goal early in the sixth quarter to bring the AFL championship to Dallas.

Several thousand fans met the Texans at Love Field upon their return later that evening. There was reason to believe the Texans had seized the advantage in their war with the Cowboys. "I thought we were really set," Stram said. "We had a good team, we had established an identity, and we had a following. The Cowboys were having trouble winning an intrasquad game. I was naive enough to think that the team that won on the field would be the team that survived."

Such was not the case. Even as his team was winning the championship, Hunt was plotting to move. Finances dictated his decision; he was losing a million dollars a year. The Cowboys' bottom line was helped by a cut of the gate from road games in New York, Cleveland, and Philadelphia, but the Texans received no such boost from their AFL brethren. The Cowboys were better armed for a long war.

The Cowboys had not won the war; the Texans had sold 1,100 more season tickets and averaged 200 more paid fans per game in '62. (The figures were used as evidence in an antitrust suit that led to the AFL-NFL merger several years later.) But Hunt, as the founder of the AFL, framed the situation in a larger context.

"We were at a point in the development of the league where we needed success stories," Hunt said. "Other teams were starting to make progress. The Bills and Patriots were starting to draw some pretty good crowds. You could see there was a chance for us to succeed if there was no competition. I decided, hey, the smart thing to do was to try to find a place to make our own name and destiny. Emotionally, I would rather have had us succeed in Dallas. But I couldn't see it happening. I didn't think that winning the championship was going to have a big impact. If we had stayed it was going to be a long, hard battle and probably a long time before anyone won."

After flirting with New Orleans, Hunt decided to move the franchise to Kansas City. "I was crying like a baby as I drove out of town, just thinking about the fact that we were having to leave," Stram said. "I was the last guy to leave Dallas. Lamar had explained the economics to me. I understood.

But I was just hoping against hope that he would change his mind. I felt like Dallas was our town."

It was not—not anymore, at least. The war was over. The Cowboys had Dallas to themselves.

Between attending college in Philadelphia and moving to Baltimore to work, I have lived half of my life in the "enemy" camp, among fans of the Eagles, Redskins, Colts, and Giants. This has enabled me to see the Cowboys from the other side, through the eyes of fans who boo them as heartily as I cheer for them. I have made bets with these fans, traded jibes, and developed friendships. The root of their distaste is the conviction that the Cowboys and their fans are arrogant, spoiled, flushed with an unwavering sense of superiority. It is hard for me to argue.

These rival fans tend to ascribe the Cowboys' attitude to Texans' belief that everything in Texas is bigger and better. Jerry Jones and the brash '90s Cowboys certainly lend credence to this view, but the superior attitude of the Cowboys and their fans has more complicated roots than that. The franchise's early days are telling. The Cowboys were born superior by destiny and necessity. The NFL hatched them to try to bury the AFL, thrusting them into a war with an unknown entity from a new league. Knowing they would lose most of their games, the Cowboys had to assume a snob's pose; the NFL's tradition was their only weapon in their war with the Texans. The Vikings, Falcons, and Saints did not have to assume the same pose when they joined the NFL later that decade. Only the Cowboys had an AFL rival at home. Only the Cowboys had to put on airs.

In addition, the Cowboys utilized a playing style that implied they thought they were smarter than their opponents. The prevailing fashion in pro football in those days was to ram the ball down your opponents' throats, as Lombardi's Packers did. The Cowboys, with their multiple-set offense, insinuated that they were going to beat you with their heads instead of with their hands. It was as if they were private schoolers intent on keeping their clothes clean against public-school brutes. Even when they were losing and taking beatings in their first few seasons, the Cowboys seemed to suggest that they were intellectually superior. After only three seasons, when the Cowboys had won just nine of 40 games, Landry said, "This is going to be the next great team in pro football."

There also were other ways in which the Cowboys implied that they were cut from a rarer cloth. They were the only team in the league that wore their white jerseys at home, as if they were pure. They spent money on scouting, used a computer to discern talent, and established an expensive training camp far from home, in Thousand Oaks, California. Murchison was wealthy enough not to have to borrow from the team's coffers, unlike other owners. Schramm was a former colleague and close friend of Pete Rozelle, giving rise to jealous concern in the league that the Cowboys were a favored son.

Brandt's scouting apparatus was particularly annoying to the rest of the league. Teams invested little time and money in scouting in the early '60s, but Brandt set up a national network of regional scouts, each of whom was paid $2,500 a year to scour their area for quality players and any athletes who could be converted into football players. Cornell Green was discovered playing college basketball for Utah State and converted into a defensive back. Gaechter played just one year of college football; he was better known as a sprinter.

On draft day, some teams relied on little more than all-conference lists and *Street and Smith's* college guide. The Cowboys used private information they had purchased, and they galled the rest of the league when they began feeding the information into a computer in '62 to more accurately evaluate players' skills. When the Cowboys delayed the '64 draft for four hours while waiting for a doctor in Oregon to evaluate an injury to Mel Renfro, Lombardi stood up and walked over to Brandt's desk at draft headquarters in New York. "What happened, Gil?" Lombardi asked with a smirk, "did your computer break down?"

The entire Cowboy endeavor smacked of an elitism that was passed on, however unwittingly, to the fans. No one would have accused my grandfather of arrogance, yet his disdain for the Texans and the AFL was the seed of his support for the Cowboys. He looked down on the new team and the new league. Most Cowboy fans did. "There is no question that we were looked down upon," the Texans' E. J. Holub said.

Landry was right about the Cowboys becoming pro football's next great team: They have had only five losing seasons since '64, spoiling their fans beyond reason. Cowboy fans expect success and settle for nothing less. Defeats are rationalized more than accepted. I speak from experience. It is the definition of arrogance.

The presumption of today's Cowboys has different roots. The bravado of Michael Irvin and Deion Sanders, the smugness of former Dallas coach Jimmy Johnson, the gall of Jerry Jones—today's Cowboys luxuriate in their lack of humility. It inspires them to play better. As Irvin said before the Cowboys defeated the Steelers in Super Bowl XXX, "When we win, oops, I mean if we win . . ."

That is different from the desperate arrogance of the franchise's early days, yet it belongs in the same continuum. The presence of the Texans provoked a stance of superiority that invaded the minds of the Cowboys and their coaches and fans in the early years, and it never withered. The Texans were far from just a rival in the Cowboys' early days; they were a force that changed the Cowboys forever.

Chapter Three

When Mickey Mantle died in 1995, baby-boomer baseball fans were confronted with their own mortality. Raised on the Yankees, General Motors, Elvis, and the early days of television, they watched Mantle swagger toward the Hall of Fame with a wink, a limp, a hangover, and a cascade of long home runs. As the years passed, they came to equate that vision of Mantle with the joy and light of their childhood. Conversely, they found a symbol of lost youth in the cancerous Mantle who faced death as a liver-transplant patient, regretful alcoholic, and failed parent. Grown men wept when he died.

I had interviewed Mantle once, briefly, on the telephone, when I was a summer intern in the *Times Herald* sports department in 1978. Mantle lived in Dallas; my father knew men who played golf and cards with him. On the phone that day, I asked for his reaction to George Steinbrenner's latest stunt with the Yankees. He professed a total lack of interest, apologized, and hung up. I wrote columns in Baltimore about his death, but from the cool perch of an emotional distance; our lives had overlapped at the edges, but I had not known him well and I could not grieve for him on any symbolic pretext. I was born too late for that; his skills had deteriorated and the Yankees' dynasty had ended by the time I was a baseball fan.

I understood the lingering fascination with him, but it would have been disingenuous for me to join the sad chorus his death precipitated.

Still, I was touched in a way I had not anticipated. I realized I was old enough now to have my own heroes leave me vulnerable to such emotions. The early Cowboys were my Mickey Mantles. Years later I still felt a sentimental attachment to Meredith, Lilly, Perkins, Hayes, and the others. They defined my boyhood for me, in all its innocence. The very mention of their names summoned thoughts of bicycle rides to the 7-Eleven on Northwest Highway, minor-league baseball games at Turnpike Stadium, cold cherry Slurpees on hot summer days, Herman's Hermits, and the early, uneasy stirrings of girl craziness.

Just as Mantle's fans had not allowed him to age beyond his baseball days in their minds, I still saw the early Cowboys in their dusty incarnations as football players. I had not allowed them to age, either. I knew I would have to interview them in the course of writing this book, and I faced the task with conflicting emotions, a mixture of excitement and dread. Confronting them now, years later, would blur my innocent's vision of them; I would see them more as equals, fellow adults with careers, families, schedules, and bills. I was not sure I liked the idea of disrupting the happy text of my childhood mythology. Nothing is grander than a child's admiration for a football star, and no one is more vulnerable than a jock whose time has come and gone. Converting my heroes into flesh and blood would render me less a child; as inevitable as that passage was, it was sad.

At the same time, I felt tingles of excitement, much as I did before my twentieth high school reunion, at which I encountered classmates I had not seen since graduation. I had continued to frame them in my mind as 18-year-olds, even though I knew they had charted the same course into adulthood that I had. Holding them captive at 18 was satisfying—those were good years—but learning what had become of them also was satisfying, like getting to the end of a good mystery novel. Interviewing the early Cowboys would be much like that experience, I figured; I would fill in the later chapters of the novel of their lives.

Some of their stories were well-known. Meredith became a TV football analyst and a Hollywood star. Lilly ran a beer distributorship. Dan Reeves became an NFL coach. Roger Staubach owned a real estate company. Bob Hayes was busted for selling drugs to an undercover agent, and went to jail. But what about the others? What had become of Don Perkins and Pettis Norman and George Andrie and Amos Marsh and Cornell Green and Sonny Gibbs and the rest? What were their memories of the days I recalled so vividly? Did they look back with fondness? How had they meshed as a team beyond the public's view? What were their secrets? Their locker-room politics? What did I not know about them?

After compiling a phone list with the help of other sportswriters, the Cowboys' publicity department, and the phone book, I made a series of calls, sat back, and waited. The phone began ringing. Like a time machine, voices on the other end of the line transported me from the reality of my current life's routine to the simplicity of the Cotton Bowl days. Sitting in my office in Baltimore 30 years later, I could almost smell Pop's cigars.

Bob Lilly called from his home in Graham, Texas, west of Fort Worth; he was as casual and friendly as a next-door neighbor and invited me out to see him. Andrie, who owned a small business outside Dallas, was surprisingly emotional and opinionated. Eddie LeBaron was a lawyer in Sacramento. Lee Roy Jordan owned a lumber company near Love Field. Ralph Neely was in the insurance business in Dallas. Pettis Norman owned a small business in Oak Cliff; we discovered a mutual love of horse racing when we spoke in his office. He told me about Amos Marsh, who became an optometrist, and died of diabetes at age 48.

Cornell Green was a scout for the Denver Broncos, one of the few still making a living in football. Jethro Pugh owned a string of shops at the Dallas-Fort Worth International Airport. Herb Adderley, who had played for the Packers for most of his career but proved a critical addition to the Cowboys in '70, lived in the New Jersey suburbs of Philadelphia and owned a company that laid cable-television wire. Mel Renfro split his time between Dallas and Portland, Oregon; he owned a business in Dallas and was trying to build up The Bridge Center, a Christianity-based community center, in Portland. Chuck Howley owned a uniform-rental business in Dallas; trucks with Howley's uniform number on it scurried around town.

Calvin Hill lived in the Virginia suburbs of Washington, D.C. His son, Grant, born in Dallas in the late '60s, was a star forward for the Detroit Pistons of the National Basketball Association, more famous than Calvin ever was. Calvin and I had run in the same circles when he spent several years working in the front office of the Baltimore Orioles, a baseball team I cover extensively. I had always refrained from telling him that I could recite his Cowboy statistics from memory; hero worship is an awkward pose for a big-city columnist. "I had no idea," Calvin said, smiling, when we spoke.

Walt Garrison had filmed TV commercials selling smokeless tobacco while still playing, and he was still pitching smokeless tobacco 20 years later. His office was a kitschy converted movie house in Lewisville, with walls lined with autographed pictures of football players, country singers, and movie stars. His whittling knives lay against one wall, his spittoons against the other. He was the Cowboys' cowboy.

I interviewed Dave Manders in his immaculate home in North Dallas; his commercial landscaping business had thrived. Mike Gaechter had done well in the outdoor advertising business; he lived in Dallas and owned plants in Amarillo and New Mexico. Warren Livingston, a starting cornerback on the Cowboys' first playoff team, had retired after 27 years as an electrical engineer. Pete Gent lived in Michigan, where he was raised, and wrote books.

Colin Ridgway, the Australian-born punter who had flopped amid much fanfare, had met a tragic fate: After marrying a Dallas girl in the '60s and flourishing in the travel business for almost three decades, he was murdered in his University Park duplex in 1993. The police publicly stated that his wife was a suspect, but she was never arrested.

Frank Clarke was living on social security and his NFL pension in his hometown of Beloit, Wisconsin; unemployed since the late '70s, he had aborted careers in television broadcasting and real estate to follow what he called a "personal growth program" aimed at enhancing his self-esteem. "It's the handbook to higher consciousness," he said. "It outlines the path to happiness and unconditional love."

At 62 years old, he had spent the past decade drifting from California to Kentucky, back to California, and finally to Beloit, where he was taking care of his elderly mother. He lived in a friend's house as a caretaker. "I call myself a householder," he said. "I do it as a work exchange. I baby-sit. I shop. I live in the house, take care of it. I keep a damn good house. It's very much a solitary life. I don't have a female relationship. I don't have friends that I hang out with a lot. I read. A lot of my hours are spent in contemplation. Almost like a living meditation."

Sonny Gibbs had lived all over the world servicing contracts in the oil business for 30 years; now a grandfather, he was back in Fort Worth with a wry take on how he had spent his signing bonus in 1963, the only year he wore a Cowboy uniform. "I could be very crude and say that I invested in lots and houses," he said, "meaning whorehouses and lots of whiskey."

As I expected, my childhood visions were jarringly updated. I was older, and so were they. Jordan, number 55, was 55 years old now, a gray-haired grandfather. Pugh was a lanky figure standing behind a cash register. Neely had a belly, wore glasses, and filled a room with self-deprecating wit. "I had a well-deserved reputation for holding," he said when we spoke in his office on Central Expressway. Lilly was a landscape photographer and weighed less than he did when he played; most of the others weighed more.

They were a fraternal group, intensely loyal to each other. "There was no free agency when we played, so we were teammates for a lot of years," Pugh said. "Basically, we grew up together, played together, had our kids together. Now we're having grandkids together. We made friends for life. We didn't make the money that they're making today, but I still feel we were lucky. Today's players will never have what we had, a group of guys coming together, staying together, and building something. I consider myself lucky to have had that experience."

Some had better memories than others of their days in the Cotton Bowl. "I gave a speech in East Texas the other day and a guy came up to me who knew more about me than I did," Neely said, laughing. I could relate; fans remember scores, statistics, big plays, and history, while players remember teammates, opponents, and the methodology of playing. The Cowboys and I shared those years, but in different ways. They were on the inside looking out, and I was on the outside looking in.

I interviewed Landry in his living room in North Dallas. We were supposed to meet at his office, but he slipped on ice that morning and had to go to the emergency room to get stitches in his hand. Polite and relaxed, he seemed excited to talk about the old days and relieved to be out of coaching. "Some of the stuff the players do today turns your stomach," he said. His eyes shone when he smiled, at odds with his image as a stone face.

The phone number I had for Don Perkins was outdated, so I called information in Albuquerque, New Mexico, where Perkins had lived since his retirement from the Cowboys before the '69 season. There were two listings for his name. I took down both and called the first. I knew I had the right Perkins as soon as he answered the phone. My father had admired Perkins's deep, kingly voice, the thespian's measured cadence, the proper grammar, the absence of slang. "He sounds like Ronald Colman," my father said, referring to the actor from the '30s. It was a voice more suited to a debate teamer than a football player.

I explained that I wanted to come see him in New Mexico and talk about the old days. He was 57 years old and working for the Albuquerque police department as a community liaison, coordinating crime-prevention programs and helping indoctrinate cadets at the academy. He agreed to meet. We arranged a date and I flew out in February of '96, several weeks after the Cowboys had beaten the Steelers in Super Bowl XXX in neighboring Arizona.

We met at his house on a cool, clear morning. Divorced, with four grown children and six grandchildren, he lived alone in a square, adobe home with a pool in the backyard and mountains rising in the distance. The air was clean and free of humidity. Perkins opened the door and offered his hand. Dressed in olive jeans and a white sweater, his black hair now dappled with gray, he could almost have passed for a current NFL player. He was trim and tightly muscled through his neck and chest. He also was small, barely taller than me and maybe 20 pounds heavier. I immediately wondered: How had someone of such average size gained all those yards?

He put on a pot of coffee, suggested we talk in the den, and immediately apologized for what he would not remember. "I put my football days behind me a long time ago," he said. It seemed true: An unknowing guest in his house would have no idea that he had played, much less starred. Not a single football photograph or trophy was displayed on his walls or mantel. "I don't go around wearing a letter jacket," he said, the first evidence of a droll humor. His eyes turned down at the corners, giving him a sad countenance, but they flared when he lifted his stentorian voice. His face beamed when he smiled.

The phone rang just as we began. A friend was on the line. "Not right now," Perkins said into the receiver. "I have a writer here who wants to talk about my . . . football thing."

He paused, listening, then burst out laughing. "Yeah, you know how much I like to talk about that," he said.

"I never see a game in its entirety," he told me after hanging up. "I do better listening on radio. I'm a radio buff. A National Public Radio buff. Me and Garrison Keillor go back a long way. *Sixty Minutes* is the only TV show I faithfully watch every week. I go to concerts. I went to El Paso last week to see Rod Stewart. I would do that, but would I go to Phoenix to see a Super Bowl? Of course not. I'm not going to sit eight hours in a stadium watching a game. It's not a judgment about what people do with their lives. But I get bored watching baseball or football."

He was a hidden jewel as a player, ranked fifth on the NFL's career rushing list when he retired, having gained 6,217 honest yards, mostly in small chunks in between the tackles. He played with purpose and consistency: He never had a thousand-yard season, but he had six seasons of 700-plus yards, almost never fumbled, and had no equal in his day as a backfield blocker. His opponents respected him enormously; they voted him onto the Eastern Conference Pro Bowl team in six of his eight seasons.

It took me a while to sort out why I had felt so compelled to take a special trip to interview him, but I finally did. Meredith, Lilly, Hayes, and the other prominent Cowboys from the old days were more famous; they belonged to the rest of the football world as well as to Cowboy fans. Perkins was different. He was all ours, the quintessential Cotton Bowl Cowboy, a gritty, underappreciated player who was long gone by the time the team moved to the glitter and glare of Texas Stadium.

"He was a great player," Sam Huff said. "Very smart, very dedicated, very tough. He played with so much heart, and never stopped coming. That sucker got me one time at RFK Stadium, I mean, I was blitzing Meredith and he stepped out and whacked me but good. Knocked the breath out of me. Not many people could get me, but Perkins did. I said, 'I can't believe you did that.' He just gave me a little smile."

His blocking was still the stuff of legend among his former opponents and teammates three decades later. On play after play, year after year, Perkins took on linebackers outweighing him by 30 pounds and rarely failed to drive them out of the play. One year, Ermal Allen, a Cowboy assistant coach who graded game films, ascertained that Perkins had completed 90 percent of his blocking assignments. No other back in the NFL graded higher than 75 percent, Allen said.

"Perk just never made an error," Lilly said. "Coach Landry talked about him every week in the film session. I remember one time when he had his worst game and graded out at like 80 percent, which was real good, and coach Landry got up and said to the team, 'If all of your worst games grade out at 80 percent like Perkins, we'll be in good shape.'"

Quickness was his antidote for a lack of size and speed. His acceleration was such that, legend had it, he could beat Hayes in the first 10 yards of a race. "I could hit the hole as fast as anyone," Perkins said. He also was imbued with old-school toughness. He played through countless injuries, took a pounding, and still produced. "He was a classic example of a player who wasn't big enough or fast enough, but still made it on true grit and determination," Pettis Norman said. "He was an inspirational player, one we drew a lot from. He was just tenacious as hell."

He was one of my favorite players because he ran with the ball, yet we had laughed at his expense in our family because of Landry's penchant for using him on first down. I asked if he had heard the jokes. He smiled. "Hey, diddle diddle, Perkins up the middle," he said, recounting the popular rhyme.

"Did it seem as predictable to you?" I asked.

"It did," he said, "but I understood it. Part of it was the club's design to let people get over the jitters. I was not a fumbler, so a good, safe play to let people get some contact and get over their butterflies was to give me the ball and let everyone hit someone and get some contact, and then we could go ahead and play the game."

His old teammates had drawn a vivid portrait of him for me before I went to see him. They remembered him as the embodiment of dependability, a quiet, serious player who led by example and never complained; his teammates, coaches, and opponents saw him as a player who personified the no-nonsense professionalism that marked their era.

"Don never said a word, but always got his job done," Landry said. "He was a great blocker, a great pass protector, an explosive runner. He gained a lot of yards and he was running behind some pretty bad lines there in the beginning."

Jethro Pugh learned about Perkins as a rookie in '65. "First day of my first training camp in California," Pugh recalled, "and coach Landry gets up at the meeting and says, 'One man has this team made already: Don Perkins. Everyone else has to fight for a job.' That shocked me. Lilly had made All Pro the year before. Renfro was Rookie of the Year. I figured this Perkins guy must be good."

I recounted Pugh's story to Perkins. He nodded without smiling. He remembered the moment. "Tom could say that because he knew I wouldn't believe it," he said. That he had been a longshot from the University of New Mexico had affected him profoundly.

"I was continually doubting myself, asking myself, 'Am I really this good?' I was always propelled by the fear that they would discover that I really wasn't that good and shouldn't be there. I always thought I had to play as well as I could or I'd lose my job. Right up until the day I retired, I never felt the comfort that I could relax and let up. I thought I had the job only as long as I produced on every snap. I played with a serious intensity. People would say, 'Hey, lighten up, Perk, smile, it's not the end of the world.' I'd think, 'The hell it ain't.' Tom knew that, which was why he could say I was the only guy who had the team made. He knew I wouldn't believe it for the next game or even the next series."

Growing up in the '40s and '50s in Waterloo, Iowa, as one of eight children, he never dreamed of playing football for a living. His father worked at the Rath Meat-Packing Plant. His mother died when he was 13. "We lived in the riverbed section of town, where all the poor folks lived," he said. "There were no paved roads, no running water. The toilet was outside. My goal was to get out of high school and get a job at the tractor factory or the meat-packing plant where my father worked, because you could make pretty good money there and maybe move to a street where you had indoor plumbing, a car, and hot and cold running water. It seemed like a pretty good goal."

Football intervened. After excelling in a single-wing offense at West Waterloo High School, he received several college scholarship offers. His family advised him to stay home and go to work at the meat-packing plant—college and football were a waste of time, they said—but he signed with the University of New Mexico. "I wanted to see some new country and I got a full (scholarship) and they said they'd pay my way down," he said. "The alternative was working in a factory. So I went. It sounded like a good trip. But the whole time I was thinking, OK, you were good in high school, what makes you think you'll be good in college?"

He was even better in college. In three years as a 175-pound halfback he set 12 school records and became the first UNM player to have his number retired. As a senior, he rushed for 2,001 yards. His coach was Marv Levy, who would later coach the NFL's Buffalo Bills and write letters of recommendation on Perkins' behalf to the Pro Football Hall of Fame nomination committee. "Don Perkins," Levy wrote in '93, "is the best football player I ever coached."

Not that his success opened every door for him. Overt racial intolerance was still widespread in '59, and Albuquerque was not exempt. Perkins got married in his senior year, and he and his new wife had to live in an apartment in the black section of town. "It was the only place the university could find," Perkins said sarcastically. "I was the star athlete, everyone's man, Mr. Everything on Campus, whatever. Then I would go shoot pool with classmates and a guy would tap me on the shoulder and say, 'You can't shoot here.'"

Yet he had prominent supporters. One was Clinton Anderson, a United States Senator from New Mexico. Anderson was a friend of Clint Murchison, who was just putting together a team when Perkins finished at UNM in '59. Anderson told Murchison about this hotshot running back in Albuquerque and suggested that Murchison sign Perkins to a personal-services contract since the Cowboys had no draft that year. Landry later recalled, "I don't know how high we would have been on him if Clint hadn't already signed him. No other team really wanted him."

His two-year contract included a $1,500 signing bonus and a $10,000 annual salary. He gained 20 pounds to steel himself for the pros and carried low expectations to training camp in Oregon in '60. His career almost ended before it began. Landry asked the players to complete a mile run at the first practice, a custom that became known as the Landry Mile. Perkins was unable to finish. He fell down several times and finally walked off. Landry had to talk him out of retiring in the locker room. "I was totally embarrassed and ready to bag it right there," Perkins said. "I told Tom, 'I'm outta here.' He said, 'Just wait and go to the All-Star Game and we'll deal with it later.'"

In those days the nation's top college players were selected to an All-Star team that played an exhibition game against the current NFL champions. Perkins was selected to that year's team, along with Meredith. It was a high honor. Taking Landry's advice, he left Oregon for the All-Star camp in Chicago, but he broke a bone in his right foot in practice and sat out the game.

He tried to practice with several orthopedic devices but ultimately underwent surgery, ending his season in early September. He returned to Albuquerque, took a job pumping gas, and rehabilitated his foot. He set no goals for the '61 season beyond finishing the Landry Mile. "That was my whole focus," he said. He accomplished his goal and never forgot the experience. "Tom gave me a second chance," he said. "I gave him my best shot in return."

Perkins took over the starting halfback job with a 108-yard performance in the second game of the '61 season. "I don't know that I was surprised to become a starter, because I had never played anything but first-team football in my life," Perkins said. "But I was a little awestruck. I'm a guy from Waterloo, Iowa, starting in the NFL. It was like, 'Is this really happening?'"

Success came quickly. He was Rookie of the Year in '61 and first-team All-Pro in '62. "He was our best player in the early days," Jerry Tubbs said. "We all admired the hell out of him. As a runner he wasn't as good as Tony Dorsett or Calvin Hill or Duane Thomas, but he was a great blocker and a really productive player overall. He just didn't blow assignments like so many other players."

Landry used him wisely. Perkins was not an adept receiver, not fast enough to run end sweeps, and not big enough to operate as an Emmitt Smith–style sledgehammer getting 25 carries a game. Landry played him to his strengths: 15 carries a game between the tackles, and a surplus of blocking assignments. In football's most complicated offense, he gained yards on simple plays such as draws, delay traps, and off-tackle slants out of the "I" formation.

"I wasn't physically built to do what Emmitt does," Perkins said. "At that time in football you went with whatever your God-given talents were. There weren't resources to draw on to give you more strength or endurance. We didn't have a weight room. You went as you were born. In the off-season the Cowboys would maybe come around once and see how you were doing, but you didn't go around running windsprints every morning. The idea was just to take care of yourself."

He stayed in shape, but his lack of size led to numerous injuries, particularly in his early years. He made the Pro Bowl in each of his first three seasons, but he took a terrible beating: broken arm, broken hand, broken ribs, broken foot. He was considering retirement after the '63 season, and told an interviewer the next year that he came back only for the money, to help his pension, and because he did not want to go out on a sour note. He was 26 years old and clearly not addicted to football.

Landry shifted him in '64 to fullback, a position supposedly requiring more size, but it was designed for a blocker and inside runner, and, thus, more appropriate for Perkins. He was challenging Jim Brown for the league rushing title with 699 yards through eight games until injuries again limited him for the rest of the season. "He is really too light to be an NFL runner," Landry told reporters after the season.

Yet he was the team's only consistently productive runner. Perkins' burden did not lighten until Dan Reeves emerged at halfback in '66. Reeves was an intelligent player, a slanting runner, superb receiver, and resourceful around the goal line. Perkins benefited from the shared spotlight; he was superb as the Cowboys drove toward their first division title in '66, gaining 111 yards in a critical victory over the Browns on Thanksgiving, after which he was interviewed on national television. In the '66 NFL championship game against the Packers at the Cotton Bowl, he gained 108 yards.

Perkins's success enabled him to pay back his father with priceless emotional gifts. "He was incredibly proud," Perkins said. "He didn't know that much about sports. He grew up chopping cotton. But when we played in Minneapolis or Cleveland he'd come to the games and sit in the stands and tell everyone around him, 'That's my boy out there, yep, that's my boy.' He'd take his newspaper clippings to the plant and show everyone. I'm glad that happened."

By '66, Perkins was a star on a dynamic young team in a city gone wild for pro football. Life seemed perfect. Yet it was not. Perkins announced his retirement after that season. He had never planted roots in Dallas, instead establishing a home in Albuquerque, where he bought a house and pledged to raise his children. During the season he lived in a rented apartment in South Dallas. When his oldest child reached school age, his family stayed in Albuquerque during the season, and Perkins abhorred the separation.

The alternative was to move to Dallas, but he could not see raising his family in a city so divided by race. Perkins could not live near the Cowboys' practice site in North Dallas because it was in the white part of town. He did not receive the offseason job offers and commercial endorsements that his white teammates received. He had to sell insurance, toys, and luggage in the offseason. At the end of the season he would not spend one extra night in Dallas; his wife would wait for him with a loaded U-haul when the team returned to Love Field after its final game, and they would drive off into the night, headed west. In Albuquerque, he could live where he chose. He felt important. During the '66 season, the governor hired him to work in the state tourism department, promising a career in civil service.

Schramm and Landry finally talked him into signing another contract, a two-year deal worth close to $100,000. He responded with two more Pro Bowl seasons. He fumbled only once in '67, and averaged a career-high 4.4 yards per carry in '68. He was at the peak of his powers, yet he insisted through both seasons that he would retire when his contract was up, and he kept his word. When he failed to report for training camp in '69, Schramm, Landry, and his teammates flooded his house with phone calls, attempting to talk him into coming back. This time, the pressure did not work. "Something is telling him to retire, and I'm not sure what it is," Landry said. It was the buildup of too much time spent away from his family, and a personal call of the wild that few people in Dallas knew about, a nonconformist streak that lay hidden beneath his solid exterior.

"I never felt a need to do anything all my life," he said as we spoke in his den years later. "That's why it was so easy for me to leave. I played in the Pro Bowl (in '68) and said, 'Bye, I'm not coming back.' I know that's not what we do in our society today. We're supposed to hang in there until the bitter end, until they have to say, 'Please go!' But I had no need to be the guy who couldn't take the hint. I wasn't going to play any better than I had already played. I was 31 years old. I wasn't going to get any quicker. I wasn't burned out. It just felt like the time to go."

Late in the afternoon on July 18, 1969, Perkins called Schramm at the Cowboys' training site in Thousand Oaks, California. The deadline for players to report was 7 P.M., several hours away.

"Is everyone there?" Perkins asked.

"All but one," Schramm said.

"Well, I called to tell you I haven't changed my mind," Perkins said. "Go ahead and tell them I have retired."

Schramm was reluctant. "I should wait until your official notification comes in the mail," he said.

Perkins said, "Consider this my official notification."

Landry later met with reporters and announced Garrison as the new starting fullback. Asked about the timing of Perkins's retirement, Landry shook his head. "His last two years were his best," Landry said. "If you ask me, Perk has retired at least three seasons too soon."

Twenty-seven years later, Perkins sat in his den and contemplated that assessment. He shrugged.

"Retiring just seemed to be the calling for Perkins, who kind of wandered into this football thing inadvertently," he said, "and then wandered back out."

Bob Lilly had told me that Perkins "walked to a slightly different drummer." It was true. He was not at all as I had imagined. My youthful rendering of him as the gritty, dependable fullback was but a caricature. The Perkins sitting with me in his den was an introspective individualist who read books on Eastern philosophy and practiced martial arts for exercise.

His search for his self had occupied him for years. Subtly, he had charted an iconoclastic course through life, rarely taking the easy routes that beckoned. His choices were unconventional in their own way. He went to college when his family thought he should go to work. His speech and manner were at odds with prevailing black stereotypes in the '50s; his ex-wife told an interviewer in '64 that her mother had liked him because he was "different from the other Negroes" and did not speak jive or dance. As a player he did not savor his talent or celebrity as the defining characteristics that other players did. His urge to explore the rest of the world was so powerful that he took a 50 percent pay cut to retire from football.

"All my life, I wanted to make a living with my hands," he told the *Times Herald*'s Frank Luksa in a 1986 interview. "But all I did was push paper, run my mouth, organize, create, and adjust. I'd like to have been a deep-sea fisherman or a mechanic. A longshoreman. But I had kids. Responsibility. All the pressures of that. I was doing what I thought I had to do. I was living the life I thought I should."

After football he continued to work for the New Mexico state government and also became a CBS broadcaster. That post-game interview on Thanksgiving in '66 had alerted television executives to his rich baritone and regal bearing. Perkins hosted a studio talk show out of New York and later provided analysis at games. After that he went through a series of TV and radio jobs: Grambling football, Western Athletic Conference basketball, sports anchor at a local station.

After his divorce, with his children grown, he quit his state job and spent six months as a trucker, just for the hell of it. He drove a 30,000-pound rig back and forth across the country, enjoying the solitude. "People get concerned and emotional when they hear what I'm doing," he told Luksa during his trucker days in '86. "First thing they think is, 'Poor Perkins.' It's like, 'Oh, you can't get another job, so you drive a truck.' The fact is that I never tried to get another job. I'm doing this because I want to.'

The police department hired him the next year. By the time I called almost a decade later, the tendrils of his life had sprouted in numerous directions. He had developed a one-man educational act in which he portrayed Frederick Douglass, the black activist from the 1830s. He had jogged five miles a day until a sore ankle forced him to quit. "I've come a long way from the Landry Mile," he said. He still dabbled in broadcasting and public speaking, and had appeared in local productions of *Driving Miss Daisy* and *I'm Not Rappaport*.

Football still occasionally calls him back to his past. He was inducted into the Cowboys' Ring of Honor in 1976, and the club always asks him to return with the other honorees every time another player is inducted.

"I usually leave after the ceremony at halftime," he said. "It doesn't do a lot for me. Lots of things do a lot for me. Not a football game. Not anybody's football game. Who am I has nothing to do with the fact that I used to play sports. It doesn't make me better or happier than the guy who didn't play sports. The fact that people gravitate to it, I don't understand it, but it's OK. I know I'm supposed to feel a lot of things, but you can walk through this house and not see one plaque or trophy. Not because I'm ashamed or embarrassed about it, but it doesn't have anything to do with me. It has to do with what I used to do. It's my former occupation. And I've never defined myself by my occupation."

At age 57, his search for his self seems less urgent. "We're all going to die, and one of the tragedies is that we don't learn how to live," he said. "We meet everybody's needs but our own. I meet your needs as a journalist. I meet the needs of the people at work as a coworker. I meet society's expectations, my kids' expectations, my brothers' and sisters' expectations, my lady friend's expectations. We spend a lot of time doing what other people think we should be doing. It's kind of nice to know that I don't have to please everybody. I want to do some things that I want to do.

Life is fun. I'm almost 58. People say, 'Don't you wish you were 27?' Not on your life. I've got things to do. I feel good. It's kind of interesting. I have a good friend who is the president of a university and he used to tell me, 'I wish I had done certain things.' I always say, 'Try it and see what it's like.'"

Chapter Four

The Cotton Bowl was a landmark by the time the Cowboys became a tenant. In a sport that was sovereign in Texas, it was the crown jewel. Houston, Austin, Fort Worth, and College Station also had large stadiums, but the Cotton Bowl was the big stage, the setting for so many high moments of college football history in the '40s and '50s. Doak Walker won a Heisman Trophy playing there. Bobby Layne accounted for all 40 of Texas's points in the '46 Cotton Bowl Classic. SMU lost a thriller to Notre Dame in '49 before 75,457 fans, then lost again to the Fighting Irish before an even larger crowd in '54. Tommy Lewis came off Alabama's bench to tackle Rice's Dicky Maegle in the '54 Classic. Syracuse's Jim Brown rushed for 132 yards and three touchdowns and kicked three extra points in the '57 Classic, but still lost to TCU and halfback Jim Swink. Bud Wilkinson's legendary Oklahoma teams won six in a row against Texas in the '50s.

Dallas was a mecca for college football in those days, spawning several generations of fans. "I was a fanatic," said Adlene Harrison, a Dallas native who later served on the city council. "I remember Dicky Maegle getting tackled off the bench. I remember that SMU–Notre Dame game with Johnny Champion blocking Leon Hart. SMU was in that one until the last second, and I have never screamed and carried on and been so emotional in all my life. Doak Walker was somebody I followed, even made weekend trips to see. To this day some of my friends call me 'The Doaker.'"

The early Cowboys were almost an affront to the Cotton Bowl with their losses, small crowds, and lack of stature. "I grew up listening to Doak and Kyle Rote on the radio, thinking the Cotton Bowl was the greatest place in the world," said Jim Harris. "My hands shook when I played in the Texas-Oklahoma game in '56, coming down that tunnel and hearing the stadium split in half. Playing pro ball there a few years later wasn't nearly as exciting."

The allure was the history, not the stadium itself. The Cotton Bowl was just a big concrete tureen, a Depression-era project incorporating none of the amenities that would become standard features in stadiums around the country in the '70s. The scoreboards provided only the score, time, down, and distance; no highlights, statistics, or advertisements. The concession stands sold hot dogs, peanuts, and sodas; no nachos, ice cream, or sausages. There were no luxury suites, no escalators, no plush premium seats.

By the early '60s it was an aging temple in a fraying pocket of town, a dowager down on her luck. The neighborhood around it had decayed as the money moved to the suburbs. There were bars on the windows of businesses and homes. Many Cowboy fans would not have ventured near Fair Park if not for the games.

Conditions were almost as tawdry inside the stadium. Many of the more fashionable fans who would later inhabit Texas Stadium would not have braved the spartan environment. "The bathrooms bordered on barbaric," said Don Hullett, a supervisor at a medical company in Dallas, and an early Cowboy fan as a teenager. "You had to go down a flight of stairs from the main concourse and it was kind of rank. The bathrooms were hot in the summer and cold in the winter. I got sick at a game once, chucked it right there at the doorway to the bathroom. I don't think it got cleaned up for awhile. That was the way it was at the Cotton Bowl. You would see things from game to game."

You did not go to Cowboy games at the Cotton Bowl for the convenience or luxury, or to chat with friends, eat fussy food, drink beer, or be seen. The concept of a football game as a social setting would arrive in Dallas with the opening of Texas Stadium in '71, but the Cotton Bowl was a place for football, and for football fans. "The whole deal was blue collar," said Jack Anthony, an attorney who grew up in Abilene and became a Cowboy fan when he moved to Dallas in the '60s. "The stadium was blue collar. The team was blue collar. The fans were blue collar."

The public-address announcer was A. K. Quesenberry, a physical-education teacher at a Dallas high school. His job description exemplified the Cotton Bowl's simple ambiance. "I worked for the Cotton Bowl Association, not the Cowboys, and they were strict," said Quesenberry, who earned $25 a game. "They didn't play music (over the sound system) during time-outs. They wanted no cheerleading or showboating. Strictly play-by-play. I didn't announce my name and I wasn't listed in the program. No one knew who I was. The only thing I said that was out of the ordinary was, 'third down and a little bit.' That was my call to fame, my signature. It just came to me one time. Someone had less than a yard to go and I said, 'third and a little bit.' The Cotton Bowl office liked it."

Tickets to the games were cheap: three dollars for an unreserved end zone seat, six dollars for a reserved seat closer to the 50-yard line. The result was a different crowd from the wealthy flock that would fill Texas Stadium.

"The Cotton Bowl fans were just average people for the most part, ordinary people who could afford a season ticket or two," Bob Lilly said. "You had doctors, lawyers, and architects, but also guys from the post office, auto mechanics, the basic blood-and-guts guys. They were loud and emotional. Even when there weren't many there in the beginning, the ones who were there really cared. They lived and died with us."

Vernell King was a season ticket holder; she supervised reservations agents for Braniff Airlines. "I'd drive down and park right on the fairgrounds near the roller coaster, or I'd take the bus if it was raining because the bus dropped you off right in front of the stadium," King said. "You came because you were a sports fan and you liked football and you wanted to follow the team. The fans that came out to the Cotton Bowl were the true Cowboy fans."

Inestor Surrells, Jr., was one. He worked as a fitter for a plate glass company. "It didn't cost much money to go down there on Sunday and enjoy yourself," said Surrells, now retired and living in the Oak Cliff section of Dallas. "I'd take two of my sons. Pay a dollar to park on a vacant lot. Buy an end zone seat for three dollars. My sons got in free. You could sit just about anywhere you wanted."

Johnny Minx was a middle schooler from Pleasant Grove in those days. He sat in the end zone. "It was a great crowd down there, all sports fans, all colors," said Minx, now a physical-education teacher at an elementary school in Mesquite. "In the real early days they hadn't thought to put up the fences to keep the extra points and field goals from going into the stands, so there was a mad fight for balls. People just about killed each other going after those balls. They finally put up the fences to put a stop to it."

The end-zone sections often were packed because of the cheap prices, but the reserved sections, between the goal lines, were nearly empty. "My dad had 12 reserved seats in the upper deck, but you didn't need reserved seats," Adlene Harrison said. "We were up there by ourselves. You could roam around, sit anywhere, talk to people. It was very casual, relaxed, a lot of families. Like a college game."

Chicken-wire fences separated the reserved and unreserved sections, but not all fans remained in the sections for which they had purchased tickets. "The fence was four feet high with just one old guy guarding it," said Doug Alexander, an early fan, now an accountant in Dallas. "We were in high school. We'd wait until the old guy turned his back or went to the bathroom and we'd scale that fence and go sit on the 50 in the upper deck."

Johnny Minx found another way to sneak into the good seats: "We had a friend who sold Cokes and had a pass to go back and forth between the good seats and the end zone. We would take turns using his pass to get into the reserved seats. I think we got caught one time in five years. And they didn't kick us out or anything when they caught us, they just told us, 'Get back over there and stay there.'"

The Cowboys could not afford to alienate any of the few fans willing to come out to watch them play. "People called me and asked for tickets," George Andrie said, "or they'd call and say, 'What time does the game start?' I'd tell them, 'When do you want it to start?' There weren't many fans out there. It seemed like one big, happy family. The players and fans were a lot closer. You talked to them, saw friends and neighbors at the games, stuff like that. The team would pay us $25 to go to a social club during the week and show a highlight film or give a little talk. We would go out and make friends on a one-on-one basis. We knew a lot of the fans. We would go to a Shakey's Pizza Parlor after the game, and people would buy us pizza. It was just a lot different then."

After games, the players showered and dressed in their cramped locker room and met their friends and families outside. Dozens of fans waited around for autographs. The players always obliged them.

"I signed for two hours sometimes," Lilly said. "My family came to every game and they waited out there for me. My dad would get me a beer or two to drink while I signed. You just stood out there and talked and signed until the people were all gone. Then we'd have a team party afterwards. It was really kind of fun. We didn't make any money, but we had a blast. We were all very close."

Pettis Norman said, "I don't think the players on other teams experienced the real love and admiration of those fans that came out every Sunday to the Cotton Bowl, come hell or high water. There weren't many of them, but they thought they were part of the team. They thought it was their team. It was a love affair. I still have people coming up to me today saying, 'I got your autograph when I was four.' I stood there and signed for hours, just talking with people and developing that love affair. You'll never have those days again."

The Cowboys and their fans were optimistic before the '63 season. The Texans were gone. Landry's multiple-set offense had averaged almost four touchdowns per game in '62. Season ticket sales were up. The outlook was so promising that *Sports Illustrated* picked the Cowboys, in just their fourth season, to beat out the Giants, Browns, and Eagles, and win the NFL's Eastern Division. The story, written by Tex Maule, who had worked at the *Morning News* before *Sports Illustrated,* was headlined, "Cowboys Can Ride High on Better Defense." Wrote Maule: "If they can achieve even mediocrity on defense—and they should achieve even more—the Cowboys will win the first of their Eastern championships."

It suddenly seemed they had a wealth of talented players; backing up Meredith and LeBaron was Sonny Gibbs, a rookie quarterback from TCU, so celebrated that the *New York Times* had profiled him in a long article titled "The Tallest Quarterback in Captivity." He was six-foot-seven and in-

stantly a heroic figure in my eyes. Captivated by his size, I said to my uncles on our annual family vacation to North Carolina that summer, "The
Cowboys are going to be great because they have Sonny Gibbs!"

TCU coach Abe Martin had said Gibbs had the greatest potential of any
TCU quarterback, including Sammy Baugh and Davey O'Brien, but Gibbs
lasted only a year with the Cowboys; he sat on the bench throughout the
'63 season and was traded to Detroit after the Cowboys decided he was
neither as dedicated nor as talented as they had thought. He never threw a
pass for the Cowboys in a regular-season game.

Gibbs' aborted career was an appropriate metaphor for the Cowboys'
season in '63: It was far more promising in appearance than reality.
Maule's exhilarating prediction of a division title set up the Cowboys for
their first meaningful pratfall. Their late-season collapses of '61 and '62
seemed minor compared to their early-season collapse of '63. They lost
their first four games, including two at the Cotton Bowl. Maule's prediction was in tatters by the middle of October. Division champions? The
Cowboys were too young. After the fourth loss, Landry said, "I wish all
those magazine stories had put it on someone else's back. The expectations were just too great."

The offense came down from the high of the year before. Perkins and
Marsh rushed for 700 fewer yards than they did in '62. Clarke had another
solid year, averaging 19 yards on 43 catches, and Howton caught 33 passes
for 514 yards to break Don Hutson's career NFL records for catches and
receiving yardage; he retired after the season with 503 catches for 8,459
yards. Still, the pieces just did not fit as neatly as they had in '62. The Cowboys were ranked in the bottom half of the league in offense.

The defense was Landry's major problem. The Cardinals scored 34
points in the opener. Jim Brown rushed for 232 yards the next week. The
Eagles passed them silly. The Giants scored 68 points in two games. Even
the mediocre 49ers scored 31 points. The Cowboys were a sieve; they
could not stop the run and they could not pressure the passer. Landry's 4-3
alignment worked for other teams, but not the Cowboys. "Everything was
a problem," Jerry Tubbs said.

Landry remained loyal to his creation; he was convinced it would work
one day in Dallas. In fact, he began installing an updated version called the
4-3 Flex. Having watched Lombardi's Packers dominate the league with a
running game based on a "run-to-daylight" philosophy, in which backs

had the freedom to scan the line and choose a hole, Landry devised a scheme in which each of the front seven defenders was responsible for filling a gap, creating a broad wall of defensive humanity that left no "daylight."

"The Flex name came from it being a 'flexible' 4-3," said Dick Nolan, who finally retired in '63 and joined Landry's staff as a full-time defensive assistant. "The goal was to control the line of scrimmage. Not penetrate it, just control it. The goal of any defense was to stop either the run or pass. Lombardi's plan was to stop the pass and make you run the ball the length of the field. The goal of the Flex was to stop the run and force you into long passing situations on third down. It was a hell of a defense, a combination of the 'inside' and 'outside' 4-3. You put one (defensive) tackle right over the ball, and an end two or three feet off the line. The rest of the defense keyed off that."

The Flex emphasized agility and intelligence more than raw speed and power. Enormous discipline was required; even if a play went away from a player, the player had to remain in his gap. "You had to learn not to chase the ball like you had in college," Bob Lilly said, "and you had to learn to depend on the guy next to you to do his job. It was a sophisticated defense. You couldn't just pick it up and go."

Nolan said, "We had a hard time getting players going with it. We had some guys that weren't the greatest football players in the world to begin with."

The '63 Cowboys had a volatile mixture of veterans and young players. "A lot of the older guys were continually bad-mouthing coach Landry," Lilly said, "talking about how the Flex and multiple offense weren't worth a crap and weren't going to work and that kind of stuff. They were in the twilight of their careers and they thought they knew how things worked in the NFL. I think it hurt Tom. If he had been smart and known it was going on, he should have gotten rid of the older players. We had some good young players, and the older guys kind of destroyed our confidence in Tom for awhile. It happened to me and it happened to Meredith."

Landry did not help himself with his cool personal approach. "He was a very good coach and we didn't have the direction he had," George Andrie said, "and he wasn't very good at steering us in the right direction. He wasn't the kind of guy to come out and say everything and tell you what to do. Some guys needed to be told what to do."

No one could see it yet, but a top defense was slowly taking shape. Chuck Howley, a wily linebacker, had joined the team in '61 in a trade with the Bears. He had retired after suffering a broken leg in '59 and was running a gas station when the Cowboys called. Cornell Green, the basketball star converted into a Pro Bowl defensive back, did not even know how to wear hip pads at his first training camp. Andrie was a sixth-round draft choice who had missed his senior year of college football because his school, Marquette University, dropped the sport. Lee Roy Jordan and Dave Edwards joined the team in '63, Jordan as a number-one draft pick and Edwards as a free agent; they would start as linebackers for a decade.

"We were starting to put together a defense," said safety Mike Gaechter, a rookie in '62. "I don't think it was the players so much as the system. The Flex was complicated and it took us a long time to believe in it, but it was the system that made us good more than the talent. Howley was an exceptional player, but the other linebackers were 25 pounds underweight. We didn't have the speed and size of some other teams. Landry made the best of what he had."

Lilly was shifted from end to tackle midway through the '63 season, with the team floundering at 1–5. It was one of the most important decisions of Landry's career, one that fortified the defense for years. Lilly had made the Pro Bowl as an end, but he was out of position there. He was quick for his size, but not fast. His assets were better utilized playing inside.

"Bob wasn't emotional at all in his first two years with us," Landry said. "It was just a natural move for us to move him inside and see what happened. He really had the knack of escape in the middle of our 4-3. He was so quick and strong. It was a completely different thing than playing end. At tackle he was in the middle of things all the time."

Said Lilly: "I was thrilled when they made the change and immediately began playing better. I was never really an end. I had never played the position before coming to the Cowboys. I had played tackle all my life going back to sixth grade. Playing end was totally different. You were responsible for containment, reverses, rollouts, trap plays. It was awkward to rush the passer from there if you weren't used to it. You never got hit much and sometimes didn't even get blocked. It was just too slow for me. I liked to make things happen. I probably would have been an average end if I had stayed there. But at tackle I could use my quickness and I had two ways to rush the passer and I could make things happen. I didn't have to worry about containment. I just read my responsibility and I was gone."

Lilly made All-Pro for the first time the next year, then made it six more times before he retired after the '74 season. Landry had uncovered the cornerstone of a championship defense.

My world as a boy in North Dallas was an *Ozzie and Harriet* idyll, a simple, happy place without anger, crime, or violence. Fathers worked, mothers drove carpools, people lived comfortably. Blacks knew their place; Dallas had an undercurrent of hatred flowing through it, but I had no idea. My idea of hostility was a war between GI Joe and the flinty-eyed Russian, German, and Japanese "enemy" figures available at the toy store.

Our house was in a neighborhood with few other children, so I imported friends to play. We ate canned spaghetti for lunch, raced my "Hot Wheels" cars, and listened to a Davy Crockett album and re-enacted the Battle of the Alamo. Television was not an option; it was still just an occasional fascination, not a daily obsession. My viewing was limited to *Captain Kangaroo,* Saturday morning cartoons, and local kid shows. A hobolike oddball named Icky Twerp hosted *Slam Bang Theater* on Channel 11; we made fun of him at school. The weekend sportscaster on Channel 8, Jerry Haynes, dressed up in a seersucker jacket and a hard straw hat and called himself Mr. Peppermint; he sang songs and staged puppet shows before a studio audience, and he came to my first-grade birthday party.

Sports dominated my life. My parents installed a jungle gym to encourage me to exercise, but I was a lost cause. I played imaginary games for hours, football and baseball and basketball and tennis, all accompanied by dramatic play-by-play monologues. Once a basketball net went up in the driveway, my beloved SMU Mustangs took on all comers. Baseball games were played on a pitchback, a tightly strung net that returned thrown balls; I staged Texas League games involving the Dallas-Fort Worth Spurs. My parents thought I was developing a work ethic when I spent one summer pounding tennis balls off the garage wall, but I was secretly staging an imaginary pro tournament.

The backyard was my private sanctuary, a place to play out my sporting fantasies. It was a rectangular yard that sloped away from the driveway down to a grove of trees at the back edge. It was secluded, surrounded by trees and the house, and I felt comfortable "announcing" at a high volume as I ran around and rolled around in the grass.

"What were you doing out there?" my sister asked, voice dripping with disdain, when I came inside.

"You wouldn't understand," I said, embarrassed.

When I had a friend over, we played catch and waited for my father to come home from work and throw us passes. We took turns as the receiver and the defensive back, and worked up a sweat running pass patterns. My father would draw the ball back by his right ear, like Sonny Jurgenson, and snap passes with a flick of the wrist. "Do I look like Sonny?" he asked.

The Dallas I knew was safe and pleasant, as comforting as spring sunshine. I rode my bicycle to the 7-Eleven on Northwest Highway, bought baseball cards, and drank a Slurpee in the parking lot; there was little danger on the streets, and no sense that parents had to keep their children in sight at all times. On weekends I went with my cousins to Lake Dallas and rode around in a ski boat, or went with friends to Six Flags over Texas, the amusement park in Arlington. I dressed up in a coat and tie and went with the family to summer musicals at the State Fair Music Hall; Pop had season tickets and bought me candy during intermission. Fast food had not come to Dallas yet, so we went out for hamburgers at Goff's on Lovers Lane.

I was a first grader on November 22, 1963, when President John F. Kennedy was assassinated while riding in a motorcade downtown. I was enrolled at the Greenhill School, but our class was meeting at Temple Emanu-El because our school building had burned in a fire several weeks earlier. Soon after lunch, the door at the back of the room creaked open and a janitor poked his head inside.

"Pres'dent done been shot," he said.

We all turned and looked at him, then turned back to look at Mrs. Harrell, our teacher, who was sitting at her desk at the front of the class, her hair swept up in a majestic Jackie Kennedy bouffant. She dropped her head to one side, put her forehead in the palm of her hand, and looked up at the janitor. The room was silent for a long heartbeat.

"You are kidding," she finally said, knowing he was not.

The janitor looked at her blankly and closed the door.

School closed early after we learned that Kennedy had been murdered just a few miles away. My sister and I waited in bright sunshine for our mother to come pick us up; she had heard the news at her regular Friday session at the beauty parlor. My sister, a sixth grader, jumped into the front seat and suggested we move to North Carolina, where our other grandmother lived and no one shot the president.

The city was a still-life painting that weekend; stunned and ashamed, people holed up in their houses. My parents spent the weekend in front of the television. I sat at their feet on Sunday morning, staring up at the set, and watched Jack Ruby step out of a crowd and shoot Lee Harvey Oswald in the basement of the Dallas city jail. It happened too quickly for me to understand that I had just seen a real murder and not a fake filmed in Hollywood.

The Cowboys played in Cleveland that Sunday, barely 48 hours after the assassination. Pete Rozelle would regret his decision to let the NFL's games go on, a decision he later called the worst of his long tenure as commissioner. I was upset mostly that the television and radio broadcasts had been canceled. Late in the afternoon I sneaked into my parents' bedroom and flipped on a radio to hear a final score. The Browns had won, 27–17, and I was naive enough to care.

My grandfather had been among the crowd waiting for Kennedy to give a speech that day at the Trade Mart. He gave me his recollections years later. He had voted for Nixon in '60, but, ever the loyal citizen, was supportive of any president willing to grace Dallas with a visit. He arrived at the Trade Mart early. The crowd swelled and grew impatient at the delay, then recoiled in horror when two busloads of confused journalists arrived without the president; they had lost track of the lead car in the motorcade when it sped off toward Parkland Hospital. Soon, Erik Jonsson, a civic leader and future mayor, announced to the crowd that shots had been fired but it was not "serious." He returned to the podium within minutes to report that the president had been shot. Pop told me later that the assassination and Oswald's murder had sent him into a depression; he had worked all his life to build Dallas, and now he knew it had been shamed in the eyes of the world.

My father knew several doctors who went into the emergency room with Kennedy at Parkland, where my father had served his residency. Just about every doctor in Dallas would later claim to have been in that room, my father said. (When Jack Ruby was ill with cancer several years later, a television newsman whom my parents knew socially called trying to uncover news about Ruby's care; my father's answers were vague.) Twenty years after the assassination, a teenager hired to work the cash register at my mother's bookstore in the Preston Royal Shopping Center turned out to be the grandson of Abraham Zapruder, the dress manufacturer whose eight millimeter film of the assassination showed the world all its gruesomeness. Zapruder's shaky celluloid was analyzed exhaustively by investigators, who built theories around the number of times the camera shook, each shake supposedly representing a gunshot that caused Zapruder to flinch. His grandson laughed; every film his grandpa ever took shook like that, he said.

Such was life for those of us raised in Dallas in those years; the assassination was always around us, our tragic opportunity to root around inside history. When I joined the staff of the *Times Herald* in '79, I found myself working alongside former customers at Ruby's nightclub; Ruby, who died in '67, had courted cops and newspapermen, and the *Herald*'s sportswriters snickered at the dramatic brushes with which historians painted him.

I never did accept that, as a Dallas native, I was supposed to feel guilty about the treachery of Dealey Plaza. Oswald had lived in Dallas and Fort Worth periodically as a child and been back for more than a year when the assassination occurred, but he was not a Texan as we knew it. He had defected from the United States to live in the Soviet Union for awhile as a Marxist. Dallas was a hotbed of right-wing fervor in those days, so angry that Kennedy's advisors had warned him not to come, but Oswald was on the far left politically, not the far right. Dallas might have deserved blame had its right-wing anger contributed to Kennedy's death, but that seemingly was not the case.

The rest of the world did not see the situation so logically, of course. Dallas was widely blamed for the death of a president. The mayor's office and the police station were flooded with hate mail and angry calls. A sign at the Cowboy game in Cleveland two days later called the Cowboys "The Assassins." The overt hatred soon waned, but a vague hostility existed for years. At a conference of mayors in the early '70s, after a long evening of dining and drink, the mayor of Toledo, Ohio, interrupted a conversation to berate Wes Wise, then the mayor of Dallas. "What do you know about anything?" he said to Wise. "Your city killed Kennedy."

As I grew older, I came to understand that my childhood vision of Dallas was incomplete. There were parts of the city that bore no resemblance to mine; my childhood Dallas was just a small part of a divided city marked in many places by closed minds and mean spirits. It was a Sun Belt boomtown with a seething dark side.

Oswald lived in a city that was rife with hatred, a city the rest of the country saw as disturbed and dangerous in the wake of Kennedy's death. Right-wing extremism had a foothold in many cities around the country in those days, but Dallas seemed particularly warm to it. The conservative John Birch Society had a large chapter that included some of the city's wealthiest citizens, most notably Bunker Hunt, Lamar's older brother. On the day before Kennedy's arrival, handbills were spread around downtown with his picture printed beneath the words, "Wanted For Treason." And on the morning of the assassination, a stunning full-page ad with a funereal black border ran in the *Morning News;* devised and funded by conservatives, the ad posed rhetorical questions to Kennedy: Why was the Communist party supporting his reelection? Why was his brother, the attorney general, soft on Communists?

As the years passed, Dallas slowly rebuilt itself out of the emotional rubble of the assassination. New images cast the city in a more favorable light. The Cowboys started the process with their rise to the NFL's elite; suddenly, Dallas was no longer just the city that had killed Kennedy, but also the home of one of football's most glamorous teams. "That was the greatest contribution the Cowboys gave Dallas," Landry said. The Dallas-Fort Worth International Airport, which opened in 1972, added a progressive sheen. The hit television show "Dallas," which ran from 1978 to 1991, reinforced the big-money stereotype so popular before the assassination. "Dallas" was also a hit show in Europe. The city became known around the world as J. R. Ewing's hometown, not just the place where Kennedy was killed.

By the time I returned from college in '79 and began working at the *Times Herald,* the city had undergone a stunning transformation. It was self-confident now, not self-conscious, a city of big dreams and big money filled with young, talented, beautiful people working hard and playing hard. There was still the sadness of segregation and an intrinsic distrust of change, but real estate was booming and money was falling out of the sky. The beady-eyed city in which Kennedy had been assassinated had rebuilt itself into a sophisticated Oz, a center for fashion, media, and commerce, a little Los Angeles with glass skyscrapers shooting into the sky and shiny cars careening down new expressways. The assassination seemed a piece of ancient history, or perhaps some other city's burden.

It was not, of course; it was a grim reality that hastened change, and left a scar on those of us who lived through it. Its impact on my life was neither direct nor dramatic, but I grew up with the embarrassing understanding that others defined my hometown—and therefore me, to some extent—by the events of November 22, 1963. I never felt guilty, and I later came to see Dallas more honestly and critically than I did as a boy, but I was still relieved when time passed, new history was written, and the world no longer thought only of Abe Zapruder's shaky film when it thought of my hometown.

When he moved Bob Lilly to tackle in the middle of the '63 season, Landry also named Meredith the starting quarterback. Meredith's apprenticeship was over after three-plus seasons of alternating with LeBaron, who retired at the end of the year. It was immediately clear that Landry had made a wise decision: Meredith passed for 290 yards in a loss to the Steelers and a stunning 460 yards in a loss to the 49ers, then completed 25 of 33 passes in a victory over the Eagles. The league saw why the Cowboys had waited so patiently for "Dandy Don" to develop. He had a strong arm, a classic delivery, and ran the team with intelligence and style.

The victory over the Eagles, before 24,694 fans at the Cotton Bowl, gave the Cowboys a 3–7 record. They were playing out the string of what LeBaron later called "a real downer year." Near the end of their week of preparation for a game in Cleveland—they now practiced at the Texans' old facility on Central Expressway, having bought it when the Texans left town—trainer Jack Eskridge came running out to the practice field shortly after noon on Friday. He told Landry that he had heard on the radio that President Kennedy had been shot.

"I was standing by Tom because the first-team defense wasn't on the field at the time," Jerry Tubbs said, "and I heard him say something and I went over to him and asked him what happened. He turned to me and he said, 'Oh, some crazy nut just shot Kennedy.'"

Word spread quickly from the sidelines to the practice field. "We were trying to run plays and we were getting sidetracked because we could see that the coaches weren't really giving us their full attention," Perkins said. "Finally we found out what had happened. A pall settled over the team."

Pettis Norman felt a shiver go through his body. Just minutes earlier, while practicing pass routes with Frank Clarke, he had wondered aloud about someone harming Kennedy in Dallas. "Having been here for a year, I had developed a sense of what Dallas was like, and it was really not a very open city at that time," Norman said. "Frank and I were running routes and I said, 'Wouldn't it be something if something happened? If some nut tried to shoot the president?' Because in Dallas there were a lot of nuts around. It was one of those incredible off-the-wall statements. Somewhere in the back of my mind I had formed the impression that somebody was capable of that, that there was enough hate here. Of course, I never really thought it would happen."

Practice continued, but the players' minds were not on it. "No one wanted to hit anyone," Lilly said. Landry finally cut it short. The players went into the locker room and huddled around a radio. Sprawled around the room in silence, they listened to updates on Kennedy's condition and the police search for the gunman. The air was thick with emotion. The players were from all over the country. Some supported Kennedy, others despised him.

"It was a lot like the rest of the country," Norman said. "There were (players) who thought the Kennedys were responsible for all the bad things, all the civil-rights gains. Then there were those who felt love and care for the Kennedys and held them up at the highest level. I was aware that we had that kind of split on the team."

Said one player, who asked not to be identified, "I told one guy that the president had been shot and he said, 'I hope they kill the son of a bitch.' I mean, there was a lot of animosity. The (player) wasn't stupid. But there was just that mentality toward Kennedy and all the things he was doing."

The news of Kennedy's death sent a chill through the squad. "It was a very touching thing," Don Perkins said. "The whole team was consumed by it. All of us, black, white, Republican, Democrat, abolitionist, Whig, Tory, whatever, we all felt he was our president. I think the feeling is different today. If it happened now it would be 'your president' and there would be people out there dancing in the streets. But back then it was a very emotional thing that I don't think we as a country feel anymore."

Pettis Norman said: "When we heard that he had passed away we just stood there in total disbelief. I felt loss and anger and frustration and every emotion in the book. I felt doomed and violated and felt there was no way we could survive this incident as a country. It was like there was a dark cloud hanging over me. I was in a daze and in depression for a long time, just thinking that something like this could happen just a few miles away from where I was standing."

There was talk that the Cleveland game would be canceled, an idea the players supported. "No one wanted to play; our minds were not on football," Lilly said. Rozelle chose to play the games after consulting with White House Press Secretary Pierre Salinger, his classmate at the University of San Francisco. Salinger suggested that Kennedy, an ardent football fan, would have wanted the games to go on.

The Cowboys flew to Cleveland on Saturday, arriving some 28 hours after the assassination. "The baggage handlers wouldn't take our bags off the plane," Lilly said. "Then the porters at the hotel wouldn't take our stuff upstairs. We had to take it up ourselves. I didn't blame 'em. Until the facts came out about Oswald not even being a Texan, it didn't look too good for Dallas."

Said Perkins: "We felt like we were some real hated bastards. The sentiment was that Dallas had killed the president. It wasn't a good time to be a Dallas Cowboy. You wanted to go, 'Hey, I didn't do it, I was at practice.' But we felt tainted. We felt the whole country indicting us."

The next morning the players went to the stadium, went through their pregame routine, and returned to the locker room for final instructions. "In the corridor outside the locker room there was a guard watching a little black-and-white TV," LeBaron said. "Just before we went back out to start the game, we stood there and watched Ruby shoot Oswald. Unreal. As we started out I passed the word back, 'Boys, put your helmets on and keep 'em on.' It was scary."

When the Cowboys ran onto the field, in front of 55,000 fans on a sunny, windy, 40-degree afternoon, they were greeted with silence: no boos, no catcalls, just silence. "Deathly quiet," LeBaron said. The starting lineups were not introduced. The Browns were barely cheered as they ran onto the field. A small band played the national anthem, after which the fans and players stood for a full minute in silent prayer as the wind racketed through the stadium.

Cowboy officials had learned of Oswald's shooting when they arrived at the Browns' offices before the game. They huddled around a television as the game began and the Browns moved downfield on their first possession. When the Browns reached the 22-yard line, a Western Union operator in the press box yelled, "Oswald is dead!" Though no announcement was made, thousands of fans in the stands heard the news on transistor radios. When the Browns scored on a pass from Frank Ryan to Gary Collins, the fans applauded but only a handful stood.

They began to cheer more loudly as the game progressed, but the atmosphere never approached that of a normal Sunday. The public-address announcer made no commercial announcements. A planned halftime ceremony honoring retired Browns receiver Ray Renfro was canceled, replaced by a Pee-Wee football scrimmage. The Cowboys played creditably in a 27–17 loss, but their minds were not on the game.

"We were really kind of worried about getting killed," Lilly said. "We stood there going, 'I wonder if there are any snipers around here?' We wore our helmets the whole time and wore those big parkas."

Said Pettis Norman: "The game should not have been played."

Meredith had his first poor game since becoming the starter. He completed 13 of 30 passes, with four interceptions. "I couldn't hit anybody and we couldn't score," he said in the locker room after the game, "and it's a shame because we had as much drive, fight, and hustle today as we've ever had since I've been a Cowboy."

The team flew home to a city overwhelmed with shock, embarrassment, and sorrow. None of the players were from Dallas and only a few were Texans, but they, too, had to confront the assassination. They were representatives of Dallas, and, thus, were marked by what had happened.

"I think the assassination affected the Cowboys for at least another year," Lilly said, "as far as feeling guilty about our city. A little ashamed. Dallas was kind of a coming star and then all of a sudden it was tarnished. It took Dallas a long time to get over it, of course. It didn't take the team quite as long. Meredith and I, as Texans, probably felt it a little more. Coach Landry, too. We were kind of ashamed of our city. It's not the best mentality for playing football. Somehow, emotionally, it did something."

After Cleveland, the Cowboys played two home games and finished the season in St. Louis, where they were booed. "We got booed the next season, too," Lilly said.

"I don't know that people blamed us as a team for what had happened," Perkins said, "but nationwide Dallas retained a stigma as a volatile place. As a team we had to contend with that. You couldn't come from Dallas in those days and not have the assassination somewhere in the back of your mind."

Chapter Five

My infatuation with the Cowboys did not just materialize without explanation. It was almost inevitable. I was born into a family of football fans, ushered toward the Cowboys by my father and Pop. With gentle tugs, and with affection more than intention, they turned me into a fan, too. Pop bought my tickets to the games, a generosity that underwrote my infatuation; the great, noisy crowd was the element that first whetted my interest. My father took it from there. He was my guide and exemplar. Camping, cars, and fixing up the house did not interest him; he came home at night, read the *Times Herald,* worked on his golf swing, and threw me passes before he settled down to read his medical journals. He was into sports. I followed his lead.

In the early years at the Cotton Bowl, I sat next to my father. I was a child out in an intimidating world for the first time; I needed his hand. After a few years, I moved down the row and sat next to Pop. It was his idea. He loved the idea of the family's youngest and oldest sitting together, but he also wanted me nearby because I knew so much about the Cowboys. He listened to the radio broadcast during games, but often pulled out his earplug to ask me questions.

"Who's number 75, Johnny?"

"Jethro Pugh, Pop."

"Who's that?"

"Defensive tackle. Eleventh-round draft pick. Been in the starting lineup about a month."

Or (shouting amid the cheers following a touchdown):

"Who scored there?"

"That was Reeves, Pop!"

"Rentzel?"

"Reeves, Pop!"

"Reeves?"

"Reeves!"

He was 72 years old when the Cowboys joined the NFL, too old for emotional displays. He was an impassive fan, and increasingly demanding as he grew older. When the Cowboys soundly defeated the Miami Dolphins to win their first Super Bowl in '72, he grumbled after the game about Calvin Hill's meaningless goal-line fumble in the fourth quarter.

Yet the Cowboys had few fans who were more loyal. The 10 season tickets that he bought for their first season represented almost one-half of one percent of their entire season ticket base. When they announced they were moving to Texas Stadium seven years later, Pop, at 79 years old, stood in line almost all night to buy eight bonds and accompanying season tickets. He was proud that his bonds had cost $250 while those across the aisle cost $1,000.

By then he had been going to football games for 50 years. His life encompassed the entire history of organized football in Dallas. Born in Dallas in 1888, he was 12 when high schools began fielding teams at the turn of the century, and 27 when SMU began fielding a varsity during World War I. He was 40 when SMU lost gallantly to Army at West Point in 1928, sealing their popularity around town. He bought season tickets, donated to the Mustang Club as though he were a proud alumnus, and shepherded family and friends to games at Ownby Stadium.

In 1935 he drove to Fort Worth for one of the biggest games in Texas history: SMU against TCU for the national championship and a trip to the Rose Bowl. Both teams were undefeated, TCU led by Sammy Baugh, SMU by Bobby Wilson. The Mustangs took an early lead and held off a rally to win, 20–14. Pop then took the train to Pasadena to see them lose to Stanford in the Rose Bowl.

In the '40s he expanded his loyalty to include Texas and Rice, the universities from which his sons had graduated. He took road trips to see those teams and SMU play, traveling with his sister's grandson, Jack Wertheimer, Jr., a middle schooler. They took the bus to Fort Worth. They took the train to College Station. They took the train to Houston. Pop rode the train at a reduced rate, as a director of the Denison and Pacific railroad, a tiny Texas and Pacific subsidiary that, he joked, could always get you halfway to anywhere you wanted to go.

Jack Wertheimer, Jr., told me years later, "I became a football fan because Pop took me to the games when I was a boy." It was a simple equation, and still true for me a generation later. Ticket prices for Cowboy games at Texas Stadium were much higher than the prices for SMU games in the '30s, but there was no doubt that Pop would invest the thousands it took to reserve space for the entire family at Texas Stadium. I took it for granted, never considering the possibility that we would not go to the games.

Our seats in Texas Stadium were on the 30-yard line in the lower deck on the Cowboys' side. We had the first four seats on consecutive rows. When our Sunday clan dwindled a few years later and it became difficult to fill eight seats—the old guard, including Pop, got too old, and the new guard went off to college and beyond—Pop gave four season tickets to Temple Emanu-El and split the other four between my father and Uncle Milton. They, along with my mother and Milton's wife, Beverly, carried on the tradition through Pop's death in '82, the disappointing Danny White days, and into the euphoric Jimmy Johnson era in the early '90s. My parents were accustomed to the angle of the game from their seats and knew many fans around them.

In the spring of '93, my father forgot to renew his two season tickets. He was 74 years old, still working a full week, and had missed fewer Cowboy games than he could count on one hand in 33 seasons at the Cotton Bowl and Texas Stadium. His failure to renew his tickets was a mistake; he wrote the $1,000 check, slipped it into an envelope, and put the envelope in his coat pocket to mail. Somehow the envelope wound up between the front seats of his car instead of in the mailbox. He then forgot that he had not mailed the check and did not come across it until he was cleaning out his car after the renewal deadline.

Horrified, he immediately phoned the Cowboy ticket office and spoke to an assistant.

"Well," she said, "we can get you two other seats. But not the ones you had."

He was immensely disappointed. His seats were ancillary members of the family, comfortable and familiar. Having to leave them might well have caused him to stop going altogether. But the woman in the ticket office searched the data base on her computer and discovered, to her surprise, that his seats were still available. Even though the Cowboys were sitting on back-to-back Super Bowl victories that spring, their popularity at an all-time high, none of their thousands of new fans had swooped in and taken my father's seats.

"You can still have them if you want them," the woman said.

"Marvelous," my father said, relieved. "We've been coming to the games since 1960, you know."

"That's interesting," the woman said indifferently.

After taking several minutes to finalize the deal, she issued my father a warning before hanging up: "You're on probation now. If you miss the deadline again, you forfeit the seats."

Click.

My father was not thrilled with the rebuke, but he did not argue because he had gotten his seats back. When he told me the story I was pleased that he had been able to renew his tickets under the circumstances, but galled at the Cowboys' lack of respect for him. Probation? That was no way to treat a fan who had supported them for so long, through the bad times as well as the good.

My father's probation sentence was a small, meaningless matter in a billion-dollar industry, but it was emblematic of the attitude searing pro football's soul. Loyalty had become a worthless currency, with players jumping from team to team, and teams jumping from city to city. Tradition was dying in the rush to make money. Teams no longer wanted fans; they wanted clients, wealthy customers who could finance luxury suites and purchase premium seats with extra fees attached. Those tickets paid for skyrocketing player salaries. Those fans were the future. Loyal fans such as my father, and those who inhabited the Cotton Bowl, had become irrelevant. He was just another faceless customer to them, an account number. The loyalty in the relationship ran in one direction.

When I heard that my father had suffered the indignity of having some faceless functionary in the Cowboy ticket office put him on probation, I was happy that Pop was not alive to hear about it. Those were still his tickets, even though he had been dead for more than a decade. He was the one who had stayed up all night to buy them. He was the one who had instilled the Cowboy habit in all of us.

Those tickets represent an epic tale that not only spans the entire history of the Cowboys, but also, through Pop, almost the entire history of Dallas itself. My family was established in Dallas before the turn of the century. Pop saw the first car come down Main Street, and he spent his life helping build the city. He bought Cotton Bowl bonds and original Cowboy season tickets. He had lived in an ordered world in which such loyalties mattered. People in Dallas were supposed to work together, he thought, not against each other. Heaven help the Cowboys if he had been the one they tried to put on probation.

Dallas was still a trembling child of a city when Isaac Tobiansky, my great-grandfather, arrived in 1884. It had emerged as more than a sparse frontier outpost only 12 years earlier, with the arrival of the Houston and Texas Central railroad. When other railroads followed, a city of banks, businesses, and families sprouted by the Trinity River.

Isaac was a Lithuanian who had immigrated from Cherkasse, a small town in Ukraine located on the Dnieper River, south of Kiev. When the czarists initiated a pogrom—a campaign of anti-Semitic terror, all but sanctioned by the government—he left his family to find a home in a safer part of the world. His brothers settled in South Africa. He entered the United States through New Orleans, crossed into Texas, and worked his way north, scratching out a living as a carpenter and Hebrew teacher in Sulphur Springs and Jefferson. When he settled in Dallas he sent for his wife and three children. His wife, Hessie, came only after being assured that she could buy kosher meat and grow watermelons in this strange place from which her husband beckoned. She brought along a bag of watermelon seeds, just in case.

The family moved into a house on Elm Street and joined a small, strong Jewish community. The Sangers, already entrenched as leaders of commerce, provided Isaac with goods to sell in a small store across from the railroad station on Main Street. The family moved to Jackson Street for a while and then to a house on Hickory Street as Hessie delivered four more children, expanding their brood to four boys and three girls. The Hickory Street house had no running water, gas, or electricity, and no sewage system. Water came from a cistern. The boys cut wood to keep the stove running. The family traveled in a buggy pulled by a horse named Bessie. The Tobianskys were barely making it.

Isaac died on Thanksgiving in 1895, several months after the birth of his seventh child. The tightly knit Jewish community suggested to Hessie that she ease her burden and send her four youngest children to the Home for Jewish Orphans in New Orleans. She would not hear of it, and the family remained intact in Dallas. The two oldest girls, Jennie and Minnie, gave piano lessons in exchange for milk. The child who assumed the most responsibility was the second-oldest boy, Louis—my grandfather, Pop.

As a youngster, Pop played in the storm sewers and rode the mule cars that served as public transportation at the turn of the century. He halted his education after eighth grade to help support the family; he took a job with Western Union, delivering messages by bicycle for four dollars a week. The streets of Dallas still were not paved. In time he became a telegraph operator, and proved so proficient taking the presidential election returns for the *Times Herald* in 1904 that the rival Postal Telegraph Co. hired him for its regional office.

When the telegraphers struck in 1907, he worked for a brokerage firm, a cotton merchant, and finally caught on with the Santa Fe Railroad, operating their telegraph wire and working as a stenographer. He rose to the position of chief clerk and was sent to the main office in Galveston, where, in 1915, he lived through a hurricane that flooded the train depot with 12 feet of water. He rode out the storm on high ground, then quit his job and returned to more comfortable surroundings in Dallas. He took a job as a traffic manager for a cottonseed products firm, Texas Cake and Linter Co. His boss was fired for smoking too many cigarettes, leaving Pop in charge. He began trading cottonseed, and did not stop for the next 50 years.

The family shortened its name to Tobian, and Pop joined the Army when World War I broke out. He was a private in a signal battalion based on the West Coast. He decided to get married before his tour began in 1916. He had dated a young lady named Isabelle Franklin, whom he had met at a party at the Oriental Hotel. Pop was streetwise, jaunty, and rakish. Isabelle was delicate, reserved, and intellectual, the first Jewish valedictorian at Ursuline Academy, a Catholic school in Dallas. They were married in Los Angeles; Isabelle took the train to California with her mother. The wedding party consisted of the bride and groom, the bride's mother, the rabbi, and two strangers as witnesses. From this humble beginning came a marriage that lasted 66 years.

World War I ended before Pop went overseas; he returned to Dallas and resumed trading cottonseed products, and he soon decided to go out on his own. He found a patron, borrowed $5,000 from a bank and a few dollars from his mother-in-law (who never let him forget it), and opened Louis Tobian and Co. He was a dealer, not a broker; instead of matching buyers and sellers, he bought cottonseed meal and soybean assuming he could find a buyer. The risk was his; in essence, he was a commercial gambler. Years later, his nephew, Jack Wertheimer, Sr., would eschew the business to run a garage and a tire company. "I can't gamble like that," Jack said.

Pop thrived on it. Cottonseed meal was used to feed livestock or fill oil wells. Soybean was used as feed for hogs. Pop bought from seed mills in Arkansas and Texas and sold all over the country to ranchers, oil drillers, and companies such as Ralston-Purina. He sat behind a battered second-hand desk in a small office, ate barbecue for lunch every day, and spent the day negotiating purchases, sales, and freight rates. Although his education had stopped early, he was fast with numbers and adept at determining when the odds favored him. As he often said, the school of hard knocks had served him well.

Louis Tobian and Co. never had a year in the red, not even during the Depression. In 1921, Pop moved into a new house in the South Dallas neighborhood where Temple Emanu-El was located and many Jewish families lived. Isabelle gave birth to boys named Louis, Jr. and Milton, and then a girl, Jean. Twenty-nine years after she was born, Jean delivered a son of her own—me.

As a child I played at the feet of Isaac and Hessie's children. We celebrated birthdays and holidays with spirited parties, usually at Pop's house on Swiss Avenue. The elders sat around the dinner table long after the food was cleared, the conversation growing louder and leading to a raucous domino game. As a youngster these nights left me feeling safe and wrapped in a bosom of love.

I remember my great aunts and uncles mostly as frail, dusty figures in fancy dress, almost impossibly old. This does not do them justice. They were elderly—six lived into their 80s, two into their 90s, one past 100—

but they were a family of strong personalities, sharp minds, fierce independence, and a quality many Jewish immigrants brought from the Old World: an intense sense of family.

There was Simon, disabled early in life by asthma. Told he had a year to live, he lived another 40. He had a brilliant mind and was mulling long-term investments at his death at age 89. His sister, Minnie, was an independent woman long before it was fashionable. Widowed early, she got into the insurance business, became one of the nation's top saleswomen, and put her earnings into real estate. She died at 88. Her younger sister, Bayla, was the surrogate mother even though she had no children herself. She played in club, city, and state golf tournaments, and donated her trophies as scrap metal to aid in the production of bullets during World War II. She read Jane Austen's *Pride and Prejudice* every year, and Plato's *Republic* every four years during the presidential election season. She lived to be 101.

Bill, Pop's younger brother, was the ultimate old-fashioned Texan. He flew biplanes in World War I, played semipro baseball, ran track, and made a living scouring the oil fields of East Texas for gushers. He drilled his share of dry holes, but hit enough to get by. He was an incessant talker, a famous exaggerator, and a font of cornball wisdom. How far was it to St. Louis? "Oh, about two axle greasings," Bill said. If you offered him a soft handshake, he grabbed your hand and warned, "Don't gimme no fish." One day he sat down with a group of men watching a baseball game on television at the Columbian Country Club. "Pitcher's got a no-hitter going, Bill," someone said. Bill watched for a few moments, until a lopsided score flashed on the screen. "That ain't no no-hitter," Bill said. "A real no-hitter is when no team gets no hits."

His friends challenged him when he went so far as to claim that he had run in the Olympics.

"Actually, I ran against some people who ran in them," Bill said. "Beat 'em, too."

The truth may have been that he ran against some people who ran against some people who ran in the Olympics. Anyway, he beat 'em.

Watching a football game with Bill was more than Pop could stand. He loved his little brother, but Bill spent the whole game exhorting the coaches to use certain strategies, as if they could hear him. Pop would stew in silence until he could take it no longer. "Shut up, Bill!" he would shout.

Chastised, Bill would sit quietly for a few plays and then start chattering again. ("Give it to Bur-nett!" he yelled over and over during a Texas–Arkansas game we all watched together. My father could barely stop laughing watching Pop turn purple.)

Of all the elders, Pop loomed the largest to me. He was an old-fashioned patriarch, the family's protector and benefactor. He gave many of the men in the family their first jobs in his office at the Cotton Exchange Building. He invested in Bill's oil wells and helped set up his nephew, Jack, in the garage business. He was proud that his wife did not have to cook or drive; her only forms of identification were a library card and a Neiman-Marcus charge plate. To my wide eyes, he was the very embodiment of authority. I saw him as an imposing wall of circles: a roundish body, a round face, round eyeglasses as thick as aquarium glass. He dressed formally and nattily, and drove a Cadillac with shark fins and vanity license plates he had arranged through a friend in the Department of Public Safety. The plates read "Pop 88," the number signifying the year he was born. He wore expensive silk ties, smoked Cuban cigars, and told corny, clever jokes. "I'm glad you met me," he said upon meeting someone new. Or: "Did you hear about the two peanuts that went for a walk in the woods? One was a-salted." Ha! "Is there a doctor in the house?" he cried, to his own infinite amusement, when my father brought a group of doctors to the Cotton Bowl one Sunday. I was amazed to learn, years later, that he was slope-shouldered and of average height. He seemed enormous.

He took me on a vacation to Santa Fe, New Mexico, when I was five; I hurtled all the way across Texas and back in the back seat of his big Cadillac. When I slept over at his house I had to get down on my knees and pray before going to bed (unlike at home) and assure him I had done my "lessons" for school. In the morning I awoke to a radio booming in the kitchen downstairs. He was busy fixing breakfast: a creamy rice-and-milk mixture I gulped down. Years later, when he gave his grandchildren copies of his civic awards and programs from the dinners held in his honor over the years, he wrote on mine: "Johnny, you won't find these in the *Sporting News*." He knew where my life was headed.

In the bloom of his life he was fun-loving, guileful, and wry. He won a movie camera in a poker game in 1929 and began chronicling his family on film—enabling me years later to see my mother, at age two, dancing on the running board of the family car. When a car he had sold wound up in the parking lot of a Ku Klux Klan meeting, and an enterprising reporter wrote down the license plates and printed the accompanying names in the newspaper, he wrote a letter to the editor denying his involvement with the Klan. "The only clan I belong to," he wrote, "is Rabbi Lefkowitz's clan." David Lefkowitz was the rabbi at Temple Emanu-El.

His honesty was so formidable that the local cottonseed merchants entrusted him to set the market prices even though he was a trader. He rose before dawn and called in the prices to radio stations, then went to work and traded the products whose prices he had set. The conflict of interest never tempted him; he was the soul of rectitude. When Internal Revenue Service auditors spent a week at his office studying the books after a particularly profitable year, the only mistake they found was a small donation to the League of Women Voters that had been incorrectly written off. They never again wasted their time on Louis Tobian and Co.

Although he was a political conservative, his instincts were humanistic. After he handed over his business to Milton in '48, he turned to a life of civic work. His goal was for the Jewish community to belong to the mainstream of Dallas life, to be accepted, not to be an island. He ran the Dallas Housing Authority from 1951 to 1968, an era during which much of the city's public housing was built. He underwrote blocks of season tickets to the symphony, opera, and theater, and supported any other endeavor that gave Dallas broader shoulders. He served on the boards of the Dallas Citizens Interracial Committee, the National Jewish Hospital, and the National Conference of Christians and Jews.

His knack for leadership engendered admiration throughout the city, among Jews and Christians, blacks and whites, laborers and leaders. He was like a prairie flower, a child of comfortless times who became a man of great accomplishment. He was an honest, capable man who could get things done. Temple Emanu-El turned to him when it needed someone to oversee the construction of a new temple at Northwest Highway and Hillcrest Road in the '50s; the auditorium in that temple is the Louis Tobian Auditorium. Embedded high in the graceful dome of the sanctuary is one of his silver dollars, minted in 1888, the year he was born.

At a testimonial dinner given in his honor in 1964, I asked my father what Pop had done to deserve the attention.

"He's like a Robin Hood, he helps people," my father said.

"Does that mean he robs from the rich and gives to the poor?" I asked.

My father relayed the story to Pop, who thought it was so funny that he gave it to Paul Crume, the *Morning News* columnist, whom he knew. At age seven, I made the front page for the first time.

He was a self-made man who left an enormous footprint on Dallas. I knew Pop only in his crankier old age, but even then he remained an indomitable figure. He established the rituals in the family; everyone else followed his lead. On his birthday, we all went to his house for a dinner of chili and champagne: a menu that summed him up, tough yet cultivated. To this day, even though Pop is long gone, I always try to eat chili and drink champagne in his honor on the fourth day of December—such was the force of his will. I still feel compelled to do it. I suspect I always will.

My father taught me about football. He never played it as an organized sport, but he followed it, knew it, and explained to me its infinite mysteries and complications. He had a profound influence on me as a fan. His habits, qualities, and attitudes became mine. We sat three seats apart at the Cotton Bowl, close enough to share cheers and knowing glances. When the Cowboys were on the road, we were locked into the same airtight compartment at home, riveted to the television in the den, our moods rising and falling with the twists of the game.

He was 38 years older than I was, but we were twins as first-generation Cowboy fans. A passion for the Cowboys was an understanding between us, our private language. We talked about them over meals, while we played catch, and during the winter, summer, and spring as well as during the season. We looked forward to training camp and the return of Cowboy stories in the newspapers. We counted down the days to the Salesmanship Club game in August, a sweltering night affair; driving home, we aimed the air-conditioning at our faces and devised the starting lineup.

He was more analytical than emotional watching a game, more pragmatic than impulsive. Rather than greet a touchdown run with a whoop, he would lean over with a smile and ask if I had noticed the block that sprung the runner. A clinician in his medical work, reliant on logic and deductive reasoning, he saw football through the same scientific lens, as a tactical puzzle more than a physical test, a game of minds more than muscles. His favorite players were elegant and clever, not rough. He loathed the game's inherent violence. I never saw him more repulsed than the day at Texas

Stadium when a fan near us exhorted the Cowboys to "give a Stingley" to an opposing receiver. Darryl Stingley, a receiver for the Patriots, had recently been paralyzed on the field by a hard hit. "That's the worst thing I've ever heard," my father muttered.

Not that he was impassive during a game. He was intense. He would lock himself into a studious pose as the game unfolded, lean forward with his elbows on his knees and his chin in his hand, and deliver a soft, steady monologue of reactions and suggestions, almost a conversation with himself. When a game was slipping away he would allow his emotions to take over. "Come on, Cowboys," he would say with exasperation. He would cheer, too; on long touchdowns he jumped to his feet and cheered the ball-carrier down the field, "Go! Go! Go!"

My mother was the third member of our "club" on Sundays at home; caught in our web of attachment to the Cowboys, she became a faithful fan who fretted about injuries and cared enough to have to leave the room at the end of close games, unable to watch until she heard the cheers or groans in the den. It was a fate that befell many women in Dallas in the '60s. My mother was an insatiable reader who later owned a bookstore, a Wellesley College graduate who organized our world and kept it running. In time, she could trade Cowboy talk with anyone.

When they won, we sailed through Sunday on a high, went to an early dinner at Vincent's or Campisi's, and stayed up to watch the highlights on the 10 o'clock news. When they lost, my father lamented their shortcomings. Their lack of a right cornerback—a hole that tormented them during their first decade—nagged at him. When I came in from my imaginary games in the backyard, he asked if I had beaten the ground with my fist after giving up a touchdown pass, as the Cowboys' Warren Livingston did so often.

His stance on Meredith was firm: He was a fan. While the rest of the city booed and called for other quarterbacks to play, my father admired Meredith's gallant playing style and wicked humor. He laughed uproariously at the stories about Meredith breaking up teammates and opponents by telling jokes and singing country songs at the line of scrimmage. My father would have been a Meredith had he been a quarterback; humor was his touchstone. He was a kidder, always looking for a laugh with a light-hearted touch and an impish deviousness. He asked his nieces and nephews to call him Wonderful Uncle Seymour. He asked to play the role of the Wicked Son at the Passover seder. He claimed he had been kid-napped as a boy and raised by Indians. His nicknames for me were Cath-cart and Jughead. Coming out of Campisi's one Sunday evening he was mistaken for Yul Brynner, the actor, and asked for an autograph; he signed it without giving himself away.

He told everyone he had taught me how to cheat at tennis—he had, sort of—and feigned admiration for athletes who could get away with skim-ming the rules. As the team doctor at my high school's football games, he claimed to relish sending the opposing team's quarterback to the hospital for precautionary tests even if the boy was not badly hurt. ("You can never be too careful," he said, "especially if it helps our defense.") He told his medical students that my mother was a drinker even though she barely touched a drop, and he often claimed that Landry did not understand foot-ball. He was just kidding on all counts, just looking for a laugh. It was easy to see why he admired Meredith, who taunted Landry with irreverent hu-mor.

His father, Isadore, had immigrated just before the turn of the century, a 12-year-old alone and unable to speak English. Isadore came through El-lis Island, married a girl from Baltimore named Molly, moved to North Carolina, and established a successful business: the Arcade Fashion Shop, a women's clothing store in downtown Winston-Salem. My father was Isadore's third and last son, the baby of the family. He was, he claimed, an unmotivated student at R. J. Reynolds High School during the Depression, and was mostly horizontal for four years as a frat boy at the University of North Carolina. He became a serious student and shot to the top of his class when he went to medical school. His older brothers followed their fa-ther into the clothing business.

He served in the Navy during World War II as a doctor in the South Pa-cific, spent a year in China after the war, and came back to finish his med-ical education. He came to Dallas for his residency at Parkland Hospital, following his mentor, a legendary professor named Tinsley Harrison. A fellow resident named Louis Tobian, Jr., invited him to dinner one night; he met my mother at the dinner table on Swiss Avenue. He was 31 and she was 22 when they married in 1950 and moved into a house on Joyce Way, just south of Park Lane. My sister was born two years later. I was born four years after her.

When I was two we moved to Rockbrook Drive, a long street that wound bumpily from Northwest Highway to Walnut Hill Lane in North Dallas. Pop had bought a parcel of land to be divided into two lots, one for us and one for Milton's family. Both families built houses, and I grew up next door to my cousins in what amounted to a family compound with four adults and five kids. I was the youngest, and often overshadowed. My older cousins were accomplished and popular, and my sister was a life force, an A student, a stage star, a head cheerleader, pretty and extroverted and sure of herself. I could not compete, so I retreated to my room with my Lego and my Strat-O-Matic. I was the follower, the little eyes looking up; it was no accident that I would one day feel comfortable in a profession requiring unobtrusive observation. My parents worried that I was too introverted, but they did not try to roust me; they, too, had been the youngest in their families.

My parents were postwar boomers, part of a generation that thrived on long days at the office, Johnny Carson's monologue, and the search for the perfect martini. They went to cocktail parties on Saturday nights. I stayed home with a baby-sitter, whom I invariably talked into playing Lego football. During the week the lines were clearly drawn. My father left for the hospital every day at 7:30, dressed in a coat and tie, and came home before dinner, around 5:30. My mother drove us to and from school and various practices, did volunteer work, and went to the beauty parlor on Fridays. Our dinner schedule was inviolate: steak on Monday, chicken on Tuesday, spaghetti on Wednesday, takeout on Thursday, roast on Friday.

We never knew what my father did at work other than teach students, interns, and residents at Southwestern Medical School and treat patients at the Veterans Administration Hospital. Over the years he took part in landmark clinical studies and trained hundreds of doctors, including a Nobel Prize winner, but he said little about his work at home. He had former students across the country who almost idolized him as a medical role model, but we heard about it from them, not him. Years later, one of his students wrote a glowing tribute in a newsletter headlined, "A Fine Example," drawing a portrait of a wise and compassionate teacher who felt it was a joy and honor to care for patients. Flattered, my father said the praise was overdone. He had no ego. We knew little about his upbringing, his war experience, or his father. Typically, he only told the funny stories. We heard about his best friend the juvenile delinquent, his homely high school flame, and the times he took $20 to the store to buy a carton of milk and kept the change, much to his mother's delight. The only war stories he told were about the knockout martini parties in China.

His avocation was golf, which he took up in a big way, like a lot of men in those days. He was long off the tee, but never overly concerned with his score. He was an aesthete, more interested in his swing than par. Every night after dinner, he spent a few minutes tinkering with backswings and arm extensions in the backyard. Occasionally he would come inside, sigh, and say, "I just retired." He enjoyed the game, but he understood that it was a maddening addiction. He retired a dozen times a year, and always took it up again the next day.

As I grew up and got into sports, I wanted to go to the local college and pro basketball games, minor-league baseball games, hockey games; in the Cowboys' absence I needed to hear the roar of a crowd. My father was a soft touch. At SMU's Moody Coliseum we bought general admission tickets for a dollar and sat on concrete slabs high in the end zone. One night we went to see the Cowboys play the Redskins in a charity basketball game. That interested him. Minor league baseball did not. When I dragged him to see the Spurs play at Turnpike Stadium, he brought a stack of newspapers and magazines to read while I sat on the edge of my seat, glove on, waiting for the foul ball that never came.

In the summer of '65 we drove to Houston to see the amazing new Astrodome. My father was not a serious baseball fan, but he enjoyed the game and wanted to see it played indoors. The Houston Astros played the Los Angeles Dodgers on the day we went. Don Drysdale pitched for the Dodgers. We sat in the upper deck and gaped at the field far below.

A few years later, we were in Boston on vacation, looked out our hotel room window, and saw the lights of Fenway Park. My father and I grabbed a cab to the ballpark and watched the last seven innings. The Boston Red Sox played the New York Yankees. The game turned for the Sox when a ball bounced off Mickey Mantle's glove and went over the fence for a home run.

I was lucky to have him as a father. He was neither stern nor pedantic, but he taught me many lessons. His work ethic was remarkable; I do not remember him ever failing to get up and go to the hospital with enthusiasm. He found the humor in situations; there was laughter in our house, unlike many others. He never complained about money or life's unfairness. Most of all, he supported his children. He came to my football, baseball, and basketball games, which were many and often ill-timed. Every son should feel so important.

Over the years he was consistent in his interests: family, medicine, Cowboys, golf. He was not one to chase a fad. The Cowboys' popularity rose and fell and rose again, but his attachment never wavered. Their Christian image in the high days of Landry and Staubach did not sway him as a Jewish fan. Nor did the antics of Jerry Jones, or the probation sentence from the ticket office. When the opening kickoff was in the air, he was always in line behind the Cowboys, week after week, year after year. He was my role model as a fan. I learned from the best.

A passion for sports is passed down through the generations in many families across the country, of course; young fans become adults and groom new generations of young fans, tutoring them in the traditions and lore of the family's favorite team, just as their elders tutored them. Yet there was no such recycling of attachments in Dallas until my generation came along. The Cowboys did not exist until 1960, and there was no major-league baseball until 1972. As popular as SMU football was, that tradition was difficult to sustain for the simple reason that many people in Dallas attended other colleges. For decades, Dallas was without the intense passions that pro teams encourage. In 1939, my Uncle Milton spent a summer as a camp counselor in Maine and was astonished to hear his campers spend hours discussing the Red Sox. His support for SMU football was tepid by comparison, and he could not fathom the force of a Boston baseball fan's interest.

Young fans in Dallas now take their many home teams for granted, but the city was not always so blessed. Pop had no home teams to cheer for until after he was married. My father's youth was similarly empty of the fan's experience. Minor-league baseball and high school football were his options in Winston-Salem, and football was out because his father was the president of the local temple and the rabbi ate dinner at their house on Friday nights. ("Not only did I have to stay home and miss the football games, but the rabbi ate all the white meat," my father recalled.) My father's career as a fan did not begin until he arrived at the University of North Carolina as a freshman in 1935 and began cheering for a star quarterback named Snuffy Sternweiss.

Check the timeline: Pop did not become a real fan until he was 40. My father began in his late teens. Me? Almost as soon as I was out of diapers.

My world was different. Sports were booming in the giddy aftermath of World War II, becoming commonplace, accessible, and wildly popular. Television was beginning to deliver games into living rooms. Pro football was emerging from the shadows to challenge baseball as the national pastime. Sitting at a confluence of change in sports and society, my father, Pop, and I grew up together as Cowboy fans. We were of three different generations, but we were all first-generation Cowboy fans. We built a tradition together, bringing different assets to the mix. They passed down to me the ability to go to the games and the knowledge to know what I was seeing. I passed up to them the youthful, tunnel-visioned zealousness that would become a staple of life in Dallas, existing in all generations of Cowboy fans that followed mine.

Today, Stephen Wicker Eisenberg, five years old and full of life, is testament to the power of genetics. Thirty-five years after I began following the Cowboys at the Cotton Bowl, I am watching my son re-create my life as a young sports fan with stunning exactitude. Wick already knows the teams in the major leagues, NFL, and NBA, as well as the names of the players and which teams are winning and losing. He spends hours alone in the backyard playing imaginary football, baseball, and soccer games, complete with play-by-play broadcasts. His favorite reading tools are the standings in the sports section. His "dolls" are electric football players painted in NFL team colors. He is his father's child.

He has more natural athletic talent than I ever did, and a gift for baseball and tennis, so he is going to play sports, too. But he also is going to watch, and cheer, and care deeply; I can see it already on his freckled face. His older sister, Anna, is a sportswriter's daughter who knows more about her hometown Orioles than most of the boys in the third grade, but she has other priorities. To Wick, teams and games and players are already a higher calling, an all-encompassing passion, just as they were to me when I was his age.

One Saturday night we entertained another couple for dinner and laughed about Wick's precocious bank of sports knowledge. After dinner I brought him to the table and gave him the names of a dozen major league ballplayers, Orioles, Yankees, Indians, and Braves. Wick stood in the doorway, slightly embarrassed, and answered whether they batted left-handed, right-handed, or both. I was showing him off, just as Pop and my father did with me. He knew his stuff, just as I did.

As I watch him racing around the backyard "broadcasting" the home runs and touchdowns bursting forth from his imagination, I wish I could give him what I had, the weekly ritual of going to Cowboy games with a noisy tumble of uncles, aunts, cousins, parents, and grandparents. It was a warm experience that underlined for me the importance of family. I do not know who would cherish it more, Wick or his grandfather.

Wick will not experience that, for a number of reasons. He is growing up in a different world, one that is infinitely faster, more mobile, and complex. His predecessors, the Tobians, could not have envisioned it. Families do not stay together so readily anymore. We live where we can find work. My cousins, with whom I was raised, have lived all over the country, from California to Maine. My sister spent a decade in New York before returning to Dallas to have a family. I have put down roots in Baltimore. Our family has come apart—not emotionally, but physically. Wick is not a Texan. He is not growing up with the Cowboys all around him. Oh, he knows that his grandparents go to the games at Texas Stadium, and that his father yells at the television when the Cowboys are on. He has a few Cowboy T-shirts, and he dressed as Troy Aikman one Halloween. But he lives in a town mad for baseball, not football, and the Orioles are his religion.

He will inherit a sports world radically different from mine. The Southwest Conference does not even exist anymore, an unsettling reality for Texans raised in the '60s. All traditions are for sale, it seems, stampeded in the rush for TV gold. I have already had to explain to Wick why Cleveland's football team moved to Baltimore, why so many of his favorite baseball players get "switched" to new teams every year, and why there was no World Series in 1994. He is not an expert on collective bargaining just yet, but he is learning about economics as he becomes a sports fan. There is no choice. "When is Cal Ripken's contract up?" he asked one day as we threw grounders in the front yard. I do not recall having that conversation with my father.

The temptation is to say that my world was simpler and better. Wick would disagree. I did not have cable television, with its dizzying array of sports, games, and highlights every night. I did not have sports videos, Nintendo, designer baseball cards, Michael Jordan, or bedsheets covered with the logos of all the major league teams. I did not have a VCR, or a 35-inch color television showing five slow-motion instant replays of every big play. When I tell him what I did not have, he looks at me with pity, as if to say, "How did you live?"

His interest in sports is driven by television. I became a Cowboy fan because I went to the games; Wick has become a sports fan and an Oriole fan because the games have come to him, at home. I take him to see the Orioles now and then, but we scramble for tickets and sit too far from the plate. He is just as happy at home. Television pulls him in as surely as going to the games pulled me. I memorized the players' faces by studying the game programs my father bought for 50 cents; he memorizes them by watching them on television. I took for granted that I would get to go to the games; he takes for granted that every game is on some channel somewhere. The means are as different as the '60s were from the '90s, but the end result—his youthful passion and premature knowledge—are the same. It will be interesting to see if Wick maintains his interest in sports without often getting to experience the sound of the crowd and the thrill of belonging. That was what made me a fan. Maybe he does not need it. Maybe he is of a different generation, with different expectations, and television will keep him interested.

The sports world he is inheriting is an exuberant rainbow of names, colors, and teams, but it is also a cynical place with expensive ticket prices, rapacious owners, and arrogant players who will not sign autographs unless they are paid to do so. Throughout this century, from the time of Pop's life to my father's life to mine, sports was always a growing enterprise, becoming more prominent, more available, more important. In the time of Wick's life, people are beginning to wonder if it is all too big, too expensive, too available, too important. My son has the spark right now, the simple joy of cheering, just as I did. I can only hope that his world does not disappoint him.

Chapter Six

After the Cowboys lost three of their first four games in '64, a fan held up a sign at the Cotton Bowl that read "Five More Years?" Landry and Schramm had said it would take that long to build a quality team when they started from scratch in '60. With gentle sarcasm that spoke for many around town, the fan with the sign was reminding the Cowboys that their original trust had been violated; the team was five years old now, and still losing.

Through the rest of that season and the one that followed, there was no way to know that the Cowboys were in the final stages of developing from a winless expansion team into a championship contender. They finished with a 5–8–1 record in '64 and broke even in '65 at 7–7, but they had long losing streaks in both seasons and defeated just two opponents who finished with winning records. A gradual improvement was evident, but it was impossible to see two decades of prosperity on the horizon.

Such was the meaning of the '64 and '65 seasons, the most important of the Cowboys' developmental period. The team was transformed in those two years. Landry's strategic blueprint, Brandt's scouting apparatus, and cornerstone players such as Lilly, Perkins, and Meredith were already in place, but three new elements introduced in '64 and '65 enabled the team to answer the question that the fan with the sign had posed: No, it would not take five more years to start winning. The three elements were Landry's 10-year contract, two superb rookie crops, and a locker room incident in Pittsburgh midway through the '65 season.

The '64 draft initiated the process. Held in December of '63, just weeks after the Kennedy assassination, it was not a numerical success: Only seven of the 18 players drafted ever wore a Cowboy uniform. But three of those seven were Renfro, Hayes, and Staubach, players who were crucial to the Cowboys' lasting membership in the NFL elite. Renfro provided the ballast in the defensive secondary, Hayes revolutionized football with his stunning speed, and Staubach emerged as the guiding light to the Super Bowl when the team was on the verge of collapse in '71.

Remarkably, none were drafted in the first round. The Cowboys' first choice in '64 was Scott Appleton, an All-America defensive tackle from Texas. His rights then were traded to the Steelers in a deal arranged before the draft; in return the Steelers sent the Cowboys a veteran receiver, Buddy Dial. The trade prove particularly wise when Appleton signed with the AFL's Houston Oilers.

Renfro was selected in the second round. He was an All-America halfback from the University of Oregon with sprinter's speed and darting moves, but he was small and fragile and scouts were concerned about his durability; he wasn't selected until the ninth round of the AFL draft. He had cut his hand shortly before the draft; angry at hearing the news of Kennedy's assassination, he smashed a mirror and accidentally sliced his wrist. There were concerns about his ability to carry the ball.

Hayes was taken in the seventh round, Staubach in the tenth. Their selections were buried in the sports pages, deemed of little importance. That seems absurd now, but both were "future" selections. Hayes had to play another year at Florida A&M before he could turn pro, and Staubach not only had to play another year for Navy after winning the Heisman Trophy as a junior, but he had a four-year Naval service commitment to fulfill before he could become a full-time pro. In those days teams often passed up the immediate benefit of a draft pick to make such long-term personnel investments. The NFL–AFL war was raging, and front offices were obsessed with procuring the rights to players and getting the jump on the other league in contract talks. The Cowboys chose a dozen "futures" in their first four drafts.

Six weeks after the draft, on February 6, 1964, Landry signed a 10-year contract to go into effect when his original five-year deal expired after the '64 season. The Cowboys were committed to him as their head coach for the next 11 years. The football world was incredulous; long-term contracts were unheard of, and Landry, though indisputably bright and innovative, had flopped so far as a head coach. His record was 11-38-3. Cotton Bowl fans were booing him. Some veteran players were disdainful of his ideas, undermining his attempt to sell younger players on his vision. There were rumors that he might be fired.

The 10-year contract was ownership's answer to such rumbles, a statement of Murchison's faith in the struggling young coach. It relieved the growing pressure on Landry to win sooner than later, gave him a mandate in the locker room, and provided the latitude for him to maximize his powers of innovation. It was far more than an unproven coach could have asked for, and it enabled Landry to develop into a Hall of Fame coach.

To go along with their new commitment to the head coach, the Cowboys introduced new uniforms in '64. Schramm, always keenly attuned to images and appearances, was displeased with the old look. "It wasn't classy," he said. He borrowed from several sources to arrive at the new look. "I wanted to get away from white pants," he said. "I liked Green Bay's uniform, with the gold pants. Then I saw Georgia Tech. They also had gold pants, but they had a real good-looking white jersey with the numbers on top of the shoulder pads rather than on the arms. I thought that look was terrific. I copied Georgia Tech for the Cowboy uniform."

The Cowboys' new home uniform consisted of a white jersey with royal blue numerals on the shoulder pads and three royal blue stripes on the arms; metallic silver pants with a white stripe down the side; and a metallic silver helmet with a large royal blue star on either side.

"The metallic color was a new color," Schramm said. "The manufacturers had to make a new dye with new materials. It was a unique color that became associated with the Cowboys. The new uniform was a big deal in the image and popularity of the Cowboys; it was classy and original and people loved it. Whenever there was a poll picking a favorite uniform, we won easily."

The Cowboys were the only team in the league that wore white jerseys at home. "Several factors went into that," Schramm said. "One was the heat in Texas early in the season. Our players were a lot cooler wearing white. The other teams wore dark at home, so, as a result, we wore white every week; fans saw us in the same jerseys every week, home and away, year after year, and that helped us establish our identity. Plus, the dark blue jerseys didn't look too good with the metallic pants."

The switch to more appealing uniforms coincided with a major improvement on the field, particularly on one side of the ball: In '64, their fifth season, the Cowboys finally began playing capably on defense. The younger players were becoming accustomed to the Flex principle of filling a lane instead of chasing the ball. Lilly, properly positioned at tackle, made first-team All-Pro. Renfro was converted to safety because of concerns that he could not take the pounding at running back, and he proved so adept that he was named the league's Rookie of the Year. Renfro and Cornell Green gave the Cowboys two pass defenders who could cover any receiver, a key component of the 4-3 Flex, which utilized seven players to stop the run and left pass defenders in single coverages.

During the '64 season, the Cowboy defense allowed 89 fewer points, 55 fewer first downs, and almost 1,500 fewer yards than it had in '63. Only three teams allowed fewer points. "The improvement," Lee Roy Jordan said, "was just a matter of us getting to know each other and the defense. Just basic growth and maturity."

Renfro added another dimension with his kick returns. His season total of 1,017 yards in kickoff returns set a team record that stood for 25 years, and he also ranked among the league leaders in punt returns. He was a swirl of darts and feints with the ball in his hand, and the fans, media, and even Renfro's teammates wanted it in his hands more often. Landry's refusal was highly unpopular.

Despite the improvements, the Cowboys made no headway in the standings; their 5–8–1 record in '64 was identical to their mark from two years earlier. The problem now was the offense, which finished 13th in the league in scoring. Landry had hoped the passing game would soar with Meredith throwing to Dial and Tommy McDonald, a Pro Bowl receiver obtained in a trade with the Eagles, but Meredith struggled and Dial was injured. Don Perkins and Frank Clarke saved the offense from complete collapse; Clarke's 65 receptions set a team record that would stand for 19 years.

Meredith had a terrible time in his first full season as the starting quarterback. He strained knee ligaments when hit by the Packer's Ray Nitschke in a preseason game, and the injury bothered him all season. He reinjured the knee in the regular season opener, a loss to the Cardinals, and it buck-led in the final moments of a 23–17 loss to the Steelers in the third week. He suffered shoulder and collarbone injuries later in the season. He still took most of the snaps, but he completed less than half of his pass at-tempts, threw almost twice as many interceptions as touchdowns, and made critical mistakes in the clutch. In two close losses he was penalized for crossing the line of scrimmage before throwing touchdown passes that would have given the Cowboys the lead. Cotton Bowl attendance was ris-ing—the average crowd in '64 was 38,380 fans, up 42 percent from the year before—but there was frustration in the stands, much of it aimed at Meredith. He heard as many boos as cheers.

In the draft that followed the season, the Cowboys responded to the boos by selecting Craig Morton, a tall, strong-armed quarterback from the University of California, with their number one pick. The front office in-sisted that Morton would be groomed to take over when Meredith was done, but no one was fooled; Morton would be an alternative if Meredith continued to struggle. So would Jerry Rhome, an All-America passer from the University of Tulsa, who had been drafted as a future selection the year before and joined the team in '65.

The rookie crop of '65 would prove particularly bountiful. Aside from Morton and Rhome, there was Jethro Pugh, an 11th-round pick who would start for a decade at defensive tackle; Dan Reeves, a free agent who played little as a rookie but became a key figure beginning in '66; and Ralph Neely, an All-America offensive tackle from Oklahoma, who became the best lineman in Cowboy history as soon as he suited up.

Getting Neely suited up was a major endeavor. He had signed contracts with the Cowboys and Oilers, and not until June did a U.S. District Court judge rule that he was Cowboy property. That ruling was later overturned, forcing the Cowboys into an out-of-court settlement in which they gave the Oilers several draft picks and agreed to play several exhibition games in Houston.

Colin Ridgway, a punter who had represented Australia as a high jumper in the 1964 Olympics, joined the team as a free agent from Lamar Tech. His leg was so powerful, according to Cowboy assistant coach Er-mal Allen, that he might average 50 yards per punt once he mastered the technique. Nicknamed "Boomer," he kicked an 86-yarder in practice and a 52-yarder in an exhibition game at the Cotton Bowl, for which he was given a standing ovation, but he was still raw and wildly inconsistent; he hit Landry, Schramm, and Murchison in the head with practice punts and shanked several in exhibition games. (He spent most of that year on the taxi squad and the next year in a minor professional league after kicking a ball straight up into a stiff wind in a San Francisco exhibition, and the Cowboys waived him in 1967.)

Hayes had by far the biggest impact of all the rookies who joined the Cowboys in '65. Few rookies in NFL history have had a bigger impact on his team or on the entire league. Anointed the "World's Fastest Human" for winning the 100-meter dash at the '64 Summer Olympics in Rome, Hayes came to the Cowboys as the swiftest man ever seen on a football field. He was too fast for man-to-man pass coverage; no single defender could keep up with him. His routes were neither precise or intricate, but who cared? He just sprinted by defenders on his way to the end zone. As a rookie he averaged 22 yards a catch and caught 12 touchdown passes, both league highs. He caught 46 passes in all, including one for 82 yards. His speed would change the very face of the game in the coming years, forcing teams to adopt zone defenses.

As the '65 season began, it appeared the Cowboys finally were arriving as a popular playoff contender. The largest crowd in their history, more than 59,000 fans, watched them rout the Giants, 31–2, in the season opener at the Cotton Bowl. The next week, more than 61,000 fans watched them beat the Redskins, 27–7, with Hayes scoring one touchdown on a pass reception and another on an end-around.

But the two wins were just a tease. The Cowboys lost in St. Louis the next week, came home and lost to the Eagles, then lost three straight road games in Cleveland, Green Bay, and Pittsburgh. That was five losses in a row, their longest losing streak since their first season. Landry benched Meredith and started Morton in one game, then tried shuttling Morton and Rhome in another. Meredith returned in Pittsburgh and completed only 12 of 34 passes.

In Pittsburgh, Landry broke down in the locker room as he addressed the team after the game. His team was 2–5. His career record was 18–51–2. His quarterback situation was a mess. The Cowboys were going home to play three straight games at the Cotton Bowl, where the fans would boo Meredith and anyone else with a star on their helmet. It was hard to fault the fans for their displeasure. The Vikings, who had begun play a year after the Cowboys, had gone 8–5–1 in '64 and were 4–3 midway through the '65 season. The Cowboys were floundering.

"Coach Landry really broke down in the locker room that day in Pittsburgh," Lilly said. "He told everyone to get out except the players and coaches. He told us, 'You all give me 100 percent and do everything I ask. I studied the Flex and the multiple offense going back 50 years and I believe it's the way of the future, but it isn't working.' He took the blame himself. He really started crying, got all choked up. It was the turning point of the Dallas Cowboys."

Said George Andrie, "Landry basically said he was quitting. He said that he wasn't going to coach anymore, that he was going to turn the team over to someone else. It was a very emotional speech, a motivating speech. We turned it around after that. Until then we were just a bunch of young guys having a good time. Landry shook everybody up in Pittsburgh. Everybody started to address their own situations. I think we kind of realized that this was a serious thing. We picked it up after that, and not just a notch. I think we picked it up a number of notches."

Three days later, Landry said Meredith would start at quarterback for the rest of the season. He would later say it was his toughest decision in 29 years as the Cowboys' coach. The fans were tired of Meredith. They thought he was a loser, and wanted Morton, the young gunslinger. But Landry had made the right call; making Meredith the starter was the beginning of the last phase of the Cowboys' development into contenders.

They broke the five-game losing streak with a 39–31 win over the 49ers, and more than 57,000 fans watched them beat the Steelers the next week to improve their record to 4–5. The next week, a crowd of 76,251 fans jammed the Cotton Bowl to watch the Cowboys play the Browns. It was the first sellout in franchise history, in the 39th home game.

The Browns were an attraction. They were the defending NFL champions, they had Jim Brown, and they were running away with the Eastern Division title with a 7–2 record. The game was nationally televised. The Browns built a big lead on a long punt return by Leroy Kelly, but the Cowboys rallied. Late in the game they reached the one-yard line with a chance to score the tying touchdown, but Meredith called a pass instead of a run and threw an interception. The Browns won, 24–17.

Gary Cartwright's game story in the next day's *Morning News* began: "Outlined against the gray sky rode the Four Horsemen: Pestilence,

Famine, Death, and Meredith." The interception on the one-yard line became an infamous play for Meredith, an affirmation of his reputation as a quarterback with a knack for making devastating mistakes.

"I was sitting in the stands that day," said Jack Anthony, an attorney in Dallas, "and I'll always remember the look on Meredith's face on the sidelines after he threw that interception. It was a look of pain and depression I had never seen in him before. I'd never seen anything like it. He was standing there next to Landry, and Landry never said a word to him. The fans were all over him."

A loss the next week put the Cowboys at 4–7 with three games to play, their season seemingly lost, but they defeated the Eagles and Cardinals and suddenly had a goal to play for: A victory in their last game would give them a 7–7 record and second place in the Eastern Division, qualifying them for the Playoff Bowl, a postseason game matching the runners-up from the two divisions. The Cowboys went to New York and beat the Giants, 38–20, with Meredith throwing three touchdown passes. In their sixth season, with a .500 record, they would grace the postseason for the first time, playing the Colts in the Playoff Bowl at Miami's Orange Bowl.

The players flew to Miami and spent a week preparing for the game. "We had arrived, that was how we saw it," Neely said. "Never mind that this was the losers' game. It was the playoffs. We didn't know any different. I mean, we were just so happy to be there. Lilly, Don Talbert, George Andrie, and I, we rented a white Cadillac convertible and partied all week. We drove that sucker straight from practice right on to Miami Beach, buried it up to the axle, and had beer iced down in that thing all week long. We were too naive to be serious."

Lilly said, "We went to the dog races, we went to jai alai. We called it 'j-eye, a-lie.' We had never been out of Dallas, basically. We were the youngest team in the league. We shouldn't have been there. We weren't good enough. But there we were."

Though Schramm later said that making the Playoff Bowl in '65 was "one of the happiest, greatest thrills we ever had," the front office was unaccustomed to success. Colts owner Carroll Rosenbloom paid for his players' wives to come to Florida, staged a team party at a dog track, and had an open bar and free food at the team hotel. "We had none of that," Lilly said. "No wives. No food. We just ate at (team) meal time."

Jordan called his college coach, Alabama's Bear Bryant. "We had played in the Orange Bowl when I was there and gotten treated much better," Jordan said. "I called coach Bryant and told him, 'Coach, they're not treating us real good down here.' I mean, we went to the dog races on our own and looked behind us and there was this big roped-off section for the Colts. I asked coach Bryant if he could set up something like that for us. He called someone and took care of it."

At the team hotel, Meredith put everyone's drinks on a tab and signed Schramm's name. "Don was offended by what was happening," Lilly said. "He said, 'Don't worry, I can sign Tex's name.' So we all just helped ourselves. Well, after about a month we got these letters from Tex saying we owed him two hundred something dollars apiece. I don't think he ever collected, but he was very angry."

The Colts were a veteran team led by Johnny Unitas, Lenny Moore, Raymond Berry, and Jim Parker. They had gone 10–3–1 during the season and lost the Western Division title on a controversial last-second field goal in a playoff with the Packers. They had played in the championship game the year before. They were far more accomplished and experienced than the Cowboys. But both of their quarterbacks, Unitas and Gary Cuozzo, were injured. A halfback, Tom Matte, would have to play quarterback against the Cowboys.

"I think a lot of people on our side felt, 'Well, we'll just go out there and win because they don't have a quarterback,'" Tubbs said. "But people weren't really motivated. I was kind of disgusted. Everybody was worried about who was getting this and getting that, and they voted on postseason shares and stuff like that. We tried to prepare. We had meetings and worked out and all, but we just didn't do well. We weren't motivated and it showed. We got out there and stunk it up on both sides of the ball. It was a shock."

Calling the plays with the help of a cheat sheet taped to his wrist, Matte played solidly at quarterback. The Colts won, 35–3. A sportswriter asked Landry whether the offense or defense deserved the blame for the defeat. "It was a team effort," Landry said. The Cowboys had been put in their place—but not for long.

My parents hosted a party on the day of the Playoff Bowl. It was a sunny, cool afternoon. My mother served chili and champagne, and my father invited the chairman of his department at the medical school. We ate lunch and watched the game in the den. The whole city was excited; 2,000 fans had traveled to Miami to watch the game in person. No one cared that it was just the Playoff Bowl; it was a postseason game and we were certain the Cowboys would win. In our provincialism we never considered that the Colts were the better team, and we had no idea that the players had spent the week drinking beer on the beach and gallivanting around Miami. The Colts' lopsided victory was a shock—not that it should have been. My parents' party broke up long before the final gun. I went outside to play football in the backyard. An imaginary game was preferable to the real thing.

The day was disappointing, but I was growing up. For six years I had gone to games, admired the players, memorized their statistics, and emulated them in the backyard. I was a cute fan, wise beyond my years. Now I was beginning to understand what was happening. I turned 10 years old the next fall, graduated from the school of hero worship, and entered the prime years of my loyalty. I became a real fan, able to comprehend, converse, and criticize. The Cowboys became a championship contender at the same time; we had experienced our infancies together in the early days at the Cotton Bowl, and in 1966 the Cowboys and I came of age together.

The complicated outline for success that Landry had stuck by so doggedly suddenly leapt off his blueprint and became a reality. The core players on defense were experienced and comfortable in the 4–3 Flex; the defense allowed the fewest rushing yards in the league, and only 17 points a game. On offense, the Cowboys were a multidimensional fury; between Landry's multiple sets and motion, Hayes' speed, Meredith's big-play touch, Perkins' stubborn running, and the emergence of a new and unlikely star in halfback Dan Reeves, the offense overwhelmed the league.

Strangely enough, it all started with an injury to Mel Renfro. Frustrated that he could not develop an outside running game to complement Perkins inside, Landry finally relented and put Renfro at halfback when training camp began in '66. "There was this thing Steve Perkins (of the *Times Herald*) got going, the 'Move Mel to Offense' campaign," Renfro recalled. "The fans really got into it. Tom called me in during the offseason and said, 'What do you think?' He told me to put on some weight and he would try me at halfback."

Renfro was a sensation in the exhibition season, averaging almost eight yards a carry, and he started the regular-season opener against the Giants at the Cotton Bowl. But then Landry's worst fear was realized: Renfro was injured on a run near the goal line. "Henry Carr was chasing me and fell over the back of my foot and broke a little bone in there," Renfro said.

Reeves replaced him in the backfield. It seemed a sizable diminution of talent; Renfro was a spectacular threat, and Reeves was a slow, obscure second-year player who had failed as a receiver and defensive back the year before. He had starred in college as a quarterback at the University of South Carolina, but he seemed to lack the speed to excel in the pros. "They had almost cut him three or four weeks earlier," assistant coach Dick Nolan said.

They were fortunate they didn't; Reeves caught three touchdown passes from Meredith as the Cowboys wiped out the Giants, 52–7, and was installed as the starting halfback. Renfro never played another down on offense. "I was out for six weeks," Renfro said, "and by the time I came back Danny was doing great. I went back to defense."

The offense was fine without him. Reeves was an unusual player who helped in many ways. He could run with the ball. He could catch passes coming out of the backfield. He could throw option passes, utilizing a skill left over from his days as a college quarterback. "He wasn't fast at all, but he was big enough to play as a running back and he had great balance and elusiveness," Nolan said. "And he was a smart player. He knew his assignments. He could throw the ball. He would give you a good day's work."

He gave the Cowboys many good days of work in '66. He rushed for a team-high 757 yards, 31 more than Perkins, and caught 41 passes for 557 yards. He scored 16 touchdowns. He completed three option passes. "We didn't think he would be any good at all," Landry said, "and he really helped the offense. He was a great receiver, a really smart player. He made a lot of big plays."

The whole team made big plays that year, particularly in the first month of the season. After beating the Giants so decisively in the opener, they came from behind at the Cotton Bowl to beat the Vikings and scrambling Fran Tarkenton, 28–17, went to Atlanta and beat the Falcons, 47–14, and returned home to devastate the Eagles, 56–7. What a month! The Cowboys were 4–0. They drew more fans in the three Cotton Bowl games than they had in any of their first four seasons. They scored 24 touchdowns. They were stretching the limits of the fans' imaginations. Meredith passed for a combined 752 yards and 10 touchdowns against the Eagles and Giants.

Hayes caught 195 yards in passes against the Giants, and scored three touchdowns against the Eagles. Howley returned a fumble 97 yards against the Falcons. Les Shy, a reserve halfback, broke a 68-yard run against the Eagles.

Their pace slowed, inevitably, with a tie in St. Louis and a loss in Cleveland, but it picked right back up again. Meredith completed an 84-yard touchdown pass to Pete Gent, and Renfro returned a kickoff 87 yards for a touchdown in a 52–21 defeat of the Steelers at the Cotton Bowl in late October. Meredith threw a 95-yard touchdown pass to Hayes in Washington in November. Wild and wonderful things were happening every Sunday.

I was in fourth grade, and madly in love. I doubt I would have become so fanatical about a losing team, but the Cowboys were losers no more. Not only were they winning, they were winning with big plays and thrilling players. Just the sight of Hayes and Renfro dropping back to return kicks sent a charge through the Cotton Bowl. I lived for the jubilation of Sunday afternoon. Making it through the school week was a test of my limited patience.

It was the year I discovered the sports sections in the newspapers, and my life would never be the same. My parents took both local papers, the *Morning News* and *Times Herald.* The more liberal (and less popular) *Times Herald* was their preference, but they read both. So did I, beginning in '66. On Monday mornings I jumped out of bed, dressed quickly, and ran to the breakfast table to read the *Morning News* before leaving for school. My father had arisen earlier, fetched the paper from the driveway, and left the sports section at my place at the table. Eating a Pop Tart and Cocoa Puffs, I experienced Sunday all over again as I read the stories and studied the pictures and statistics.

On Monday afternoons I waited in the driveway for the paperboy to deliver the *Times Herald.* It arrived shortly before my father came home from work, in the shadowy early-evening light. I ran inside with it, pulled off the rubber band, yanked out the sports section, and spread it on the floor in the den. As dinner cooked in the kitchen, with its smells drifting through the house, I flopped on my belly, kicked my legs in the air behind me, and took one final trip back to Sunday, savoring the words and pictures and committing the statistics to memory.

The rest of the week's papers were never quite as dramatic, but there was a steady stream of news, profiles, and columns. Until then I had used trading cards and game programs to bring the Cowboys home, but the sports sections were even better. There were always pictures and quotes from the players that made it seem as if they were talking directly to you. My appetite was insatiable. Much of my vast body of Cowboy knowledge began to come from the papers.

The sportswriters became almost as familiar to me as the players. Bob St. John covered the beat for the *Morning News.* Sam Blair wrote columns. Steve Perkins covered the beat for the *Times Herald.* My father's favorite writer was Blackie Sherrod, the *Times Herald's* columnist. He wrote with a singular flair, making points with ironic humor instead of overwrought prose. You could tell he was not a typical sportswriter, interested only in box scores; he made references to literature, movies, and politics. Sportswriters were "ink-stained wretches." The Cowboys were "Your Heroes." His "Scattershooting" column, a long gathering of facts and opinions, was the best part of the Sunday paper. My grandmother, who had studied Greek and Latin, thought Blackie's columns were wonderful. "I loved reading him," said Calvin Hill, who joined the Cowboys as a rookie from Yale in '69.

Blackie and the other sportswriters had a powerful effect on me. I began typing up accounts of my imaginary games. For awhile I went next door to my cousins' house and used a typewriter in their study, but then my father brought home a small portable and I retreated to my room to write game stories, with phrases and styles stolen from my favorite writers. There was always a statistical chart at the bottom; no game was legitimate without statistics.

It was the first stirring of a love affair with newspapers that would shape my life unlike any other affection. Later on, I became the editor of my high-school paper, and then in college worked long hours as a sports reporter and columnist at Penn's school paper, the *Daily Pennsylvanian.* My column was titled "The Lone Star."

When I went to work at the *Times Herald* in '79, my main job was covering high school sports, but I also helped cover the Cowboys on Sunday afternoons at Texas Stadium. The *Herald* ran a dozen stories, columns, notebooks, and features on every game, a Herculean task requiring almost the whole staff. I was a minor figure assigned to write a non-Cowboy sidebar or a notebook, but I still felt like a king sitting in the enclosed, air-conditioned press box at the center of the Cowboy world. My parents sat just below the press box, and I always took a walk downstairs to see them before the game. I wore a press pass, a slip of cardboard attached to my waist, and my father always managed to mention to those sitting around him that I was covering the game for the *Times Herald*. He could have disapproved of me for using my Ivy League education to become an "inkstained wretch," but he beamed at his son who was important enough to cover the Cowboys. I can only hope I will treat my son with as much respect when the time comes.

Blackie was still the columnist at the *Times Herald* when I began working there. He had a gruff demeanor and spent his days holed up in his office, venturing out only to ask questions about old movies, World War II, or other esoterica. The answers to his questions inevitably appeared in his column the next day. (Ida Lupino!) The joke among the young staffers was that the older editors and writers would jump out a window if Blackie demanded it. We all idolized him, of course; he was a Texan's Texan, raised in Belton, a World War II veteran, and I feared he saw me as a spoiled son of privilege, but he was nice to me and occasionally asked me questions, and I could tell he respected my work. Years later a friend of his told me that I was one of two young writers Blackie had said he would use if he were building a sports section from scratch. I considered that the highest possible compliment. Out of the blue he quoted me in a "Scattershooting" column one Sunday—a line from one of my *Baltimore Sun* columns—and my mother called that morning as soon as she saw it. It was as if I had finally succeeded.

On autumn Friday nights in the '60s, I went to high school football games. My school, Greenhill, ran from nursery school through 12th grade, and all the students were encouraged to support the high school varsity. We went to every game after my older sister became a cheerleader and my father agreed to serve as the team doctor.

There were dozens of high school games around Dallas on Friday nights. Driving to ours, I sat in the backseat of our station wagon and picked out the light standards of the other games in the distance, rising into the night like giant illuminated insects. I followed the big public school teams in the papers and often knew which teams were playing under which lights. I wondered what was happening in those games.

Greenhill played its home games on a dimly lit yellow-green field located behind the gym. Several hundred fans packed into bleachers on either side of the field. There was a soda stand behind one end zone and an electric scoreboard behind the other. A few bulbs usually were blown out on the scoreboard, making it difficult to differentiate between a five and a six. Our team, nicknamed the Hornets, wore uniforms identical to those of the Green Bay Packers, with gold pants, green jerseys, and a large G on the helmets. The players dressed in the gym and ran onto the field through painted paper banners held up by the cheerleaders. ("Let's cheer the Hornets onto the field!") We could hear the public-address announcer and the roars of the big crowds at nearby Loos Stadium, a major high-school venue.

My friends and I watched the first few plays and then headed for an open field behind the end zone, where we picked sides and played a touch football game in the dusky fringes of the artificial light. We stopped to watch the varsity when the crowd cheered or the play came to our end of the field. At the end of the night I fell into the backseat of the car, sweaty and exhausted. The next morning I turned to the high-school pages in the sports section and located the small story about the Greenhill game, phoned in by a stringer.

Football was all around me, an impassioned, secular church. It was inevitable that I would play myself. My parents outfitted me in second grade with a red jersey and pants, a red helmet, and a set of shoulder pads. I put them on and raced into the backyard, glowing with pride. Imitating the players on my football cards, I cradled a ball in my right hand and thrust my arm out to fend off a tackler. My father took a picture. I was smiling behind the plastic bars of my face mask; my baby teeth had not fallen out yet.

My dream was to play the game, not watch it or write about it. I closed my eyes and saw myself coming down the ramp at the Cotton Bowl in a Cowboy uniform, cheers raining down. I saw myself skirting the line of scrimmage with the ball in my hand, turning the corner, and sprinting down the sidelines. I was young enough to believe it could happen.

Organized football did not begin until fourth grade. My friends and I could barely wait; we played at recess, on Saturdays, any time we could. We even played one-on-one if no one else was around.

Organized baseball started first, in the summer before third grade. We played in a slow-pitch hardball league sponsored by the Town North YMCA. I was put with my classmates on a Greenhill team. I was a second baseman, and a dead pull hitter. In one game I caught a line drive and tagged out a runner for an unassisted double play, and the parents gave me an ovation. My parents came to every game, and Uncle Bill, the old semi-pro outfielder, even came out a few times; he stood behind the backstop and hollered at me to keep my body in front of ground balls. We didn't win many games that first summer, but we won the championship the next summer. Our coach pitched whiffle golf balls during batting practice and kept elaborate statistics, which thrilled me. We were credited with a hit every time we reached base, regardless of whether the other team had made an error (which it usually had). I hit .820 that summer and went home with a big trophy.

With that triumph fresh in our minds, we started fourth grade and arrived at our reckoning point as young athletes. It was time for organized football; time to merge my fantasy world with the reality of putting on a helmet and getting hit. The league was also sponsored by the Town North YMCA. Most of my classmates signed up. On a crisp Saturday morning in September we met at the Y with the other teams for an organizational day. Uniforms were handed out. The field turned into a rainbow of red, blue, yellow, orange, and green uniforms. We did calisthenics and ran pass routes as the parents who had volunteered as coaches began positioning us. Then a Y official came by and told us we had so many players that we had to split up into two teams. We looked at each other in disbelief; this was not what we had planned.

The officials motioned over two other men with clipboards. They watched us practice for a few minutes, talked briefly among themselves, and split us into two teams without asking for suggestions from the parents. A disaster occurred; my best friends Greg and Joe were with me, but all the good players were on the other team. The division of personnel had left our team horribly undermanned.

Alas, there was no turning back. We received our schedule and began practicing after school for our first game. Several fathers left work early to coach us. They did their best; one of them diagrammed a few plays on a piece of paper and sent copies home for us to memorize. (Our playbook!)

The rules called for six men on a side and four six-minute quarters. It all sounded impossibly exciting.

I was the quarterback. I gathered the team in the huddle and barked out a play, and we clapped our hands in unison, yelled "break," and raced to the line of scrimmage, all but growling with feigned ferocity. Sometimes we ran the plays reasonably well. I took the snap from center and handed off to a back, or I retreated and threw a short pass to an end. There was no way of knowing that we were smaller, slower, and weaker than the teams we would play. In the solitude of practice, behind the school building in the late afternoon, we did not seem so terrible.

Reality struck with devastating force in our first game. We had to play the team from St. Mark's, the private boys' school on Preston Road. One of their players was Lamar Hunt, Jr., the son of the owner of the Kansas City Chiefs. The Hunts still lived in Dallas, and even though many of the fourth graders at St. Mark's surely were Cowboy fans, their team was out-fitted in full Chiefs regalia, with red uniforms, white pants, and red helmets with the Chiefs' arrowhead insignia on the side. When they ran onto the field before a game, we stared in amazement and looked down at our paltry green YMCA jerseys. My father said later that he expected to see Hank Stram, the Chiefs' coach, pacing the sidelines calling plays.

The Chiefs were crisp, organized, and physical. We were small, unorganized, and afraid of getting hit. When we kicked off to start the game, their halfback picked up the bouncing ball and returned it for a touchdown, easily breaking through our harmless attempts to stop him. When they kicked off to us, Greg fumbled the ball and fell on it at the five-yard line. In the huddle I called an end sweep. The introduction of real opposition smashed the illusion of competence we had fashioned in practice. Our linemen's faces were pushed into the dirt as soon as the ball was snapped. Greg was buried in the end zone for a safety.

The tone of the game was established. The Chiefs never needed more than two or three plays to score. I lined up at defensive end, weighing all of 75 pounds, and experienced the intimidating sensation of larger muscles pressing against mine. All those hours in the backyard had not prepared me for that.

When we had the ball, their defenders often tackled me almost as soon as I took the snap. My only escape was to turn and run. I darted back and forth across the field, dodging tacklers to keep from getting pounded. Our little playbook was quickly rendered irrelevant. "Set up in the pocket!" Joe's father shouted once, sounding annoyed. I was too harried, and polite, to yell back, "What pocket?"

The final score was fifty-something to nothing. I was supposed to be beaten, bloodied, and profoundly discouraged, but I was not. I was 10 years old and covered with dirt and grass stains. I had just played my first football game. I was a quarterback, a warrior. Years later my father would recall that he was far more upset than I was.

There were five more games on our schedule. My weekends now consisted of four football games: Greenhill on Friday night, mine on Saturday morning, SMU on Saturday afternoon, and the Cowboys on Sunday. Life could get no better. On Sunday nights I toted up the wins and losses and gauged the success of the football weekend. My four teams never went undefeated; Greenhill, SMU, and the Cowboys won their share of games, but I always lost on Saturday mornings. The St. Mark's game was a foreshadowing of the rest of the season. We could not block or tackle. Our games were an exercise in abject futility. We never got close to the end zone. We played five more games without scoring a point. Our only show of life was my scrambling, and I usually was running away from the line, not downfield. The parents cheered me because it was exciting, but I was running for my life. One time I darted and dashed between three defenders, wound up 30 yards behind the line, and tossed a pass to Joe. He dropped it.

We continued to practice and maintained relatively high spirits considering the circumstances. There was much about the experience that I relished: the clattering of my shoulder pads as I pulled them over my head; the acrid smell of my uniform, washed clean yet still redolent of perspiration; the starchy feel of my long white socks on my bony ankles; the clacking of my cleats across the locker room floor; the tightness of my chinstrap against my skin. I treasured the postgame aches in which I luxuriated, a football player at last. As horrible as the season was, I did not want it to end. It was a thrilling moment when the Y announced that each team would play one more minigame: two quarters "under the lights" at a high-school stadium. Our eyes grew wide. Under the lights! A night game! A stadium! What could be better?

We practiced once more, giving attention to our trick play: an end around. I handed the ball to Greg, who ran to his left on a sweep and handed the ball to Aubrey Haltom, our split end, who peeled back from the line of scrimmage heading in the opposite direction. It was a clever play that we had tried several times in games without success; opponents just tossed aside our blockers, stormed into the backfield, and crushed us in the midst of our pale trickery.

We played under the lights on a chilly weeknight in early November. Some two dozen parents were scattered through the first few rows of the bleachers, their cheers echoing thinly through the empty stadium. We cast long, jerky shadows in the artificial light. We gave up three touchdowns in the first quarter and another early in the second. Mercifully, only a few minutes remained in our season.

The other team kicked off after its fourth touchdown. I kneeled in the huddle and called for the end around. We clapped our hands, shouted "break," and raced to the line, fearsome to the end in our minds, if not in reality. I took the snap and handed off to Greg, who was running to his left. The defenders brushed aside our blockers and swarmed after him, but at the last moment, just as he disappeared beneath a pile of orange shirts, he pitched the ball to Haltom. The defenders buried Greg, but he no longer had the ball. Haltom headed in the opposite direction and turned upfield, toting the ball in his right hand. The reverse had worked!

Haltom eluded one orange shirt, broke into the clear at midfield, and sprinted for the goal line. He was our only player with any natural athletic assets. He was fast. He could broad jump 10 feet. The players on the other team started to chase him, but they had no hope of catching him. Haltom was gone. After 26 quarters, we were going to score. We sprinted downfield laughing and jumping as if we had won the championship. Our parents stood and cheered this stunning development. The other team scored again before the final whistle, but we barely noticed. We were floating. We had scored. It was the smallest victory imaginable, but it was a victory, our first and only.

As much as I enjoyed playing, the trauma of the season ultimately scarred me. Intimidated by our crushing failure, I did not play Y football in fifth grade—we won another baseball championship that summer—before returning for one more season in sixth grade. We fared only slightly better in sixth grade. Once again the Y divided our class into two teams, and I was reunited with Greg, Joe, and many of the same players. We scored an occasional touchdown, but still lost every week leading up to our last game. Early in the first quarter I threw a pass to Greg, who picked up a blocker and ran for a touchdown. I had the lead for the first time in my football career. Before halftime I threw a second touchdown to Greg, then a third early in the fourth quarter. Our opponents lost several fumbles, one of which I recovered. We won, 20–6. I did not know it at the time, but it was my last organized football game. I went out a winner.

Seventh grade marked the beginning of school-sponsored teams, and I opted out, as did most of my teammates on those Y teams; we had had enough. Greg played another year before quitting. (His pants fell down as he ran with the ball in a junior varsity game, hastening his retirement.) I turned to basketball and tennis, and spent hours shooting at the basket in my driveway and playing tennis with Greg. Football was not for me; I was too small and too afraid of getting hit.

My aborted career rendered me a failure of sorts, but I never felt I had failed. I had played football with a reasonable degree of skill. I was adept at other sports. The rising popularity of soccer and basketball made it less imperative for a young boy in Texas to succeed in football. I went in other directions. I covered the varsity for the school paper. I filmed the games for the coach from my vantage point in the press box. I was on my way to becoming a sportswriter.

My retreat from football started from the moment I began playing in fourth grade, in the fall of '66. It was a momentous autumn for me as well as for the Cowboys. The fantasies of my early childhood were dashed as I began to realize I was destined to watch the game, not play it. At the same time, the Cowboys emerged as a championship contender. In my agony and the Cowboys' ecstasy, the course of our futures were charted in the fateful autumn of '66.

Chapter Seven

The first rush to glory is a time of unmatched joy for a team and its fans. It's the sporting version of a first kiss, a sweet, elevating interlude in which players' self-doubts are quashed and fans' dreams are realized. It also marks the end of innocence, the last time accomplishments are not sullied by expectations and demands resulting from prior successes and failures.

The Cowboys' first rush to glory occurred in the final weeks of the '66 season, starting with a miracle in Washington, passing through an unforgettable Thanksgiving, and ending on a New Year's Day that carved pro football history. They were the best of the Cotton Bowl days, loud and fresh and bright, and they completed the re-ordering of Dallas's sports priorities. Finally, and officially, the college football king was dead. The Cowboys owned the city after '66, holding it firmly and with both hands, never to lose grip again.

It started in the ninth game of the season, in the mist and mud of D.C. Stadium in Washington, and it started with a team in trouble, confronting the possibility of another lost season. The Cowboys had won just once in four weeks, wasting the advantage of their 4–0 start. The Browns had humbled them in Cleveland—it was 30–7 at one point—and the inferior Eagles had beaten them in a demoralizing game in which the Cowboys yielded only 80 yards of offense but allowed touchdowns on three kick returns. The losses had pushed them into second place in the Eastern Division, a game and a half behind the Cardinals. A loss to the Redskins would drop them to third.

Meredith took a beating during the game that astounded even his teammates. "He got hit so hard that he could barely call the plays, but he kept getting up," Pettis Norman said. The Redskins had a 30–28 lead late in the fourth quarter, when a punt backed Meredith and the Cowboy offense into seemingly impossible circumstances: 97 yards from the end zone, 63 seconds to play, no time-outs left.

Meredith gathered the offense in the huddle and called for quiet. "Listen up and listen good," he said. "We're going to run that ball, we're going to pass that ball, and we're going to go down this field and win the game."

Norman smiled at his memory of the moment years later. "I still get chills thinking about it," he said. "Don conveyed to us his belief that there wasn't anything the Redskins could do to stop us from winning the game."

On first down, Meredith dropped into the end zone and passed to Pete Gent for 26 yards. The offense quickly lined up again and Meredith rolled out to the left for 12 yards before going out of bounds. The next play was a swing pass to Garrison, who found no running room and scrambled out of bounds after gaining one yard. Another 26-yard completion to Gent advanced the ball to the Redskins' 32 with 22 seconds to play. Meredith took the next snap, rolled out and gained six yards, and a linebacker hit him after the whistle, resulting in a 15-yard penalty that moved the ball to the 13. Danny Villanueva kicked a 20-yard field goal to give the Cowboys a 31–30 victory.

Their locker room was euphoric. "That's the greatest drive I've ever seen," Landry said. It was a critical boost to the Cowboys' fragile psyche. They had never had a winning season and still were not sure they knew how to win. An incident several weeks earlier, before the loss to the Browns, had sharpened their insecurities. Joan Ryan, the wife of Browns quarterback Frank Ryan, had written in the *Cleveland Plain Dealer* (where she was a columnist), that Meredith was "a loser." Frank Ryan tried to distance himself from the comment, but it seemed accurate when the Browns thumped the Cowboys that Sunday. No one doubted that Meredith was a fine quarterback whose teammates were loyal to him, but it did seem he had a knack for losing important games. The winning drive at D.C. Stadium changed that perception. It was Meredith's answer to Joan Ryan's criticism.

The Cowboys beat the Steelers at the Cotton Bowl the next week to improve to 7–2–1 and move into a tie for first place with the Cardinals, whose starting quarterback, Charley Johnson, had just gone down for the season with a knee injury. The Browns were right behind the leaders with a 7–3 record.

The schedule called for the Browns to play in Dallas on Thanksgiving night: a showdown with the Cowboys at the Cotton Bowl, broadcast nationally on CBS. The Cowboys had much at stake. The Browns were a veteran team that had won an NFL championship, and the Cowboys were young and still trying to prove themselves as winners. The Browns were their measuring stick. The Cowboys had beaten them only once in 12 tries. A loss on Thanksgiving would not ruin the Cowboys' title hopes, but it would crush them emotionally. Landry called it "unquestionably" the biggest game in Cowboys history.

Of all the games in the Cowboys' first decade, this one stands out in my mind most vividly. It was a turning point, "a day that changed the Cowboys forever," safety Mike Gaechter said years later. The Thanksgiving game in '66 formally introduced the Cowboys to the rest of the nation and transfixed my 10-year-old eyes. The seed that would sprout America's Team a dozen years later was planted that night at the Cotton Bowl.

Thanksgiving was my favorite holiday growing up. We celebrated with a large family party at our house. School let out at noon the day before, and my mother and I drove across town, picked up Aunt Bayla, and brought her to our house, where she spent 24 hours preparing a colossal turkey. She dressed it on Wednesday, went to bed early, and rose at 4 A.M. to put the turkey in the oven. By the time I awoke, the smell of the cooking turkey filled the house and the furniture in the den had been cleared out and replaced by tables set for the party. We ate in the afternoon. After dinner, the men listened to the second half of the Texas–Texas A&M game on the radio.

Everything changed in '66. A Cowboy game, kicking off at 5 P.M., forced us to move dinner to earlier in the day. We ate Bayla's turkey in the middle of the afternoon and lingered over dessert, discussing the upcoming game. The women laughed that the men seemed distracted, which was true. "I sure hope the Cowboys win," one of my aunts said. "The men won't be in much of a mood if they don't."

Those of us going to the game piled into our station wagon and set out for the Cotton Bowl. It was the men and the boys. The Eastern Division lead was at stake, a game for serious fans. We listened to the Longhorns and Aggies on the radio as we drove to Fair Park.

The league office in New York had come up with the idea of the Thanksgiving game. The Lions had played a Thanksgiving morning game in Detroit since the '40s, and the league had sought a team willing to host an afternoon game. "I told the commissioner we would be interested," Schramm said. "I thought, 'What the hell, we're the new kids on the block.' And I knew from my Thanksgiving experience that after you ate your turkey there wasn't a damn thing to do except flop down on the couch and watch television. I thought it was a hell of a chance to sell the Cowboys to a shut-in audience."

The problem was finding an opponent. "I tried to find someone to play, but no one else wanted to do it," Schramm said. "They all said, 'What do you mean, play on Thanksgiving?'" Browns owner Art Modell was the only one even mildly interested. "He understood the TV part," Schramm said, "but he said, 'You're liable to have no one in the stadium.' We took it to the commissioner, and Art said, 'I'll play if the league will guarantee me a certain gate.' The league agreed to pay him a certain amount if I couldn't match it (with revenue from ticket sales). So he came down, and, of course, the place was jammed. No one had to worry about any guarantees. Before the game, Art and I climbed up on top of the press box to look down on the whole scene. Art said, 'This is one of the most gorgeous sights I've ever seen.' I had to agree."

So did I. Arriving early as always, I was stunned, almost rendered breathless, by the sight that greeted me as I entered the stadium bowl. It was as if I had entered the scene from *The Wizard of Oz* in which the world turned from black and white into color—as if every Cowboy game until now had been played in gray and now, suddenly, without warning, this one was in color.

The field had been spray-painted a brilliant green by a "turf artist" from Kansas City. The end zones were stained with the word *Cowboys* in great golden letters. At the 50-yard line there was a large D in a crest, done up in the Cowboys' colors, silver, blue, and white, with a pair of stars flanking the crest. The hash marks were red, white, and blue, and the yard lines were designated at five-yard intervals by giant block numerals, alternately red and blue and trimmed in silver. The dazzling tableau, designed to enhance the television broadcast, was intensified by extra banks of artificial lights.

The Cowboys had played on national television before, but never at night, never on Thanksgiving, and never with so much at stake. The knowledge that the game was being broadcast across the country was empowering. I felt I was at the center of the universe; everyone from Alaska to Miami was watching, and no doubt wished they could change places with me. For the first time I fathomed the power of belonging to a greater whole as a sports fan. If I had not been hooked before, I was now.

The seats steadily filled as the kickoff neared. More than 80,000 fans, almost 5,000 more than capacity, came to the Cotton Bowl that night. It was the largest crowd ever to watch a sporting event in Dallas, even larger than any of the crowds that had cheered for Doak Walker and SMU in the '40s. When I interviewed other Cowboy fans from those days many years later, they all remembered the first Thanksgiving game.

"I went with my parents," said Don Hullett, a medical company supervisor in Dallas. "We rode out there without tickets, parked in a yard and told the guy, 'Don't park anyone in front of us, we might not stay.' The guy said 'No problem,' but he parked a million people in front of us. We couldn't get tickets to the game, so we sat on the hood of the car and listened on the radio."

Bill Livingston, now a newspaper columnist in Cleveland, said, "I was a bag boy at Safeway and I had asked off for Thanksgiving well in advance so I could go to the game. At the last minute, my boss decided he couldn't spare me. I called in sick. I went with a friend. We had end zone seats, but we waited until the national anthem started and the cops were standing at attention, and we slipped through a little break in the fence separating us from the good seats. The cops started chasing us, and we got separated. In the second quarter my friend paged me, 'Bill Livingston, please report to gate two.' I was later told you could hear it on the radio. I thought it might cost me my job at Safeway, but my boss never said anything about it."

At prior games a marching band had played the national anthem, but this time a lone trumpeter wearing a black suit walked to a microphone on the 20-yard line. It was a Dallas musician, Tommy Loy, a member of a nightclub band called the Cell Block 7. The teeming crowd hushed as Loy began to play the anthem in a solo. His clear, lilting notes floated through the air, a breathtaking burst of elegance. The crowd just listened, too surprised and moved to sing. There was a brief, dramatic silence as the final note faded in the gathering darkness. Then there was a roar. The holiday crowd, the painted field, the national television cameras, and the setting sun had made for a dramatic backdrop, and Loy's anthem had finished the spectacle. It was as if we were watching the filming of a Hollywood movie. The Cotton Bowl was charged with a special current.

Early in the game, a fan across from us unfurled a long banner that everyone could see: "Ryan Is A Loser" it said. The crowd roared with appreciation; Meredith had heard boos before and would hear them again, but we were all together on this night, brothers in the growing Cowboy fraternity.

The Browns were not intimidated. They were old pros, accustomed to the spotlight. Ryan led two long touchdown drives and the Browns led by a point, 14–13, at halftime. The Cowboys needed to come through in the second half or they probably would have to wait another year—again—before they could deliver on their playoff promise.

On the first drive of the second half, a pass interference penalty set up a 12-yard Villanueva field goal that gave the Cowboys the lead, 16–14. Ryan and Leroy Kelly came right back down the field, but the Cowboy defense held and the stadium shook with cheers when the Browns' legendary kicker, Lou "The Toe" Groza, shanked a 31-yard field goal attempt. The Cowboy offense again drove downfield. Deftly mixing short passes with runs by Perkins, Meredith moved the offense across midfield and deep into Browns territory, the drive encompassing 12 plays and 74 yards. When the Browns finally held, Villanueva kicked another short field goal to give the Cowboys a 19–14 lead.

The Browns were losing their grip on the game, but they still needed only one big play to take back the lead. Ryan led the offense downfield with passes to Kelly and tight end Milt Morin, setting up a first down at the Dallas 15 as the fourth quarter began. The Cotton Bowl quieted, fearing the worst, but the defense held when tackle Larry Stephens sacked Ryan on third down. Groza lined up a 20-yard field goal, seemingly an automatic three points, but Gaechter came through the middle of the line and blocked the field goal. Again, the stadium shook from the force of the crowd's roar.

The game had taken a permanent turn. Meredith and the offense took the ball and marched the Cowboys downfield and over the threshold into the NFL's elite. Again mixing short passes with handoffs to Perkins, Meredith completed five straight passes and converted two third downs in a masterful drive. Perkins, fittingly delivering when it counted, gained 22 yards on four carries up the middle. The cheers grew louder as the offense neared the goal line.

On first down at the Cleveland 11, Meredith handed off to Perkins on a draw play. Perkins zipped through the line untouched and sprinted to the end zone for the biggest touchdown in Cowboy history. A burst of camera flashes validated the moment. The Cowboys had arrived. The Browns were beaten. Meredith was not a loser.

"It was the night the Cowboys began to prosper," Schramm said. "The night of our fulfillment."

We were so excited that we stayed until late in the fourth quarter, far after our customary departure time. Not even Pop wanted to leave the Cotton Bowl early on this splendid night. Finally, we headed out, piled back into the station wagon, and drove home to end the happiest Thanksgiving ever. The headline in the *Morning News* the next day was a joy: "Happiness is Cranberried Browns."

The Thanksgiving game was a hit. Art Rooney, owner of the Steelers, phoned Schramm to congratulate him on the dramatic game and colorful presentation. Millions of fans watched, resulting in one of the highest-rated football telecasts ever. Executives at CBS, thrilled, got the NFL to move the Cowboys' next game from an early Sunday kickoff to later in the day, to facilitate another national broadcast. It was another big game: The Cardinals were coming to the Cotton Bowl tied for first place with the Cowboys. They were without their first-team quarterback now and odds-makers favored the Cowboys by two touchdowns, but it was still one of the biggest games of the year.

Cowboy madness hit Dallas in the wake of the Thanksgiving game. All 75,000-plus tickets to the Cardinal game were sold as of Wednesday at 9:52 A.M., 100 hours before the kickoff. It was easily the earliest sellout in franchise history. The newspapers were full of stories about the fans' newest craze: driving 75 or more miles to outflank the reaches of the local TV blackout. According to the *Morning News,* hundreds of fans were making plans to drive to Sherman, southern Oklahoma, or East Texas on Sunday morning to watch the game on television either at a bar or in a motel room. Before the game on Sunday came the surest sign that the Cowboys had arrived: Scalpers were arrested at the Cotton Bowl trying to sell six-dollar tickets for between $10 and $17.

CBS was hoping for more four-star theater, but the Cardinal game was not as taut or dramatic. The weather did not cooperate. A thick fog shrouded the Cotton Bowl, making it difficult for fans in the upper deck to see the field. Almost 77,000 fans came out, but they were not on edge; it was as if another *Wizard of Oz* transformation had taken place, from the brilliant Technicolor of Thanksgiving night back to the familiar black and white.

It was almost inevitable that the Cowboys succumb to the "day-after" atmosphere, and they did. The Cardinals gave them all they wanted. The Cowboys trailed early in the game, 10–7, and still led by only a touchdown midway through the fourth quarter when Cornell Green intercepted a pass to set up a decisive touchdown. The 31–17 victory left the Cowboys a game in front of the Cardinals and a game and a half in front of the Browns, with two to play.

They needed the cushion. The following week they played their third straight game at the Cotton Bowl, and Sonny Jurgensen and the Redskins upset them, 34–31. Meredith was knocked out by a Sam Huff hit in the first quarter and sent to the hospital with a broken nose. Morton and Rhome filled in ably, but Jurgensen engineered a late drive that won the game. The sting of defeat was eased by the news that both the Browns and Cardinals had also lost, eliminating the Browns from the division race and leaving the fading Cardinals in dire straits. Trailing the Cowboys by a game, the Cardinals had to close out their regular season schedule in Cleveland the next Saturday. The Cowboys would play the Giants, winners of only one game, in New York.

As expected, the Browns swept the Cardinals out of the race with a lopsided win in Cleveland. Sitting in their hotel rooms in New York on Saturday afternoon, watching on television, the Cowboys clinched their first division title. They went through the motions against the Giants the next day at Yankee Stadium and hacked out a 17–7 win that gave them a 10–3–1 record for the regular season. The Browns finished second with a 9–5 record, tied with the fast-finishing Eagles. The Cardinals finished fourth, at 8–5–1. They went 1–4 after Charley Johnson's knee injury.

Some 8,000 fans came to Love Field that Sunday night to greet the Cowboys upon their return from New York. Just before the plane landed, Murchison grabbed the microphone from the pilot and made an announcement. "Welcome to Dallas, former home of the Kansas City Chiefs," he said. The players roared. It was a night for laughter and celebration. In their seventh season, the Cowboys were in the NFL championship game.

The championship game, which rotated between the home fields of the division winners, would be played at the Cotton Bowl on New Year's Day. The Cowboys' opponents would be Vince Lombardi's Packers, the standard of pro football excellence. Having easily won the Western Division title for the fifth time in seven seasons, the Packers would try to win their fourth league title under Lombardi. They were at the peak of their powers, with Bart Starr throwing passes to Boyd Dowler and Carroll Dale, Paul Hornung and Jim Taylor running sweeps, and Ray Nitschke and Willie Davis leading a crushing defense. They had beaten the Browns in the championship game in '65 and come back to win their division with a 12–2 record. They would be favored by a touchdown over the Cowboys.

Dallas had never been more wild about football than it was in the days leading up to this championship game. The Cowboys were playing the Packers, and SMU had won the Southwest Conference championship in a surprise, on the talents of a darting receiver named Jerry LeVias, the first black star in school history. On December 31st, the day before the Cowboy game, the Mustangs would make their first appearance in the Cotton Bowl Classic since '49, against the Georgia Bulldogs. Tickets were long gone.

The newspapers were full of stories about Dallas's big football weekend, with 150,000 fans expected at the Cotton Bowl within 24 hours. Yet there was no doubt which game was a priority to most fans. The Cowboys filled their season-ticket holders' requests, then sold the remaining 40,000 tickets in one morning at Fair Park. They set up a counter with 21 windows. The line began to form 24 hours ahead of time and swelled to 8,000 people at one point. The tickets were gone in five hours.

Many hotels ringing Dallas outside a 75-mile radius sold out their rooms to fans who did not have tickets and wanted to watch on television.

"I drove up with three buddies to an aunt's house just over the Oklahoma state line and we watched on TV," Bill Livingston said.

Georgia handled SMU easily on Saturday, 24–9. After the game, we went back to Pop's house and joined the rest of the family for a holiday meal that included a helping of black-eyed peas for good luck in the coming year.

The next day dawned clear and mild, with temperatures expected in the low 50's: perfect for football. We drove back to Pop's house to eat lunch and watch the AFL championship game between the Chiefs and Bills. The NFL and AFL had merged after six years of war, and for the first time the champions of the two leagues would play an "ultimate" game being billed as the Super Bowl. The Chiefs, who had left Dallas just three years earlier, thumped the Bills, 31–7. If the Cowboys beat the Packers, they and the Chiefs—bitter rivals from the war of Dallas—would play in the first Super Bowl. The idea delighted most fans in Dallas, but not me; I had rooted for the Bills and my favorite AFL player, a running back named Cookie Gilchrist.

We drove to the Cotton Bowl and discovered with delight that the turf artist from Kansas City had returned for an encore performance. The field had again been spray-painted green, with the yard markers highlighted and the end zones painted in Cowboy and Packer colors. As it did on Thanksgiving, the colorful field and the additional banks of lights jazzed the crowd as the kickoff approached. Once again, I could almost feel the eyes of the rest of the world upon us.

The game that followed is often and mistakenly overlooked by those who weigh and measure pro football history. "The game was a classic, one of the best championship games ever," said Steve Sabol, executive producer of NFL Films. "It gets overlooked because the Ice Bowl was the next year, but it was a spectacular game."

It was the 34th NFL championship game, and a Chicago sportswriter who had seen them all later called it the best ever. It was the second installment of the holiday special the Cowboys ran that season: They had taken a huge step forward on Thanksgiving, and they took another on New Year's Day, maturing before our eyes into an elite team.

The Packers' plan was to establish immediate superiority and discourage the Cowboys; a quick start could make for an easy game against a young team untested in championship play. The Packers instituted their plan with stunning swiftness, as Elijah Pitts ran off tackle for 32 yards on the first play from scrimmage. On the eighth play, Starr threw a 17-yard touchdown pass to Pitts. Then Renfro was stripped of the ball on the ensuing kickoff return, and the Packers' Jim Grabowski picked it up and ran 18 yards for another touchdown. The Packers had a 14–0 lead with less than four minutes gone. "We were standing over there thinking, 'Man, how bad are we gonna get our asses whipped?'" Ralph Neely said.

Behind by two touchdowns without having run a play, the Cowboys finally sent their offense onto the field after Renfro returned the next kickoff to the 35. The rest of the offense waited while Meredith spoke to Landry on the sidelines and trotted onto the field. As he approached the huddle, according to Neely, he was singing the chorus from "God Didn't Make Honky Tonk Angels." He then kneeled in the huddle, looked up, and said, "Boys, we're in a heap of shit." The other players laughed. "Don got us relaxed," Neely said, "which was what he wanted."

Meredith was at his best that day. At 28 years old, after seven seasons of bruises and boos, his apprenticeship ended and his brief valedictory began. He drove the offense right down the field for a touchdown, and then, after the Packers punted the ball back, drove the offense to another touchdown in five plays. Perkins covered the last 23 on a draw. The Cotton Bowl was frenzied; the Cowboys had spotted the Packers two touchdowns and caught them by the end of the first quarter. "We grew up right there," George Andrie said. "We were men after that."

Landry said: "That was Meredith's finest hour. We weren't at the Packers' level yet, but they had a tendency to get ahead early and coast a little bit, and we jumped on that. Coming back like we did in the first quarter certainly got their attention."

The Packers, champions that they were, were not fazed. Less than a minute after Perkins' touchdown run, Carroll Dale got away from Cornell Green and Starr hit him with a 51-yard touchdown pass that abruptly turned off the noise in the Cotton Bowl. The touchdown was the fifth of the game in 16 minutes, a spectacular offensive pace. The Cowboys kept it going on the next series: Meredith passed to Gent for 10 yards, and Reeves turned a short catch into a 40-yard gain. When the Packers finally held, Villanueva kicked a short field goal. The Packers led, 21–17.

The fastbreak pace had to end, and it did. The rest of the second quarter was scoreless. The Packers drove to the Cowboys' 21 on their first possession of the second half, but Pitts fumbled when hit by Gaechter, and Warren Livingston recovered for the Cowboys. The offense came back the other way. Meredith passed to Frank Clarke for 13 yards. Perkins gained 10 on a draw. Meredith rolled out for 11, his path cleared by a crushing Perkins block. But the Packers' Willie Wood broke up a pass to Reeves in the end zone, and Villanueva kicked a 32-yard field goal—the first points for either team in 23 minutes—that cut Green Bay's lead to 21–20.

The crowd exhorted the Cowboy defense to stop the Packers, but Starr passed to Dale for 43 yards; having beaten Green to the inside earlier, Dale faked to the inside and went outside. Five plays later, the Packers' Boyd Dowler beat Renfro over the middle and Starr hit him with a 16-yard touchdown pass. Gaechter, frustrated, upended Dowler in the end zone after the play was over. Don Chandler's extra point gave the Packers an eight-point lead late in the third quarter.

A sense of foreboding infiltrated the Cotton Bowl as night fell. Meredith lost his touch, throwing seven straight incompletions, and the Cowboy defense simply could not stop the Packers. Landry's 4-3 Flex had limited Lombardi's daylight-oriented running game, just as Landry had envisioned when he designed the Flex, but Starr and the receivers were devastating the secondary. The Cowboys had fretted about Livingston, their weak link in the secondary, but Renfro and Green also were struggling. The conservative Packers were making big plays, forcing the Cowboys to utilize long drives against a tough defense.

Chandler boomed a punt toward the Dallas end zone early in the fourth quarter, and Hayes, who had been a nonfactor, drifted back to the goal line and fielded the ball, a huge mistake. The Packers swarmed him at the one. Hayes had dumped Meredith and the offense into a hole. They managed one first down before Villanueva punted to midfield, and Starr drove the Packer offense to another touchdown, converting three third-and-long plays on the way. The touchdown was a 19-yard pass to Max McGee, a backup receiver who had replaced the injured Dowler. He beat Livingston with an inside fake and a corner route.

The Packers led, 34–20, as they lined up for the extra point. Lombardi screamed at his linemen to prevent the middle of the Cowboy defensive line from blocking the kick. Proving Lombardi prescient, Bob Lilly muscled Packer guard Jerry Kramer and got his hand on the kick, deflecting it away. The lead was still 14 points with 5:20 to play. The Cowboys still had a chance; two touchdowns would tie the score. Lombardi cursed Kramer as the kicking team returned to the sidelines.

The Cowboys started a last-gasp series at their 26. Meredith scrambled for one first down, but then Reeves fumbled after catching a swing pass. Willie Wood appeared to fall on the ball for the Packers, but it bounced away crazily and rolled out of bounds. The Cowboys still had possession, but the 10-yard loss left them at third-and-20 from their 32. Meredith called a play in the huddle. Hayes would run a fly pattern, engaging Bob Jeter and Wood. Reeves would go in motion and run a pass route. Frank Clarke would take on the strong safety, Tom Brown.

"It was one of those zen moments of sports," Clarke said, "when you're elevated off into another world. As soon as I heard the play, I knew it was a touchdown. I knew it was perfect. I was on the right side, and Danny Reeves came in motion toward me and (linebacker) David Robinson went with him, and I was uncovered. I put some moves on Tom Brown, and they were so clean and sharp that Tom got twisted up and fell down, and then I knew, and I looked over my shoulder and that ball came at me like it wanted me to catch it."

Clarke caught Meredith's pass at the 30 and sprinted to the end zone to complete a 68-yard touchdown pass. "Willie Wood dove and just touched my left heel," Clarke said. "When I got into the end zone I took my helmet off and it was as though an explosion had occurred. Eighty thousand people were going wild. I had never heard that sound before. It was like someone had turned up the volume or something. I ran into the end zone and handed the ball to a fan who was sitting there. I got a note from the guy later. He was a Packer fan, believe it or not, who had come down to the game from Green Bay. He wrote to thank me for the ball."

The touchdown brought the fans and Cowboys back to life. The crowd implored the defense to get the ball back for Meredith and the offense. Starr completed an 18-yard pass to Marv Fleming, briefly dulling the Cowboys' momentum, but then Dave Edwards sacked Starr, defensive tackle Willie Townes batted away a pass, and Lee Roy Jordan ran down Jim Taylor and slung him to the ground for a loss on third down. The din was shattering. Facing fourth-and-25, the Packers had to give the ball back.

Chandler dropped back to punt, and Andrie put on a strong rush and deflected the ball. It sailed off to the side, as though wounded, and bounced out of bounds at the Packer 47 after traveling only 16 yards. Suddenly, everything was going the Cowboys' way. Meredith and the offense trotted onto the field, needing a touchdown to tie. There were 139 seconds left in the game.

On first down, Meredith hit Clarke again, this time for a 21-yard gain. After Perkins gained four yards off tackle, Meredith went back to Clarke one more time. "I was going for the corner instead of for the post," Clarke said. "But the same thing happened. I put some moves on Tom Brown and got past him. This time he just grabbed me as I went past. He was befuddled and just grabbed me. If he hadn't, it was six points. I would have been wide open and we would have tied it."

Brown's interference penalty gave the Cowboys a first down on the two. They had four plays and 90 seconds to score, seemingly an easy assignment for an offense that was suddenly unstoppable. Packer offensive tackle Forrest Gregg admitted after the game that the Packers were shaken. "It was hard to stomach as you watched," Gregg said. "The Cowboys were on a roll."

On first down, Meredith handed off to Reeves up the middle. The Packers stopped him at the one, setting up second down with one yard to go for a touchdown and, extra point willing, overtime. The Cotton Bowl was lost in pandemonium. The Packers were tilting.

Then Boeke moved.

As the Cowboys set for second down, Jim Boeke, the big left tackle, dove across the line an instant before Dave Manders snapped the ball. The Cowboys went ahead and ran the play—Meredith rolled out, stumbled, and threw a pass to Norman, who dropped the ball in the end zone—but the play did not count.

"Were they offsides?" Landry asked on the Cowboy sideline.

"We were in motion," someone said.

The impassive Landry closed his eyes and flicked his head to the side in disgust. An NFL cameraman captured his response, which would become an emblem of the Cowboys' big-game frustrations.

The Cowboys were penalized five yards for illegal procedure, pushing the ball back to the six. Boeke's mistake was little more than a muscle twitch, but it changed the game—and maybe the course of NFL history. "I knew we'd win once they got that offsides penalty," Gregg said later.

Reeves had been poked in the eye while executing a fake on the nullified second down, leaving his vision blurred. Now, on the post-Boeke second down, he drifted into the left flat and Meredith flipped him the ball. Unable to see it clearly, he dropped it. "I probably should have come out of the game after the previous play," Reeves later told an NFL Films interviewer.

The Cowboys had gone from second down at the one-yard line to third down at the six. Now they were desperate. Meredith called a pass to Norman, who was open on a square-out route near the goal line. Meredith rolled out and underthrew a pass that Norman caught at the two. Tom Brown tackled him there.

The season had come down to one play. Meredith called it in the huddle. He would roll out to his right and either run or pass. "I wanted options," he said in the locker room. He had none. Bob Hayes was mistakenly in the game—he was not part of the goal-line offense—and failed to block linebacker Dave Robinson, who blitzed and reached Meredith untouched before the play could develop.

"Frank Clarke was supposed to be in the game," Gent said. "Hayes didn't know how to run the play."

Robinson slammed into Meredith and knocked him sideways. Forced to pass with Robinson hanging on his left side, Meredith threw a fluttering ball that sailed into the end zone and was intercepted by Tom Brown.

There were 16 seconds left. Starr ran two quarterback sneaks and the Packers began celebrating a 34–27 victory, their second consecutive NFL championship, and their fourth in six years. The Cotton Bowl fell as silent as a snowy midnight. The Cowboys' first rush to glory suddenly was over. It had been delicious, dramatic, a feast of cheers and excitement, but it had fallen one yard short.

Thousands of fans remained in their seats, unable to believe that the Cowboys had come so close and lost. Only Clint Murchison kept his sense of humor. Spotting one of his favorite sportswriters heading toward the locker room to interview the players, the Cowboys' dry-witted owner put his arm around the reporter and smiled. "Well," he said, "I guess we don't want to give the fans too much too soon, do we?"

With five minutes left and the Cowboys behind by two touchdowns, Pop looked down the row at my father and gave his traditional signal that foretold our departure.

"Anytime you're ready, Seymour," he said.

My father nodded, but clung to a final lifeline. "Let's just see how they do with the ball, Pop," he said.

Moments later, Meredith hit Clarke with the long touchdown pass and the game careened toward its maddening finish. Pop never said another word about leaving. We stayed until the end. It was the only Cowboy game at the Cotton Bowl in which we heard the final gun.

I was thankful as I grew older that my father had not given in to Pop's anxiousness and ushered us out of the stadium prematurely. Even though the game ended in disappointment, it would have stained my record as a fan not to have stayed to the end of the only championship game played at the Cotton Bowl.

The drive home that night was silent. Trundling to and from the Cotton Bowl for the SMU and Cowboy games on back-to-back days had zapped us of our spirit. So had the two defeats. Cruelly, Christmas vacation ended the next day, the first Monday of the new year. I was on my way to school just 12 hours after Meredith's interception, after eating breakfast over a bold, exasperating headline in the *Morning News*: "Cowboy Season Falls One Yard Short."

The immediate hangover from the loss was surprisingly short. There were no radio talk shows to pick at the carcass for weeks. The sportswriters followed up only for a few days; they were more whimsical than critical, seemingly loath to harp on the many Cowboy mistakes. Basically, it was a gallant loss that was easy to swallow at first. The Cowboys had never led, trailed twice by two touchdowns, and struggled all day to contain Green Bay's offense. They obviously were not the better team. Victory would have been sweet, but surprising. That made defeat easier to take.

The game assumed a more notorious role only as the years passed and the Cowboys made a habit of losing in the playoffs, rendering the '66 championship game infamous as the first of many such losses. Among the fans, those of us who lived through every disappointing turn, one player came to symbolize the Cowboys' frustrations: Boeke. It is still a name that wrenches the heart of any Cowboy fan from the Cotton Bowl days.

He was a fringe figure for the most part, a big tackle who came in a trade with the Rams in '64 and stayed for four seasons. Always competent, and even exceptional as a downfield blocker, he was a backup for one year, a starter for two, then a backup again for a year. The Cowboys traded him to the Saints in '68. He came and went, but he stayed forever in our hearts, consigned to an unmatched level of ignominy among Cowboy fans because he moved before the snap at the one-yard line.

Fans of the Boston Red Sox have Bill Buckner, who booted a groundball to lose the sixth game of the '86 World Series. Fans of the Buffalo Bills have Scott Norwood, who missed a game-winning field goal at the end of Super Bowl XXV. Fans of the early Cowboys have Boeke. Other Cowboys would commit famous mistakes, such as Jackie Smith, who dropped an easy touchdown pass in Super Bowl XIII, but only Boeke's name swelled into myth among Cowboy fans as a synonym for losing a game.

Not that his penalty alone lost the game. A litany of other mistakes contributed. Renfro's fumbled kickoff return in the first quarter. Hayes's decision to field a punt on the goal line. The Cowboy's final series was riddled with mistakes. Reeves did not come out of the game with blurred vision. Norman did not run his route into the end zone on third down. Hayes was in the game on fourth down; Clarke would have known to block Dave Robinson, giving Meredith time to consider his options. Who knows what might have happened?

Still, to fans and even to the players and coaches, Boeke's mistake loomed above the rest. In an interview years later, Landry summed up the end of the game thusly: "We got down there and had a chance. It was a shame that Boeke moved. It broke his heart and broke our hearts, too."

Such was the burden Boeke assumed after his mistake. He was suited well to the task; a resolute Midwesterner raised in Cuyahoga Falls, Ohio, he took the blame after the game. "It was me; I blew the $15,000 ball of wax," he said in the locker room. When Steve Perkins quoted him in the *Times Herald* saying "someone else down the line" had moved, Boeke phoned Perkins to complain; he had never made such a statement and was worried that his teammates would think less of him for not accepting the blame. Perkins confessed that the quote had come secondhand from another reporter and been rushed into the paper on deadline. Boeke hoped a retraction would appear, but one never did.

When the team gathered for training camp the next summer, Boeke admitted he was still having trouble forgetting his mistake. "I've relived it a thousand times," he told Andy Anderson of the *Fort Worth Press,* "but it doesn't do any good. I blew it, and I knew in a minisecond as I shot out of there that I had blown it. But what can you do about it then?"

He lost his starting job to John Niland that year, spent the season on the kick teams, and was traded. A year later, the Saints traded him to the Lions, who released him at the end of training camp in '69. The Redskins picked him up, then released him after he blew several assignments. His career was over after nine years—a successful NFL life for a player from tiny Heidelberg College in Ohio.

Married with two young daughters (a third came later), Boeke retired to Southern California, where he had established his home and worked in the offseason as a substitute teacher. He became a full-time teacher after football. After working for a year at a juvenile hall, he was hired as an English teacher and assistant freshman football coach at Westminster High School in Orange County, south of Los Angeles. He taught there for 23 years, introducing sophomores to classics such as *All Quiet on the Western Front,* and also, as part of a sports-and-literature course, *Instant Replay,* Jerry Kramer's autobiographical look at the Packers. He retired in '94.

"Three-fourths of my students were minorities," he said when I interviewed him in 1996. "I didn't teach rich kids. It was Mexican-American kids, Vietnamese kids, and just a matter of trying to get them interested in reading."

To augment his schoolteacher's salary, he fashioned a second career as an actor. He had small roles as a football player in *Heaven Can Wait* and *North Dallas Forty,* the latter based on the novel written by his former Cowboy teammate, Pete Gent. Years later, he played an assistant coach in the hit movie *Forrest Gump,* in which he had a one-line speaking part. ("Say, wasn't that Gump?") Around that time he was hired for an occasional role in the television show *Coach,* portraying the father of an assistant coach. "He's a big dumb blond coach and I play the big dumb blond father," Boeke said. "It's a match made in heaven."

He also made television commercials for Taco Bell, Texaco, the Wells Fargo bank, True Value hardware, and Orville Reddenbacher popcorn. "I got into commercials because of (Don) Meredith," he said. "I had been out of football for a year or two, and Meredith was doing stuff on *Police Story.* I wrote him and said I had a Screen Actors' Guild card, and to please call if he ever heard of any roles. He gave me a call and said he had a Lipton Tea commercial and they needed football players. I thought I had the part and I wound up having to audition, but I still got the part and as a result I got a commercial agent and things grew from there. I owe it all to Don."

Hollywood is a place where dreams come true, but Boeke's take on his acting career was decidedly unromantic. "The big thing is that you get paid," he said. "Everyone says it must be fun, and it is, but I look at it more from the job angle than the fun angle. I got into it because of my size, not my acting ability. It's no big deal. It's just like me being an offensive tackle; it wasn't a glory position. I don't look at me as a star or anything. I drive an hour each way to audition, and if I get the job I go in, do the work, and get paid. It's a job. Football was different; it was a job, too, but there wasn't a day when I went out there and didn't enjoy the practices and games. I was getting paid for something I loved to do. I would still do it right now if I could."

I had procrastinated before calling him, fearing he would make for an uncomfortable trip down memory lane. He had to know that he was a fabled character among Cowboy fans, that his name conjured dark spirits. The penalty had "broken his heart," Landry said. Was he indeed tortured by his mistake? Was he bitter about the fans' memories of him?

Once we began talking, I quickly realized my fears were unnecessary. Boeke was pleased to discuss the old days, and not at all tormented by his mistake. "I kid him about it," former teammate Tony Liscio said. "I hold up my hand and say, 'Hey, I'm missing a Super Bowl ring because of you.' He's funny. It could have happened to anyone. I was lined up next to him that day and I couldn't hear Meredith calling the signals. The noise was deafening."

Not that Boeke was warmed by the memory. "It's the worst memory you could dream of," he said. "But what can you do? You live with it, you acknowledge it, and you move on. You wish it hadn't happened, but you can't get it back. You don't mull over it, don't cry over it, don't think about it for the rest of your life. It's just one incident in your life, and that's the way it goes. You do the best you can. Sometimes things don't work out."

He explained what went wrong at that fateful moment 30 years ago. It was the result of an injury, he said.

"Earlier that season I had gotten chopped down in Cleveland and had my knee torn up," he said. "I had an operation after the season. I rehabbed it during the season, missed three games down the stretch, and then came back to play at the end of the season and then in the championship game. The cause of the (penalty) was I wanted to get off on the ball and not be slow. It wasn't a matter of missing the snap count or not knowing it. It was just a matter of anticipating the count, and anticipating it too soon. I did that the whole game. My knee was so messed up that I wanted to take advantage of everything I had. On that particular play, I just moved a little too quickly."

He said he received only one letter that offseason—a supportive letter from three Dallas businessmen. He said he never received one critical letter. "I still run into people now and then who bring it up," he said, "but I put it behind me. You can't have something like that on your mind. I just made a common mistake that could happen to anyone, and it happened at the end of the game. There were lots of other mistakes in the game, like Renfro fumbling the kickoff and Hayes catching the punt at the goal line, but people don't think about those because they didn't happen at the end of the game. What can you do?"

Unlike the fans, he did not cast his years with the Cowboys solely in the dark light of his mistake. "My years with the Cowboys were my best performing years and just my best years, period," he said. "To go from winning five games (in '64) to playing in two championship games with guys like Meredith and Bobby Hayes, you just can't ask for anything more."

He had returned to Dallas for several reunions in the '70s and stayed in touch with Liscio, but his football days were behind him now, almost part of a prior life. After awhile, few of his students even knew he had played pro football. When we spoke, he was just a retired teacher with three daughters still living under his roof, the youngest a budding basketball star. He had lived a singular life, graced movie screens and football fields, elevated minds, done all he could to bury his moment of infamy. That I was calling him proved that he could never bury it entirely, that it would always come back from time to time and slap him in the face, a reminder of life's capriciousness.

"The only time I hear about it is when people like you call," he said without rancor. "I always know what the conversation is leading up to."

It was hardly fair; he was a good man without pretensions, wholly undeserving of the mythology that trailed him. But he was Boeke, just Boeke, who moved. Such was his destiny.

Chapter Eight

There was so much I knew about the Cowboys when I was young, but also so much that I did not know. I knew the players' names and uniform numbers, but I did not know that some of them played on amphetamines, smoked marijuana, and drank voluminously. I knew their statistics and the scores of their games, but I did not know that their skin color separated them in so many ways. I knew where they had attended college and when the Cowboys had drafted them, but I did not know who their friends were, what they did in their free time, what their politics were, what intangibles they brought into the locker room.

When they were on the field they were as familiar as family to me, a homogeneous assemblage of real-life superheroes who dressed alike and seemed to share all thought and purpose. Off the field they were strangers; I had no concept of who they were. It never occurred to me that they had different backgrounds and beliefs, that some were smart and others dumb, some liberal and others conservative, that some might not get along, or that they were young and wild and, as Ralph Neely said years later, "doing crazy stuff." I never thought that those with light skin might live differently from those with dark skin, or that they might take drugs, or disagree. They were teammates, Cowboy brothers. Were they not all the same?

That I would regard them so simply was no surprise. I was just a child indulging in hero worship, incapable of seeing them as real people made of flesh, blood, and vulnerabilities. I was oblivious to the complexities of race relations, the intricate mechanics of locker-room politics, the lure of drugs, and the bad blood that always existed between players and management.

I began learning about football's other side in the '70s when I read such books as Dan Jenkins's *Semi-Tough* and Pete Gent's *North Dallas Forty.* Gent's cynical tirade on drugs and cold-hearted coaches, clearly based on his years with the Cowboys, was particularly successful in illuminating the reality that players were people and not just cartoons, and that pro football was not the simplistic haven I had envisioned. I read all the antifootball books, most of which seemed to have been written by former Cowboys such as Gent and Pat Toomay. Obviously, my beloved team had a side I did not know.

At first I felt ashamed of having been so unaware when I was younger, but that was silly. I was not supposed to know the truth at that age; naiveté is an integral part of the loyalty that develops then. It also was more difficult to know the truth; the media was still uncomfortable discussing race and drugs, and also more forgiving and complicit. I was shocked when Lance Rentzel exposed himself to a young girl in Highland Park, ending his Cowboy career in 1970, but it turned out he had been involved in another similar incident while playing for the Minnesota Vikings before he came to Dallas. The Cowboys had kept that history quiet. I also later learned from a former employee of KLIF, the Cowboys' flagship radio station, that KLIF had agreed to keep the news of the 1970 incident from going public until after the Thanksgiving game, because the Cowboys wanted Rentzel to play that day.

When I began writing about sports for a living, I learned just how bare the truth really was. Behind the headlines engendered by every team, there was always another world in which egos and personalities clashed, money was an all-encompassing topic, trust was rare, and players had lives beyond the sidelines. One of my first assignments for the *Times Herald* was to take Lee Roy Jordan to see the movie *North Dallas Forty,* and write about his reaction. We met at a theater on Central Expressway, watched the movie, and retreated to a coffee shop to talk. Jordan had laughed at scenes of players taking drugs and shooting out mailboxes on off-day dove hunts. He did not try to pass it off as fable.

Not that the Cowboys stood out among NFL teams as particularly wild. They had books written about them, but not because they were exceptionally riotous. "Every team was wild," Gent said. "When Danny Villanueva came from the Rams, he told us the Rams set out drugs at the end of the cafeteria line. Bowls of Dexedrine, just sitting there. And if the amphetamines didn't kill you on the field, the really dangerous drugs were the cortisones and steroids they gave you for pain relief and inflammation. Those were systemic drugs. They stayed in your system. Getting shot up with cortisone every week could cause real damage."

Years later many Cowboys still would not confess to using amphetamines and smoking marijuana in their playing days, but it was not difficult to discern that some had partaken. They had come to Dallas straight from college at a time when many campuses were thick with marijuana smoke and a new sense of permissiveness.

"I had hair down to my shoulders and they assumed I was on dope, and the irony was, I was the only one who wasn't," said Toomay, who played for the Cowboys from 1970 to 1974, in an interview with Skip Bayless for *God's Coach,* Bayless's book about Landry. "All their 'character' guys, their Southern good ol' boys, were experimenting with pot."

Drinking was even more prevalent than drugs; it was institutionalized as part of the pro football life. Bobby Layne became a folk hero playing with hangovers in the '50s. Heavy drinking was condoned with a wink. The Cowboys had catered postgame parties at a beer company hospitality room near Parkland Hospital. They also met after practice on Thursdays at the VIP Lounge on Abrams Road. "Meredith started it," Walt Garrison said. "It was a relaxed environment where you could have a few beers and try to work out problems."

The hard partying was done privately, among the clusters of friends that formed on the team. "We'd let our hair down on a day off," Neely said, "and sometimes on the night before a game. I remember when Meredith got his nose broken against Philly one year. We had been out the night before, late, real late, and it was my guy who hit him and broke his nose. I mean, bone was out and blood was spurting everywhere and Don was leaning over and walking off the field, and he looked up at me as he went

by and he said, 'See if I ever go out with you again.' We were just young
and bulletproof. I told (*Morning News* columnist) Bob St. John that somebody ought to put together a book about the crazy things we did. Not just
the dope, I mean, the crazy stuff."

There was so much partying, Gent said, that he had to undergo a personality transplant. "So much of the game was off the field, and you had to
be a certain way," Gent said. "I had come from college basketball, a finesse
game, to this game where you ran straight into people. The violence was
accepted. It was what you were supposed to like. You needed a different
mindset and personality to get through it. Up to that time I didn't drink or
smoke. If I went out, I was the only sober one in the bar. After my rookie
year I had to think hard about whether I wanted to do this. It was such a
hard-living life, and that was the only way. I knew I would do it, of course.
I loved being a pro football player. So that next year I became a totally different person, much more aggressive, outgoing, and obnoxious. I had a
great roommate who taught me how to live like a football player. Don Talbert. He was an All-America tackle from Texas, and his reserve unit had
been sent to Vietnam. So he was really mad. I just followed his lead. I still
remember a couple of the wives who had thought I was nice, that next season they came to me and, 'What happened to you? You turned into such a
creep.' They were right. But I had to do it."

At age 10, I had no idea that drinking, drugs, and cynicism could invade
the Cowboys' locker room. And even though I knew about the Vietnam
war, which was always on the *CBS Evening News* with Walter Cronkite, I
considered it part of a different world from the Cowboys. Wrong. "We
were always scared to death that we might have to go over there," Gent
said. "They walked in one morning in '65 and said the war was going to
escalate and we had to get in National Guard units. That hadn't been in the
papers. Only Clint Murchison could have found out before Congress. They
had places reserved in units in Oklahoma and El Paso. I went down to the
examining station on Jackson Street at 4:30 one morning. There were all
these other guys waiting to go in. I flunked the physical. Every six months
they sent me back for another physical."

Race was the most predominant of the realities of pro football life that
existed beyond my knowledge. It hovered over the Cotton Bowl Cowboys,
affecting teamwork, personnel moves, almost every aspect of the franchise. The '60s was a decade of great change in black–white relations in

the United States, a decade in which African-Americans finally stood up and demanded the end of many of the inherently racist practices that the white-dominated world had nurtured for so long. The Cowboys were a mirror held up to this, immune neither from the practices nor from the struggle to eliminate them.

It all went over my head. I grew up in a tolerant household in which slurs were abhorred and change was supported, but I also grew up in the all-white cocoon of a segregated city. Racial tension did not exist in North Dallas; the only blacks I saw were the maids, cooks, and gardeners who ventured north from Oak Cliff and South Dallas in used cars and city buses. They were always pleasant and compliant, never angry. Ollie, our maid, cooked fried chicken and baked brownies for me and took me for rides on the bus. Juanita, who came when Ollie left, played Lego football with me. Our cousins had Martha, and many of my friends' families also had maids who became fixtures. That was my interaction with the black world. My classmates were white, my parents' friends were white, the other people in stores and restaurants were white.

I had no idea that blacks lived in a different world, a harsh place in which they endured an endless flow of indignities, including the inability to eat or sleep where they wanted. Black and white Cowboys alike were cheered as heroes on Sundays, but once the game was over the blacks were subjected to the same discrimination that all blacks in Dallas endured. They had to live in certain neighborhoods and eat at certain restaurants. In the early '60s they had to drink out of certain water fountains and shop at certain stores.

"It was almost like living a double life," Pettis Norman said. "You were cheered on Sundays and segregated the rest of the week. We came together as African-American and white teammates, got dressed together, practiced together, played together, and went to war together, and then we dispersed. One group went north and the other went south. That was the way it was. We were assigned roommates by color on the road and at training camp. We could not move into neighborhoods where our white teammates lived."

Many of the blacks who played for the Cowboys in the early '60s experienced the overt racism that was still common in Dallas. "Not long after I got there, I was shopping downtown and I saw colored and white water fountains," Frank Clarke said. "That was a shock. It was like, 'Wow, this is incredible.' I had grown up in Wisconsin with a lot of segregation and white superiority, so my fear was probably a little stronger. Because whereas in my hometown it was subtle, I sensed that these people in Dallas meant business. It was, 'Boy, this is where you drink from, and don't drink from that other one.'"

Don Perkins had an experience even before he began playing for the Cowboys. "After the college All-Star game in 1960, I went to hook up with the team in San Antonio, where they were practicing," he said. "I was traveling with Meredith and Gil Brandt and one other player. We stopped off in Dallas at a cafeteria and I was promptly told I could not eat there. We went to another place to eat, but Perkins had lost his appetite. It wasn't really a surprise. There were still colored and white bathrooms all over Texas and New Mexico."

Cowboy management struggled at first to find a hotel that would allow the team to rent rooms to black players. "We could only find one hotel in 1960, a Ramada Inn inside the terminal at Love Field," Schramm said. "They said we could stay there as long as the other hotels didn't retaliate and spread the word that they were letting blacks stay there. We stayed there that first year, and teams that came in to play us stayed there. We finally got the situation squared away the next year and moved to a Sheraton downtown."

The white players lived near the Cowboys' practice field on Forest Lane in North Dallas. Most of the black players lived near Bishop College in South Dallas, a half-hour away by car. Their neighborhood was so dangerous that Jethro Pugh put his stereo in the trunk of his car when he left for a road trip; he feared his apartment would get robbed while he was gone.

Landry fined players for being late to practice, a misdeed to which the black players were far more susceptible. "We had to come through town and up Central Expressway," Cornell Green said. "If there was a traffic jam, we got fined."

Calvin Hill joined the team as a rookie from Yale in '69. "Everything was geared toward North Dallas, and yet the black players lived in South Dallas," he said. "The black guys were sensitive to that and resentful of it. I used to go to a place on Forest Avenue to get my hair cut. I went to a nightclub that (champion boxer) Curtis Cokes owned where they checked for weapons at the door. As a black player you were exposed to a different side of Dallas. You had no choice. I offended Pete Gent one time after he came out with *North Dallas Forty*. I told him that it was a look at the Cowboys, but just the North Dallas Cowboys. I don't think he appreciated it."

Housing was not the only obvious inequality from which Cowboy management and the white players turned their heads. Many white players had commercial endorsements, radio shows, and comfortable offseason jobs: the perks of being a Cowboy. The black players had few such opportunities. Clarke had a radio show on KNOK, a black station, but he was the exception. "Everyone knew what was going on," Green said. "Nothing was hidden. Car dealerships used to let players drive cars. Very few black players got to do that. Then some white guy would get traded here, a third-stringer, and he'd get a new car. Meanwhile guys like myself, Renfro, and Perkins had been playing for years and making All-Pro and couldn't even get a car deal."

The Cowboys did not address these problems until the late '60s. Why? Until then it was just assumed that black players would accept a lesser lot. And since college football was still mostly an all-white enclave, the Cowboys were regarded as progressive for having blacks at all.

"It was just a completely different era then," Schramm said, "and you really can't compare it to today. Teams were operating differently, the civil rights movement was going strong, and there was an emergence of black players. There was a lot of talk about what to do, and a period of adjustment."

Officially, the Cowboys had a broad-minded philosophy. "Coach Landry stood up in a meeting and said, 'We will not have a race problem,'" Pugh said. The team used enough black players to erase any belief that discrimination existed. Some teams tolerated more hostile attitudes toward black players; the Cowboys were above that. "We had a very high percentage of African-Americans, even early on," Pettis Norman said, "and Landry's position was clear. He had a policy of, 'No matter what color you are,' and if you didn't adhere to that you could go elsewhere. His leadership helped limit trouble."

Yet the Cowboys were guilty of an inherently discriminatory practice known as "stacking" that was common in all sports then. Coaches seldom put blacks at quarterback or linebacker, positions supposedly requiring intelligence. Blacks mostly played running back, split end, and in the secondary—positions supposedly demanding speed and quickness, not intelligence. Blacks thus were "stacked" against each other, limiting the number that played. It was a quota system, born not out of discrimination so much as outdated stereotyping. The Cowboys were open-minded, but they did not start a black offensive lineman until Rayfield Wright in '68, did not start a black linebacker until Thomas Henderson in '75, and never started a black quarterback.

"I look at the team now and it has maybe four Anglo starters," Perkins said, "whereas when we played there were maybe four black starters. But there weren't as many blacks in the sport then. In the early days we didn't have one black linebacker or offensive lineman. We had one black defensive lineman, a guy named Nate Borden who had played for the Packers. That's just the way it was. I know people want to believe that we're a melting pot, which I don't believe, and that we were always a melting pot, which I don't believe, either. No one wants to remember that these things happened, that there was slavery or strange practices or that Perkins couldn't eat and sleep where he wanted when he was playing for the Cowboys. But that was the reality."

Also a reality was the separation of the black and white Cowboys into two camps that forged an uneasy truce. The core of the championship contender that the Cowboys built in the '60s was a group of white players from southern colleges with segregated football teams. Many had enlightened attitudes, but some had never played or even dressed with blacks and they brought preconceived notions with them to Dallas.

"There were players whom we knew didn't want to associate with us, and didn't," Pettis Norman said. "One white player, when he first came here, he was a young man who was very open-minded and he and his wife used to be very good friends with my wife and I, and he and I would ride to practice together and talk, and he was ostracized by some of the white players because he was associating with black players. He told me they asked him, 'What are you doing? Why do you go with the black players after the game?' We became very good friends and we still are today. But I knew there were several players that would prefer not to be in an environment with blacks. They were products of their communities. A lot of them came from hate-filled communities."

That was not unusual in the NFL of the '60s. "Those attitudes weren't any more prevalent on our team than on any other," said Clarke, who played for the Browns in the '50s. But it still was harmful to cohesiveness. According to Norman, some white players refused to hug black teammates after good plays. "They had misguided ideas that something bad was going to rub off on them," Norman said. "It was not uncommon for people from where they came from. People from there just didn't hug blacks."

Clarke said he "always heard that one Cowboy was a card-carrying member of the Ku Klux Klan." Dave Manders recalled an incident in which a white player "went wild" at a postgame party after Manders danced with Renfro's wife. The players finally stopped having postgame parties, which did as much to crystallize racial problems as solve them.

The color line did not divide all players. Many had no trouble coexisting. "Meredith, Reeves, Neely, and myself would get together and talk, smoke cigarettes and go have a beer," Clarke said. "Meredith would come to my house for dinner. My kids adored Dandy. Those kinds of things were going on."

Neely said, "We partied together. We had a Halloween party one year and we went in a white Rolls Royce, and my wife and I went as hippies, and we went down to Oak Cliff and picked up Cornell and his wife and Bob Hayes and his wife. Bob went as a white rabbit. We got some stares that night."

They could even joke about the situation, as serious as it was. "My first exhibition game, against the Rams in '65, was delayed three days because of the Watts riots," Neely said. "And then we had to drive right through Watts to get to the L.A. Coliseum. We were walking down the ramp for the game, and two weeks later we were scheduled to play a game in Birmingham, and as we were coming down the ramp in L.A., Cornell said to me, 'Ralph, I'll take care of you tonight if you take care of me in Birmingham.' That was beautiful. And then, when we got to Birmingham two weeks later, all the black guys got out and got some athletic tape, because we had city buses pick us up, and they put a big white line down in the bus and all the blacks got in the back. So we laughed and joked about it. It wasn't right, but we didn't get involved in that stuff."

On Sundays, none of it mattered. That was the miracle. Any division was washed away in the desire to win. The Cowboys were a football team above all else, not a social experiment. "Come game time, everything vanished," Gent said. "It was sort of amazing to see. In the end, it was not about that. Deep down inside these guys, football was so important that they weren't going to let any of this stuff that had been socialized into them about blacks affect their real clear thinking processes."

The black players agreed. "When I stepped onto the field, I wasn't about color or what someone said or where they lived or what they were making," Renfro said. "My desire was the prize, and that was to win. There were two or three guys I couldn't stand on the Cowboys because of their racist attitudes, but once we got out there there was only one thing on my mind and one thing on their minds, and that was winning."

The only color that mattered on Sunday was the color of their uniforms. "We were brothers then," Manders said. "One year, one of the Eagles cheap-shotted Lee Roy Jordan for something he had done in a prior game. He was standing on the sidelines in a total rage, so mad he was jumping up and down and yelling, "You better watch out, you fuckin' nigger!' The black guys on our team were standing there going, 'Yeah!'"

I met George Birdsong at our class party at the end of fourth grade. George had attended another school, but he was joining us the next year and his mother brought him to our party to meet his new classmates. The party was well underway at a friend's house when their car rolled to a stop at the curb, the passenger door creaked open, and a pair of the longest, thinnest legs I had ever seen dropped to the ground. George slowly unfolded himself out of the car and stood on the curb. He was five inches taller than any of us, a long straw with big brown eyes, a kind smile, and an innate gentleness obvious at first glance. He also was black; the first black student at my school.

Our teacher gathered us on the front lawn and introduced us to George, who nodded without saying a word, obviously wishing he were elsewhere. He then joined our soccer game and boomed a few kicks out of bounds. A rough start. My friends and I talked about him a little bit over the summer, but only because he was new, not because he was black. We were color blind, for the most part. We had no idea that he was integrating our school, or that the eyes of the school's fathers were upon us, praying there would be no trouble.

I next saw George on the first day of fifth grade, in September of '67. Our first class was history with Mr. Brennan, the varsity football coach, a tough-loving Irish bantam who had played halfback for SMU in the '50s and ran a crisp class long on discipline. George was late. Mr. Brennan had already handed out books and begun teaching when the door slowly opened and George's long head popped inside. The room fell silent; we were all scared of Mr. Brennan's famous temper, and poor George was about to feel its fury before he had even sat down.

"You're late!" Mr. Brennan shouted.

George froze by the door, paralyzed with fear.

Mr. Brennan then paused, producing a tense silence. Years later, when I understood the significance of that morning, I realized why Mr. Brennan had hesitated. He was in a tough spot. Did he adhere to his rules of order and discipline the school's first black student before the kid had even opened a book? Or did he ease up because of the circumstances and the school's desire for things to go well?

Mr. Brennan was a smart man, a powerful teacher I would never forget, and he chewed privately on his options for a moment before reaching a decision.

"Well," he said, "come on in and find a seat, son."

George exhaled, smiled, and lurched into the rows of chairs to find one that was unoccupied. He was off the hook.

"Let's get here on time, OK?" Mr. Brennan said sharply, incapable of letting a malfeasance pass without some rebuke.

"Yes, sir," George mumbled.

George's father was an inspector for the United States Department of Agriculture, a tall, kindly man who wore wire-framed glasses. His mother was responsible for their decision to send George to a private school. She was a soft-spoken woman who had graduated from Columbia University and was determined to give her children a first-rate education. They were social pioneers, imbued with extraordinary fortitude for choosing to send their son to an all-white school in Dallas in 1967.

As it turned out, their decision was more difficult than the reality of George's life at school; few racial barriers have come down as easily. George was responsible for that. He was impossible not to like; shy, gangly, and smart, he made friends easily, laughed at jokes, and fit right in. He immediately turned our YMCA basketball team into a winner, towering over everyone as he batted rebound after rebound against the backboard until one finally banked in. My friends and I had concentrated on football and baseball until then, but we quickly realized we had a winning future in basketball as long as George remained our classmate. I began spending a lot more time shooting at the goal in my driveway.

Not that George's assimilation went perfectly. A couple of punks gave him trouble from the beginning, laughing at his long, awkward gait on the playground, and calling him "nigger," at first behind his back and then, boldly, to his face. George endured their taunts impassively and with our support until he could take it no longer. Exploding in anger during recess, he pummeled one of the smart alecks with a flurry of punches before the kid could react. Bloodied and humiliated, the kid never bothered George again and transferred to another school the next year. Fighting in recess normally merited punishment, but the teachers never said a word to George.

Among all the kids in the class, I hit it off the best with him. My parents encouraged me to ask him over to play on Saturdays, and we found we enjoyed spending time together. We played records and games, shot baskets, watched television, rode bicycles. When he spent the night at my house, he would eat out at restaurants with me and my parents, just as my other friends did. We went to the usual haunts: Campisi's for spaghetti, Jamie's for hamburgers, Vincent's for fried shrimp. There was never any trouble getting George in, and it never occurred to me that there would be. Years later my father admitted he had always called ahead to make sure the restaurant would let George in. "My son has a friend who is black and we're coming to eat, and I sure hope there won't be any trouble," my father would say. Sometimes he even used my grandfather's name as leverage to insure an uneventful evening. I was stunned to hear that my father had felt compelled to do that; it spoke volumes about the tenuous state of racial progress in Dallas.

George was one of my best friends, and yet, unlike with my other friends, there were times when it was inescapably clear that we were different. He lived with his parents and two younger sisters in a tidy frame house in Hamilton Park, the lone black enclave in North Dallas, but we never played there. There was more room and more to do at my house, and, incredibly, a cross street near his house had been named Tobian Street by the city, honoring my grandfather for years of service on the Dallas Housing Commission. George and I joked about the coincidence, but in

Frank Clarke was taken in the 1960 expansion draft and stayed long enough to play a critical role against the Packers in the 1966 NFL championship game at the Cotton Bowl.

Sonny Gibbs was a bonus-baby quarterback from TCU who lasted just one year with the Cowboys. Here he is wearing the uniform that Tex Schramm hated and couldn't wait to redesign for maximum effect on television.

3

The author in full backyard regalia, January 1963.

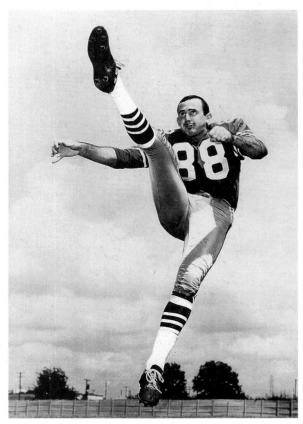

4

Colin Ridgway, nicknamed "the Boomer," was supposed to revolutionize pro football with his powerful kicking leg. Instead, he kicked the ball straight up.

Hey diddle diddle: Don Perkins runs the ball (where else?) up the middle.

6

7

8

Bob Lilly, then and now. Mr. Cowboy has changed very little.

Pettis Norman runs with a pass reception in the 1966 championship game.

9

Don Meredith, who endured incredible physical pain and endless second-guessing, yet somehow emerged with his sense of humor intact.

The author's grandfather, Louis Tobian ("Pop").

10

11

Jean and Seymour Eisenberg, the author's mother and father.

12

The facade of the Cotton Bowl, home to a lifetime's worth of memories.

13

"Some say the world will end in fire/Some say in ice . . . " Robert Frost would have appreciated the 1967 NFL championship game in Green Bay, unlike Jim Boeke, who went to extreme measures to fend off the cold, or Dick Daniels and Bob Hayes, who huddled under a makeshift tent on the sidelines. (Hayes ran his pass patterns with his hands stuffed in his pants, tipping off Green Bay that they could cheat toward other receivers.)

14

15

Champions at last: The Cowboys carry Tom Landry off the field after winning Super Bowl VI, in the season in which they abandoned the Cotton Bowl for Texas Stadium.

the back of our minds we knew it reaffirmed our differences. We cared more about our friendship than any adult symbolism, but as much as our friendship had taught me that blacks were no different from me, it also taught me the sad lesson that cultural barriers would always separate whites and blacks to some extent—even those trying to live together as though those barriers were not up.

Still, I was proud of my friendship with George as we grew older and moved through grade school and into high school, proud that I had not succumbed to the easy lure of intolerance that attracted so many. As I look back, I had no right to feel such pride. I had it easy. I did not have to learn to live in George's world; he had to learn to live in mine. The pressure was on him, not on me, and what pressure there was. By coming to my school and joining our world, George entered into a dual existence in which he was never fully accepted. In the white world, at school and among his friends, he was the token black. In the black world, his neighborhood, he was the token white who had forsaken his culture. Everywhere he turned there was a line in the sand. We were his friends, but he grew uncomfortable among us when we became increasingly interested in girls. That was a tough situation for him. Another black student, a girl, joined our class, but she and George were not close. Who else was he supposed to date in a city so uneasy with integration? He finally gave up his dual existence and quietly began dating white classmates with open-minded parents.

We remained close early in high school, but our friendship slowly waned. He enjoyed science and math, I enjoyed English. He befriended an intellectual long-distance runner, and I fell in with a popular and slightly irreverent group that spent a lot of time playing tennis and talking about girls. One boy in the group, William, was clearly of bigoted stock. "Nigger!" he screamed once, reflexively, at a car that cut him off as we rode to a football game with George in the back seat. The car fell silent.

"Sorry about that, George," William said.

"That's OK," George mumbled, still enduring.

It was clear why George chose to find friends elsewhere.

George graduated near the top of our class, when to Amherst College, and returned to Dallas to attend Southwestern Medical School, where my father was one of his professors. He specialized in pathology, took a job in Atlanta, and established himself there, ultimately joining the faculty of the

Emory University Medical School. His parents' decision to send him to my school in '67 had sent him into the white world, and he never went back. I wondered, years later, how he felt about that. The last time I spoke to him was to invite him to my wedding in 1984. He told me his father had died, and I was embarrassed that I had fallen so out of touch with him. He was unable to come to the wedding, but he sent a present and a telegram. He was touched; we had too much history between us not to feel the tug of a special bond in our hearts. As I grew older, left with only that history instead of a lasting friendship, I could not help feeling that I had let us down.

Dallas historians and observers generally agree that the Cowboys' greatest gift to the city was their part in helping erase the stain of the Kennedy assassination. Yet that was just a boost to Dallas's image, a polishing of its reflection in the eyes of others. As important as that was, it had little impact on everyday life in Dallas. Within the city itself, the Cowboys gave a more important gift: the sight of blacks and whites working together.

The city's racial history to that point was far from noble. My grandfather told a Dallas Public Library interviewer in 1973 that it was difficult to conduct business in Dallas in the '20s if you did not belong to the Ku Klux Klan. In 1950, segregationists bombed South Dallas businesses. Midway rides at the State Fair still were not integrated then; blacks could ride only on "Negro Achievement Day." By 1960 Dallas was one of the largest cities in the South with a school system that was still completely segregated. Jerry LeVias, SMU's first black football star, received death threats before games as late as 1967.

The Cotton Bowl still was segregated in the '50s; black fans could sit only in certain areas of the end zone, a custom that was abolished by the time the Cowboys joined the NFL. The Cowboys had thousands of black fans in the early days. They still sat mostly in the end zones, but not in a segregated section. "They cheered for the Cowboys, but they cheered particularly hard for the black Cowboys such as Perkins and Don Bishop," said Allen Stone, now a broadcasting executive in Dallas.

The number of black fans swelled when the Cleveland Browns came to town. "The black fans loved Jim Brown and came to see him play," said

Doug Alexander, now an accountant in Dallas. "They cheered for the Cowboys, but they also cheered for Jim Brown."

The Cowboys were among the first organizations in Dallas, and certainly the most public, to cultivate an integrated environment. As imperfect as their own house was, they set an example for the rest of the city to follow. They were ahead of the city's long, slow curve toward equality. The simple act of a touchdown pass from Meredith to Hayes, white to black, carried a great symbolic weight.

"A lot of the things that had existed in Dallas when we got there, the colored water fountains and such, came down. There is no doubt we were part of that," Clarke said.

"I came out of an environment that pushed for change in Charlotte, North Carolina," Norman said years later, sitting in the offices of Pettis Norman Incorporated, a distribution business based in Oak Cliff. "Jesse Jackson had been part of a demonstration in Greensboro, which is 85 miles from Charlotte, where they opened up lunch counters. I was among the student group from Johnson C. Smith University that did the same thing in downtown Charlotte, going, 'We are not going to go to a place where we can't sit and eat.' So I came out of that movement. Early on, when I came to Dallas, I was assessing things. But I knew I would be involved in change, that this was a place where I could make a contribution. When I spoke to the issues, I was called a rabble-rouser and all kinds of things. There are still people who believe I was traded (to San Diego in 1971) because of my political positions, leading demonstrations downtown. You have to identify the war zone before you get in and fight. Once I did that, I pushed for those changes I felt strongly about and still feel strongly about."

The first "war zone," inevitably, was the Cowboys themselves. Before they could become a symbol of integration, they had to integrate themselves. One by one, the color barriers on the team came down.

The first was the method for selecting roommates at training camp and on the road. In the early '60s there were white rooms and black rooms; veterans could choose roommates, but none chose to integrate. That changed as the team matured into a playoff contender.

"I approached Tex (Schramm) and some others before training camp one year," Norman said, "and I said to Tex, 'It is time for us to change this situation. We practice together, we play together, we bleed together, we fight for each other, and yet we go to training camp and we have to live by race. I think you miss a lot when that happens. You don't grow or mature.'"

Schramm considered Norman's suggestion and brought together Norman and Manders, who was white, as camp began. "Tex said he wanted us to become the first to live together and see what happened," Norman said. "We got along fine. Other players then saw that this was acceptable, so when we came back to Dallas to end training camp, before we went to our houses, roommates were assigned by alphabetical order. And from that point on, we lived in a truly integrated environment. I don't know of any major incidents that occurred other than the usual clashing of personalities that would occur no matter what color people were."

Schramm's memory was slightly different. "We brought the (black and white) roommates together and there were no major incidents, but teamwide it didn't really work over the long haul," he said. "Artificial methods (of socialization) usually aren't going to work. Players wanted to room with their friends, so they did."

There still was enough juggling of roommates that some blacks and whites wound up together on the road or at training camp. Jethro Pugh roomed mostly with Rayfield Wright, who was black, but also at different times with John Wilbur and Blaine Nye, who were white. "It was interesting sometimes," Pugh said. "On the road some guys wouldn't know how to react when relatives came by. You might have a white guy with a bunch of black people in his room. Some guys got kind of quiet. They didn't know how to interact. But really it worked out OK. In Washington and New York I had a lot of relatives and I would take teammates, white and black, to my cousin's house to eat navy beans for good luck. In Pittsburgh we all went with Tony Liscio because he had family and they ate lasagna. Tony had 25 people follow him home."

The next barrier was housing. The black Cowboys lived south of town until '68, when Mel Renfro was denied once too often when he tried to rent a townhouse in North Dallas. Renfro had grown up in Oregon, in a relatively integrated society, and had seethed at the segregated existence forced on him and his family in Dallas. In '68, a North Dallas builder agreed to rent to him, then reneged when Renfro returned to sign the lease. "It had happened so often before, and this time it was just so blatant and it pissed me off so bad that I just said, 'OK, this is it, I'm not standing for this anymore,'" Renfro said.

He sued in federal court, citing the Fair Housing Act, and won an injunction. He moved into the townhouse in North Dallas with his wife and children and later won one of the first permanent injunctions in Dallas supporting the Fair Housing Act. He said later that the Cowboys asked him not to file the suit, but they ultimately supported him and helped him find counsel, and Schramm testified for him.

"I opened up the doors for a lot of people," Renfro said. "I frightened those white folks to death, those real-estate people, the developers. I got a lot of positive mail from people of color that said because of what I had done they could live where they wanted. It made a mark on that community."

Rightly or not, Renfro felt singled out for his trouble. A quarter-century later, he was still angry about a remark made by Clint Murchison in the hallway of the Cowboy offices on Central Expressway. It happened in '71, after the Cowboys had lost to the Colts in Super Bowl V. The Colts scored on a freak play in which one receiver tipped a pass to another. It was illegal for teammates to tip passes to each other, but the officials ruled that Renfro's fingernail had tipped the ball in between the Colt receivers. The Cowboys went on to lose on a last-second field goal.

"During that winter Mr. Murchison cornered me in the hallway and said, 'Why did you lose that game for us?'" Renfro said. "I said, 'What game?' He said, 'The Super Bowl.' I said, 'What are you talking about?' He said, 'That tipped pass.' Craig Morton had thrown two fourth-quarter interceptions and Dan Reeves had tipped a pass (resulting in an interception) to win it (for the Colts), and I was the goat to the owner? Man, that said it all."

Murchison, who died in 1984, had a notorious deadpan sense of humor and may well have been kidding when he spoke to Renfro, but Renfro and many of the rest of the black Cowboys were not in a joking mood after being forced to live in South Dallas until 1968. After Renfro's lawsuit, the other black Cowboys moved out of South Dallas and found housing nearer to the Cowboys' practice facility on Forest Lane. "My class (of Cowboys) didn't really experience that (segregated housing) situation," Calvin Hill said. "I lived near Love Field. Claxton Welch lived by Turtle Creek. Les Shy and Phil Clark lived by Turtle Creek. The patterns were breaking down."

So was the team's fundamental racial barrier: the one dividing the locker room into black and white fraternities. "We had been through a lot of years together and times were changing, and the attitudes (of the white players) changed quite clearly in the late '60s," Norman said. "A lot of the guys who had not wanted to be around blacks, their anxiety levels began to diminish. They began to hug you after big plays; that told you we had taken great leaps forward. Southerners never wanted to give up the South, but they were losing the war."

Herb Adderley's arrival in '70 was a turning point. Adderley had played cornerback on Lombardi's championship teams in Green Bay and then clashed with Lombardi's replacement, Phil Bengtson, leading to his trade to the Cowboys. His forceful leadership brought about change. "There wasn't a black–white thing in Green Bay, but there was in Dallas," Adderley said. "The blacks and whites didn't socialize much. My input had a lot to do with changing that. I said, 'Hey, we're a team, we got to get this thing together.' I started talking to the white guys. I said to Lilly, 'Man, we got to get these guys together. If there is any prejudice, we got to get beyond that. That's not what this thing is about.' Me and Calvin Hill had a major impact in that situation."

Hill said, "Herb came in and said they had dealt with it in Green Bay. And then when (former Packer) Forrest Gregg came to play for the Cowboys, Herb went up and hugged him at a meeting. I can recall that several players, including myself, were really touched and tried to imagine doing the same thing to our teammates. The perception was that maybe they had a closeness in Green Bay that we didn't have."

Adderley's arrival coincided with that of Duane Thomas, the running back who introduced the militancy that had sprouted in the black community in the '60s. When Thomas criticized Landry as "a plastic man" in '71, he brought to a boil the long-simmering resentments of the black Cowboys—resentments not aimed at Landry so much as their second-class status and the reality of white control. Thomas ended a holdout before the '71 season by saying he was returning "for my people, the black people." His famous silences clearly had racial underpinnings; when he refused to speak to reporters or teammates during the '71 season and even once told Landry to "go to hell," he became a symbol of defiance that threatened to polarize the team: The black players admired his gall, while the white players either loathed him or did not know what to think.

"And the funny part was, Duane wouldn't talk to the black players, either," Pugh said, still laughing years later. "Bob Hayes said, 'Duane, how do you do it, I can't keep my mouth shut five minutes.'"

In the end, the players put aside their differences and built a bridge over the divide that had separated them, a bridge that held up long enough for the team to win a Super Bowl in '71. The leadership of Adderley, Mike Ditka, and other veterans was essential, as was the players' overriding determination to win a Super Bowl after years of playoff failures. That mattered more.

After that, the Cowboys were held up by others as an example of racial understanding. In '72, Pugh, Wright, and Toomay took a USO-sponsored trip to the Far East to speak to troops. "There were some racial problems over there and they thought we could shed some light," Pugh said. "They worked us pretty good. We flew on military planes, went on the radio, went to the bases, talked to the kids. It wasn't all race-related, but a lot of it was. We talked about the example of getting on the team bus and hearing the different kinds of music, rhythm and blues, country-western, acid rock. There were a lot of different personalities and backgrounds on the team. The troops asked us, 'How do you get along?' We told them, 'We just do. We manage.'"

In the '70s and '80s pro football experienced a racial revolution. The face of the game changed from white to mixed to predominantly black. The championship Miami teams of the early '70s were almost entirely white, but the championship Pittsburgh teams of the late '70s were dominated by blacks. Teams began to rely as much on black players as whites, then more on blacks than whites as coaches finally disdained "stacking" and old stereotypes and put blacks at decision-making positions. By the '90s, black players composed two-thirds of most rosters.

As the years went by, as such things will, the old tensions between the players from the Cotton Bowl days faded along with any other unpleasant memories of the days gone by. "When we get together now, it's like we have gotten older and wiser and seen through all that superficial stuff," Hill said. "There is a closeness now that perhaps didn't exist then."

Lilly said, "I have fond memories of all of my teammates, even Duane Thomas. I just think the world of him now. I didn't in 1971, but I have gotten to know him since then and he has changed and every time we see each other we have a blast talking about the old times."

The black players prefer their more pleasant memories, too, but they also can look back to the '60s with the understanding that they helped facilitate real change at a critical time in Dallas's racial history.

"It was pretty wild, in the first place, that the NFL decided to bring a franchise to a segregated area of the country," Clarke said. "There was some fear among the black players at first, but we saw this as a chance to facilitate change and be part of something important. We had a chance to exemplify blacks and whites living together, and we pulled it off. There was still a lot of crazy stuff going on, but we pulled it off."

Chapter Nine

In the Cowboys' early days you could park near the Cotton Bowl, sit where you wanted, and move around and talk to friends during the game. All that changed after the Cowboys won a division title and played the Packers in the '66 championship game. Suddenly, they were the hottest ticket in town, with a large and passionate following.

"The talk of the town on Monday morning was the Cowboy game," said Ron Chapman, then a KLIF disc jockey. "You planned your weekend around it. If you weren't going, you listened on the radio or went to a bar with friends, or had a party. And if you were an event planner and your charity function happened to fall on the same Sunday as a Cowboy game, you were dead. You couldn't get anyone to come."

The weekly Cowboy luncheons, open to the public, became major affairs. "There had been 50 or 60 people coming, and it swelled to like 500 or 600, enough to fill a ballroom at the Southland Life building," said Bill Mercer, the team's play-by-play radio voice, who emceed the luncheons.

Mercer suddenly was a busy man; besides the luncheons and his weekly game duties, he hosted the *Tom Landry Show* and *Pete Gent Show* on television and handled the play-by-play call on preseason television broadcasts, which were taped on Saturday nights and shown on Sunday afternoons. Being associated with the Cowboys was not so lucrative yet—

he earned 75 dollars for every game he broadcast in KLIF—but it made life interesting.

"When they started winning in '66 it was incredible, like the Beatles or something," he said. "I remember one time we landed at Love Field after a big road win and the fans knocked down the fence and surrounded the airplane. We all ducked our heads and went out the back door. I was hiding behind the linemen. People were just going crazy. Things were never the same with the Cowboys after that year. They were really, really big."

Surprisingly, the Cowboys still seldom sold out the Cotton Bowl. They drew 70,000 or more fans to only six of 23 regular season and playoff games at home from '67 to '69. The Cowboys played easy schedules in those years and the fans still were not willing to pay to watch just any team. The corners of the upper decks were often empty. "When Atlanta, New Orleans or Washington came, there wasn't much excitement," said Don Hullett, now a supervisor in a medical company.

Most games did draw more than 60,000 fans. The Cotton Bowl, a hallowed college football ground since the '40s, entered a new phase of its history as a loud and rowdy home field for the Cowboys.

The players would convene on Saturday afternoons at the downtown Holiday Inn, eat a team meal, and meet a curfew later that night. Some players hit the bars before curfew. Walt Garrison, a true cowboy, drove out to the Mesquite Rodeo and competed. "He'd sneak out there and ride, and make it back in time," Ralph Neely said, "until Landry caught him and made him stop."

The players rose on Sunday morning, ate a team breakfast, and dawdled around the hotel until their bus left for the stadium shortly before 11 o'clock, some two hours before kickoff. Players who wanted to go earlier took cabs. "Me and Manders and Reeves, a bunch of us, would get there at 9:30 and play cards," Neely said. "During the State Fair we would go down to the midway and play games and eat a couple of corny dogs and win teddy bears. Coach Landry would come in and start talking about the game plan and all that, and there'd be teddy bears sitting in lockers. He never said anything, so I assumed it was OK."

Their locker room at the Cotton Bowl was spartan, just rows of lockers, a trainer's table, and a bank of showers; players expected no more in the days before big salaries invaded the NFL. Many players preferred the hotel as the best place to prepare for the withering physical test that lay ahead. "Guys who went early just sat there and worried for two hours," Mike Gaechter said. "I took the bus."

As a fan you also had a routine, your own set of Sunday conventions. The team's rising popularity all but obligated you to develop a plan for beating the crowds; you could spend hours in traffic if you didn't. You navigated your own route to Fair Park through the back roads of downtown and East Dallas, a path perfected through trial and error. You parked in your favorite secret hiding place amid the warren of alleys and side streets around the stadium, leaving your car behind a pharmacy or on someone's lawn. You walked to the stadium through the graceful urban green of Fair Park. You handed your ticket to the same attendant every week, held your nose in the same clammy bathroom, stood in the same long line for a watery soda.

"On Sunday mornings my father would go to Ernie's Deli on Lovers Lane and pick up cold cuts and corned beef for sandwiches, and we would take them and my mother's cookies and eat lunch at our seats," said Leonard Epstein, a Dallas attorney who began attending the games as a seven-year-old in '65. "We carried a thing that held a metal thermos on one side and a food holder on the other. The thermos had hot chocolate in it, or Delaware Punch, a noncarbonated soft drink. We'd come down Central Expressway and weave through town on Oakland Street. We parked behind a pickle factory. There were pickle barrels in the back and we would drive through and park in the back so we didn't have to leave the car on the street. After the game, my father bought pickles."

Parking was often a test of your bravery and resourcefulness. The few parking spaces inside the fairgrounds were reserved for team and game officials, players' families, media, and well-connected fans. Everyone else had to improvise.

"I found a place no one seemed to know about," said Harry Sebel, a stockbroker. "You turned into an alley and went behind a drug store. There were four or five places back there. In all the years at the Cotton Bowl I missed only one game, because it was raining so hard that the alley flooded and we couldn't get into it. We just said, 'The hell with it, let's go home.'"

Don Hullett's father was similarly creative. "There was a gate over on the other side of the stadium, and we pulled in there and parked behind the cattle barns," Hullett said. "Didn't have to pay a dime. The gate was open almost every week. We could leave with two minutes to go and still beat the traffic. If the gate wasn't open, we had to drive around and find another place."

Many fans left their cars on the lawns of Fair Park homeowners, who cashed in on the Sunday invasions by turning their lawns into parking lots. Nearing the stadium you were swarmed by barkers standing in the road with cardboard signs offering spaces on their lawns for three dollars. Many fans grudgingly accepted invitations, lacking alternatives. "You just hoped your car was there when you got back," Bill Livingston said. "Guys would ask for five dollars to watch your car during the game. You went, 'Yeah, you'll watch my car while it gets stripped.'"

Livingston often rode the bus, as did hundreds of other fans. "I took the Junius Heights bus and transferred at Exhibition Street," he said. "Back then people didn't think twice about putting a tenth grader on a bus and sending him downtown alone on a Sunday afternoon."

Johnny Minx's mother drove him and his friends in from Pleasant Grove before he was old enough to drive. "She dropped us off at the front gate of the fairgrounds on Second Avenue," Minx said. "Then she'd come back and pick us up at a prearranged time. You didn't worry about crime or anything."

Once the adventure of commuting and parking was completed, fans walked through Fair Park toward the stadium, passing the Women's Building, the Automotive Building, the Planetarium, the 4-H Building, and the other fair exhibits. Many fans stopped and ate picnic lunches in pleasant weather. Fathers and sons threw footballs. "It was a nice communal walk that everyone made," Ron Chapman said. "Today you just go through the parking lot. At the Cotton Bowl there was the pleasant experience of walking over grass and curbs and through buildings. It was a little homey, almost like going to a college game."

The slow, pleasant roll toward kickoff was transformed when a game coincided with the State Fair in mid-October. The fairgrounds were overrun with the smell of fried food and cotton candy, blinking lights, clanging bells, whistles, and thousands of people running in every direction. The midway ran right in front of the Cotton Bowl. I always talked my father into letting me ride a few rides and play a few games, even though this was not my main trip to the fair. (That came on Fair Day, a school holiday.) "I would go ride the roller coaster at halftime," said Doug Alexander, a Dallas accountant. "They gave you an in-and-out pass."

Before you went inside for the start of the game, you stood in line for a Fletcher's corny dog, a hot dog attached to a stick, rolled in a cone of cornmeal, and fried. You knew it would fester in your stomach all day, but it was so tasty that you ate it anyway. Once you were inside, you found your seat and watched the stadium slowly fill. The players warmed up and returned to their locker rooms, and then a marching band gave a pregame show. The Cowboys relied on a rotation of high school and college bands to perform before games and at halftimes. Over the years the bands became as familiar as the Cowboy players. There were high school bands from Temple, DeSoto, Cisco, Plano, and Highland Park. There was the Tyler Junior College Apache Band, and the Apache Belles, a high-kicking dance squad, as well as the Kilgore Junior College Ranger Band and the Rangerettes. The Grambling College band drew standing ovations. There was a "Circus Day" with an Elephant Ballet, and a "traditional" Thanksgiving show featuring the Dallas Civic Chorus singing the "Battle Hymn of the Republic." The North Texas State Square Dancers Association made an appearance, as did the Senoritas, a dance group from Navarro Junior College. You knew them all if you were a serious fan. The Greater Fort Worth Lions Club Band, unofficially known as the Cowboys' band, sat in the end zone and played during time-outs.

Beginning in '67, the national anthem was played in a trumpet solo by Tommy Loy, the Dallas musician who caused such a sensation on Thanksgiving night in '66. "They told me later that Clint Murchison wanted a trumpet solo because he liked the scene in *From Here to Eternity* when Montgomery Clift played a bugle solo for his dead friend," Loy told a *Times Herald* interviewer in 1986. Loy was a compact native Texan who played Dixieland music at Dallas nightclubs. His Air Force flight leader was an aide to Gordon McLendon, who owned KLIF, and the aide gave Loy's name to Murchison. "Clint didn't know me from Adam's cat, but he wanted a trumpeter," Loy said.

Loy was paid 10 dollars a game, and an extra 15 dollars for national television. My father and I joked about him, playfully cringing on the rare occasions when he misplayed a note, but his graceful trumpet became a fundamental part of the Cotton Bowl experience. On gray afternoons late in the season, with division titles at stake and the crowd pulsating with anticipation, Loy's anthem knifed through the chilly air and elicited a roar.

These were the days before professional cheerleaders—a fashion the Cowboys would start at Texas Stadium—but you could not play a football game in Texas without cheerleaders, and the Cowboys used local high-school students. "Sunset High School, Roosevelt High School, whatever, it was a big honor for them to get to cheer in the Cotton Bowl, and the crowd would actually kind of get into it," Walt Garrison said. In '70 the Cowboys used an all-star assemblage and called them the Cowboy Cheerleaders, a pale precursor to the minimally dressed group that would gyrate on the sidelines at Texas Stadium.

The crowd was not as pretentious as the rich, refined crowd that would fill Texas Stadium. "They were loud and rowdy and right on top of you," Garrison said. "The Cotton Bowl crowd was more like the Dawg Pound in Cleveland, or the folks in Denver, or the people in San Francisco who poured beer on you when you came out for the game. I loved going down that ramp to start the game because it was open and you weren't coming out of some tunnel. I mean, it was open and everyone could see you and you could see them, and you could hear them screaming, and you were ready to play coming down that ramp. I mean, you just wanted to start hitting people."

The relationship between the players and fans was much closer than it is now. The fans had an easier time relating to the players. Players' salaries were more commensurate with fans' salaries; many players worked second jobs in the offseason. Meredith and Gaechter were stockbrokers. Andrie sold real estate. Howley owned a dry-cleaning business. Liscio sold cars. It was the days before big money in pro football, before players became millionaire swells who considered themselves superior to the fans. They still had their humility.

"The players knew they weren't going to make a million dollars, and you could relate to them more," Don Hullet said. "You saw them around town a little bit. I went to a promotion at Highlander Stadium (at Highland Park High School) and wound up catching passes from Craig Morton. You wouldn't see that today. My wife met Meredith at Sears; they had autograph sessions at Sears and her mother worked there. My wife got Meredith's autograph."

Billy Jack Smith was a boy growing up in Oak Cliff in those days. He lived down the street from the sister of Jerry Rhome, the Cowboys' backup quarterback. Rhome's nephews were his playmates. "Jerry would come over and play with us," said Smith, now a marketing consultant in Dallas. "He was just a big kid. We'd play hide and seek, or touch football. Jerry taught me the mechanics of how to throw a football. I wound up playing quarterback at Carter High School. I still have an accurate arm."

Smith went to the Cowboy games with Rhome's nephews. "My parents would come and get me out of Sunday school early," Smith said. "After the games we'd go on the field and get into the locker room. What a treat that was. You didn't realize how lucky you were. I met Lilly and Garrison and all those guys when they were taking their uniforms off. Garrison had a beer in one hand and a dip in the other. The locker room was small and jam-packed, just wall-to-wall humanity. Everyone seemed huge. but they were nice, really nice. Then there'd be dozens of people waiting around outside the locker room. It was a very friendly, open, nonthreatening atmosphere, just a different mentality from the way it is now. There was a lot of exchange, players signing autographs and talking to their families and just kind of hanging around. Jerry came out and kissed his girlfriend. It was like something out of a movie, a college scene."

She came down the aisle on the 50-yard line, behind the Cowboy bench, as the Cowboys were beating up on the Falcons at the Cotton Bowl in '67. She tip-toed down the steps atop white high heels, wearing a leopard-skin miniskirt that revealed almost all the legs there were to see. Her white-blond hair was piled high on her head. In each hand, held up to her protruding chest, was a gob of pink cotton candy.

Bubbles Cash said later that she never intended to cause a stir, that she was just hungry for a snack. That was doubtful, considering what she was wearing and where she worked: on the stages of Dallas's most popular strip joints. Anyway, her timing was perfect. She came down the aisle during a lull in the game, shaking her hips and balancing her "snack." The crowd went wild. One man whistled, then another, then a third. Soon, hundreds were ogling and shouting. The commotion was so loud that the players looked up to see what was happening. "Never will forget it," Neely said. "We were standing in the huddle during a time-out, and Meredith said, 'Oh my God.' And there she was, walking right down that 50-yard line."

Only at a Cowboy game in the Cotton Bowl, in the late '60s, could a stripper become a star. Any earlier, a woman could not have worn so little in public. Any later, once the Cowboys moved to Texas Stadium, and the crowd would have gasped; the Texas Stadium crowd was too refined to wolf-whistle at a stripper. The Cotton Bowl crowd was not. Gritty and gregarious, the Cotton Bowl crowd made Bubbles Cash famous.

Few fans knew she was a stripper when she came down the aisle that first time. She was just a knockout wearing a miniskirt. A *Morning News* photographer snapped a picture as she descended; Bubbles was smiling as the fans laughed at her bawdy audacity. The *Times Herald*'s Steve Perkins was so stirred by the sight that he wrote about her in a column titled "That Girl."

"I put it to you," Perkins wrote, "that few things are more worthy of attention than the reasons for the spontaneous combustion among a segment of the Cotton Bowl crowd Sunday when That Girl came ticky-tacking down the steps. I submit that it was a true Happening . . . The girl herself is not important, except for the fact that she was there as a saucy swatch of catalyst for the right moment. Her blonde hair towered impossibly above her head. She wore a miniskirt that had been shrunk at the cleaners, resulting in a super fit. And she was carrying two great whirls of gossamer cotton candy, frail gobs of pinkness which perfected the tableau."

She was a 20-year-old who had grown up on a dairy farm near Fort Worth, dreaming of replacing Candy Barr as Dallas's premier stripper. Her dreams came true. Her boss began promoting her as the woman causing such a fuss at the Cotton Bowl, and her legend was sealed. "She became quite a star," said Abe Weinstein, owner of the Colony Club.

Her trips down the aisle became a Cotton Bowl tradition; Bubbles promenaded at every home game as the fans cheered and whistled. Even the players turned and watched. "I saw Coach Landry looking at her one time," Walt Garrison said. "She always waited until like the middle of the first quarter to make her entrance. You knew when she was coming when you heard the crowd start going, 'Ahhh.' That was Bubbles coming down. But that was the kind of crowd there was at the Cotton Bowl. It was more of a blue-collar crowd. I loved that crowd."

She became the Cowboys' unofficial mascot, and even flew to several road games. Her picture popped up in the game program, in an advertisement for a Lear jet charter service. The ad said she was "appearing nightly at the Theater Lounge on Jackson Street."

Her celebrity was such that fans sought her autograph. "I got her to sign a little plastic football," said Billy Jack Smith, whose seats were near the aisle she made famous. "She had quite a signature. The B in Bubbles was a pair of breasts with nipples. Her last name was a dollar sign."

At the peak of her fame, she ran for governor in '68 as a "peace candidate" and appeared in two low-budget movies, *Swamp Lust* and *Mars Needs Women.* But the novelty wore off, her star faded, and she stopped coming to Cowboy games. She moved to Los Angeles and Hawaii, returned to Dallas, and "retired" because "it was too hard competing with the skin flicks and massage parlors," she told a *Times Herald* interviewer. A failed marriage and young motherhood forced her to grow up. "I didn't want to grow old wearing a G-string," she said. She became a musician, singing in gospel, rock, and country groups, then opened a jewelry store in a strip mall near Love Field. As a 43-year-old in 1990 she ran for governor again and led all write-in candidates with 3,287 votes. "It just warms my heart to know that many people wrote in my name. I'm just grateful," she said.

When I tried to find her in 1996, her jewelry store had closed and none of her old bosses knew where she was. But if she was gone, she was not forgotten. "Just say her name after all these years, Bubbles Cash, and the people who remember her break out in a smile," Ralph Neely said.

In '67 the NFL added a 16th team, the New Orleans Saints (the 15th, the Atlanta Falcons, had been added the previous year), and realigned into four divisions. The Cowboys' new home was the Capitol Division of the Eastern Conference. The other teams in the division were the Eagles, Redskins, and Saints: a weak fraternity. After striving so hard for so long to make the playoffs, the Cowboys suddenly had what amounted to a free pass; they were almost guaranteed a division title and a place in the Eastern Conference championship game. Almost overnight, the regular season was transformed from a tense proving ground into a glorified practice session for the playoffs.

Suddenly, instead of hoping the Cowboys would win, fans now expected the Cowboys to win. No longer was it enough just to beat an opponent. The Cowboys now had to win the "right way," too. The style of the victory was almost as important as the victory itself. A poor winning performance was almost unsatisfactory. "Once we started beating people by 20 or 30 points, they expected it every week," Walt Garrison said. "We'd get booed if we didn't beat people bad. Dallas has the most fickle fans in the world. As Roger said, they love you win or tie."

The Cowboys were loved most of the time in '67. Their big-play offense continued to dominate opponents. Perkins led the team with 823 yards rushing. Reeves rushed for 603 yards, caught 39 passes, scored 10 touchdowns, and completed four option passes for 195 yards and two touchdowns. Landry took some of the pressure off Hayes by trading for Lance Rentzel, a tough, smart receiver, adept at short routes, and a perfect complement to Hayes. He caught 58 passes for 996 yards in '67. Hayes caught 49 for 998 yards.

The offense made more big plays and emanated more sheer electricity than any in pro football. In one game against the Cardinals, the Cowboys scored on a 69-yard punt return by Hayes, a 74-yard pass from Meredith to Rentzel, and passes covering 59 yards and 34 yards from Meredith to Hayes. In other games, Hayes caught touchdown passes covering 64, 55, 43, and 35 yards. Frank Clarke ran 56 yards for a touchdown on an end-around, and Reeves caught a 60-yard touchdown pass against the Falcons, one of four touchdowns he scored that day. Rentzel had a 223-yard receiving day against the Redskins.

Although they struggled against weak opponents, the Cowboys won often enough to insure they did not give away their easy trip to the playoffs. Down to their last gasp against the Redskins in early October, they won when a blown assignment left Reeves open for a touchdown pass with 10 seconds to play. The next week, in a driving rain at the Cotton Bowl, the winless expansion Saints had the ball on the Cowboy six-yard line late in the game, trailing by four points; a huge upset seemed possible, but the Saints fumbled. The next week in Pittsburgh, the Cowboys again trailed late and needed 72 yards for a touchdown. Morton, subbing for an injured Meredith, completed a pass to Rentzel, who fumbled when hit. Reeves picked up the fumble and continued running, but then he, too, fumbled. Reeves finally fell on the bouncing ball for a 71-yard gain that set up the winning touchdown with 24 seconds to play.

The Capitol Division race was decided by early November. The Saints lost their first seven games. The Redskins won two of eight. The Eagles split six. A 5–1 start put the Cowboys in control and shifted attention away from the standings. Meredith became a focus; coming off his best season, in which he almost led the Cowboys to the Super Bowl, he experienced a season of pain, hardship, and criticism, a sweep of adversity that pushed him toward his premature retirement.

It started early, in the Salesmanship Club game against the Packers. The championship rematch was anticipated with a naive intensity; fans saw the exhibition game as the Cowboys' chance for redemption. Some 78,000 fans filled the Cotton Bowl, but the Packers won easily, 20–3. Booed lightly at the start of the game by fans who had not forgiven him for throwing the decisive interception in January, Meredith was booed harder as the game progressed and the offense did not produce.

He was booed again at the next exhibition game, in which the Cowboys were beaten by the Colts, 33–7, to finish the preseason with a 2–3 record that did not satisfy fans coming to expect success. Meredith assumed the burden of those expectations almost by himself. The other Cowboys were cheered in '67, but Meredith was booed—not always and not by everyone, but often enough and loudly enough to shake him.

"He wasn't beating teams by 30, he was beating 'em by three or seven, and people weren't satisfied," Garrison said. "It had to affect him. He'd say, 'They pay their money, they can do what they want.' But I don't think he really felt that way. It bothers anyone to be unpopular, even if it's just because of a game."

Meredith had physical problems throughout the '67 season. He suffered fractured ribs in an exhibition game in San Francisco, then reinjured them against the Redskins early in the regular season. He stayed in the game and beat the Redskins with a dramatic last-minute pass to Reeves, but his wife took him to the hospital that night with a 105-degree fever. His cracked ribs had resulted in a buildup of fluid in his lungs, a serious ailment. He lost 17 pounds in a week and missed three games. When he returned, a forearm smash resulted in a compound fracture of his nose. He played with a face mask guarding his nose late in the season, and suffered a twisted knee.

Morton played well in relief, winning two of three games when Meredith was in the hospital, and many fans implored Landry to stick with the younger quarterback, but Meredith kept the job. Underweight and in pain, he was erratic in the second half of the season, completing less than half of his passes and throwing more interceptions than touchdowns. Fittingly, the Cowboys clinched the division title on a day when Meredith threw four interceptions in a loss to the Colts.

The Cowboys finished the regular season with a 9–5 record. The other three teams in the Capitol Division were a combined 14–24–4. How good were the Cowboys? It was hard to tell. They had beaten only one team that finished the season with a winning record. They had led the league in rushing defense, but finished 12th in passing defense. Neely, Lilly, Howley, and Green had made the Associated Press All-NFL team, and Perkins, Reeves, Hayes, and Rentzel also had played well. What was the sum of those parts? The Cowboys obviously were one of the league's better teams, but were they of championship mettle?

The question was answered in stunning fashion when the Browns came to Dallas for the Eastern Conference championship game. The Browns had won the Century Division with a 9–5 record, and they had Leroy Kelly and Paul Warfield. But the Cowboys destroyed them. Playing on a warm Christmas Eve, the Cowboys scored two touchdowns in the first quarter, led by 24–7 at halftime, and by 45–7 after three quarters. After a long, difficult regular season, Meredith had one of his best games. He missed just two of 13 passes and teamed with Hayes on an 86-yard touchdown that broke open the game in the second quarter. When Landry took him out at the start of the fourth quarter, Meredith shook hands with each member of the offense in the huddle and slowly trotted off the field to a huge ovation. Pop suggested that we leave shortly after that, and we packed up and headed for home, chattering happily in the car about the remarkable performance we had just seen. The big-play Cowboys were back, sending the message that their lackluster regular season had been misleading.

The Western Division championship game also was surprisingly one-sided. With an 11–1–2 record and the league's highest-scoring offense, the Rams seemed a good bet to beat the aging Packers, whose starting running backs, Elijah Pitts and Jim Grabowski, were injured. But the game was a horror for the Rams. Playing in Milwaukee, the Packers limited Rams quarterback Roman Gabriel to 11 completions in 31 attempts, controlled the ball with their running game, and won, 28–7. Lombardi was so moved that he cried in the locker room after the game. "That was magnificent, gentlemen," he told the players.

For the second straight season, the Cowboys and Packers would play for the NFL championship, this time on New Year's Eve at Lambeau Field in Green Bay. The Packers were favored, but the Cowboys were supremely confident after their fearsome performance against the Browns. "It was our year; Lombardi knew, all of them knew it," George Andrie said. "We had matured as a team. We were there to replace them as the team going to the Super Bowl."

Landry said, "In '66 we weren't at the Packers' level yet, but the '67 game was totally different. We were more experienced, and we felt the Packers were on the way down. I'm sure Vince felt the same way; he never would have stepped down that next year if he didn't feel that way. From that standpoint, we were very confident we were going to win."

On Friday afternoon the Cowboys boarded a chartered Braniff plane for the flight to Wisconsin. My father got off work early and we drove to Love Field to cheer the team off. A warm sun was shining. Several thousand fans were at the airport. The experience was disappointing. We had to park hundreds of yards from the runway and stand across the street behind a chain-link fence. We never got close enough to the players to see them; they would have to win without my exhortations. All we saw was the plane rising into the sky.

That evening the players settled into a motel in Appleton, 30 miles from Green Bay, and went through a light practice Saturday afternoon at Lambeau Field. The weather was perfect for football, with a layer of high clouds and the temperature in the low thirties. The mood at the practice was almost buoyant. "We were very, very frisky," Bob Lilly said. "The atmosphere was great. The feeling was that we were on the verge of something big."

Pettis Norman said, "Had we played on that Saturday, in that weather, the score would have been 35–14. We would have beaten them. There is no question about it. We had surpassed the Packers in talent. We were so high and confident, not overconfident, but after the '66 game we knew we could play with the Packers. I have never seen a team so ready to play in a game in my life."

The players returned to the motel, ate a team meal, played cards, and went to bed. They were prepared to awaken to colder temperatures the next day—the National Weather Service's representative in Green Bay had predicted that "a cold air mass moving down from Canada will bring with it more fresh air"—but no one was prepared for the cold that arrived.

"You could actually hear it coming as the night went on, hear the air getting colder," Jim Boeke said. "You could hear the windows creaking and cracking because of the frost building up."

When the motel operator awoke the players the next morning, she cheerfully offered a brief weather report that none of them would ever forget: "Good morning, it's sunny and 17 degrees below zero."

One by one, as the operator worked her way around the U-shaped motel with her wake-up calls, players jumped out of bed and pulled open their blinds. "You could look across the courtyard and see blinds opening and noses pressing against the glass," Lee Roy Jordan said. "No one could believe it. No one had ever been in that kind of cold."

It was a surreal cold, a freakish cold. "I have lived in Green Bay since 1958, and that's the coldest day I remember," Packer linebacker Ray Nitschke later told the *New York Times*.

Lilly and Andrie were roommates. Andrie rose first, dressed, and went out to Sunday mass. When he returned, he strode across the room without saying a word, filled a glass with water from the sink, and hurled the water against the window. It froze. "Most of the guys have never played in cold like this," said Andrie, who had attended Marquette University in Milwaukee. Lilly nodded, thinking, "I sure haven't."

The players, so upbeat at practice just 24 hours earlier, met for a somber pregame breakfast. Several stayed in their rooms to avoid the cold. The prospect of playing in such conditions had sapped their confidence and enthusiasm. "We just stared at each other at breakfast," Jordan said. "We were horrified. Most of us had grown up in the South. We had never experienced anything like that. We were thinking, 'Maybe the commissioner will cancel the game.' But we never got the call."

NFL commissioner Pete Rozelle was in Oakland for the AFL championship game between the Raiders and Oilers. A member of his staff, Joe Browne, called him.

"It's thirteen below in Green Bay," Browne said.

"Thirteen below what?" Rozelle said.

"Zero," Browne said.

Rozelle only briefly considered a postponement. "My feeling was that we would go on with it as long as it wasn't a threat to the players' health," he later told the *New York Times*. "We hadn't heard anything from Vince (Lombardi). And then the doctors told us the cold as such wouldn't be injurious, so I said, 'OK, let's play.'"

Landry said later, "I thought they should have postponed it. But they haven't postponed a game yet, so away we went."

The Cowboys' bus ride to Green Bay was silent. The players' concentration was ruined. Instead of thinking about what they had to do to beat the Packers, they were thinking about what they had to do to stay warm. When they arrived at the stadium they received their second shock of the morning: The field was frozen, an icy plane. A crew had spent the morning sweeping off a topcoat of ice, but the ground beneath it was an ice-skating rink.

The Packers had spent $70,000 to install a heating element beneath the field; Lombardi had shown off the device to reporters and bragged that the field would be perfect regardless of the weather conditions. What happened? Either the cold was too extreme for the heating system, or someone shut it off. Some Cowboys would always wonder if Lombardi himself had shut it off to help his team against the speedier Cowboys. According to Tom Brookshier, who broadcast the game for CBS, Lombardi came out of the tunnel before the game, tapped the icy field with his foot and said, "Perfect." Yet there was never any evidence that he turned off the heating system. "I take those allegations with a grain of salt," Don Perkins said years later.

The Cowboys dressed in the locker room and went out to the field for warm-ups. "That was probably the worst thing we ever did," Lilly said, "because we realized just how cold it was. I went out without a warm-up jacket, but I came right back in and got it. You could hardly breathe. You went, 'Gosh, I can't believe we're going to play.' We probably shouldn't have gone out there. Tom should have kept us inside, done some calisthenics in the locker room, and then just had us run out there and start playing. Then maybe we wouldn't have realized how cold it was until the half."

Cornell Green said, "The warm-up was real cold. On the field, with the wind blowing, it kind of surprised you just how cold it was. That morning it hadn't seemed quite as cold. But in the open space it was bad. I'm a firm believer that if one guy had quit, everyone would have quit. I mean, if one guy on either team had walked off and said, 'I'm just not doing this,' I guarantee you everyone would have walked off."

That did not happen. After warm-ups, the Cowboys returned to the locker room to brace themselves for the cold. "I put on two pairs of longjohns and wrapped Saran Wrap around my feet," Lilly said. None of the defensive linemen wore gloves after defensive line coach Ernie Stautner told them not to. "Ernie said we were too tough for that," Lilly said. "I went, 'OK, whatever.' I went out that door thinking, 'You're a fool, Bob.'"

Jordan said, "Ernie had told them no gloves because they wouldn't be able to grab the lineman, so I went, 'OK, me neither, I'm a man.' After one series I came back inside and got my gloves. But they were just brown cotton gloves, the kind you might work in the yard with. They were not too effective."

The 50,000 fans who packed Lambeau Field were accustomed to cold winters and more prepared for the cold than the Cowboys. They wore thermal underwear, wool shirts, sweaters, furs, parkas, ski masks, and earmuffs. Many also had their version of a homefield advantage: flasks filled with spirits calculated to warm their insides. "The place smelled like a bar," Cornell Green said.

The fans' breath created a fog that hovered over the stadium. "All you could see was their eyes inside the ski masks," said Dave Manders, who traveled to Green Bay but did not play because of a knee injury. "It was the eeriest feeling. Almost like playing on another planet."

The Cowboys were stunned when the Packers came onto the field before the kickoff. "We were all bundled up and they came out in T-shirts," Mel Renfro said. "We knew we were in trouble."

The Cowboys were, indeed, in trouble. "The Packers were unaffected by the cold," said Bob Ryan, vice president and editor in chief of NFL Films. "The Cowboys were thinking about everything else but the game. They were thinking about staying warm. Landry was trying to talk about game plans, but they didn't want to hear it. They were just thinking about the cold."

In his book, *Instant Replay*, Packer guard Jerry Kramer wrote, "I looked over at the Cowboys and I almost felt sorry for them. As bad as the cold was for us, it had to be worse for them. We were freezing, and they were dying. They were all hunched over, rubbing their hands, moving their legs up and down, trying to persuade themselves that they weren't insane to be playing football in this ridiculous weather."

The press box window was completely fogged over; Bill Mercer could not see the field until he sent an assistant across the street to buy a can of window de-icer. CBS opened its broadcast with a shot of a thermometer hovering at 13 below. Back in Dallas, where the temperature was 50 degrees higher, Cowboys fans watching on television could not relate. I could not fathom such conditions. Thirteen below? That was just a number. A frozen field? How bad could it be if the players were running around during warm-ups without falling down? And the sun was out! How cold could it be up there with the sun shinning so brightly?

The Ice Bowl, as the game would come to be called, would never resonate vividly to Cowboy fans. We did not experience it.

The Packers' Don Chandler kicked off to start the game. "The referee blew his whistle and it froze right there on his lips," Lilly said. "He pulled part of his lip off and the blood froze down his chin. The referees all wore Vaseline after that."

After the Cowboys punted, the Packers came roaring down the field on their first possession, taking advantage of the Cowboys' eternal weakness at right cornerback. Warren Livingston, whom Bart Starr had exploited in the '66 title game, had been cut before the season, but Livingston's replacement, Mike Johnson, was similarly vulnerable. Starr immediately isolated veteran receiver Carroll Dale on Johnson. Dale caught a pass over the middle for 17 yards, then ran a sideline route and caught a 15-yarder. Starr then sent Boyd Dowler to Johnson's side, and Dowler broke free for an eight-yard touchdown pass.

After an exchange of punts, the Packers struck again. On third-and-one at the Dallas 43, Starr faked a handoff to fullback Ben Wilson; Renfro took the fake, came up to tackle Wilson and fell behind Dowler, who was sprinting downfield. Starr's perfect pass gave the Packers another touchdown and a 14–0 lead over the Cowboys for the second year in a row in the championship game.

Mental discipline had given the Packers the lead. They were playing the game; the Cowboys were thinking about the cold. "I could barely hear the defensive signals because I could hear my mother's voice in my head, almost as if she were there," Jethro Pugh said. "She was saying, 'What are you doing out in that cold weather, fool?'"

Ralph Neely said, "I was miserable. You could not run around and create enough physical heat to get warm. I put my foot in a heater on the sidelines and I smelled burning leather. I mean, if there was ever going to be a game called because of the weather, it probably should have been that one. That was the only game, and, I admit it, that I was just wanting it to get over."

Frozen, distracted, and behind by two touchdowns, the Cowboys were on the brink of collapse. Hayes, their best weapon, was no factor. Miserable in the cold and unable to use his speed, he was running routes with his hands tucked in his pants. "I had the easiest job of anyone, covering Hayes," Packers cornerback Herb Adderley said. "You didn't have to be a Phi Beta Kappa to know he wasn't going to get a pass with his hands in his pants. I was able to cheat over and help out elsewhere. I intercepted a pass and recovered a fumble in that game because I could cheat over."

The Cowboy offense produced just three first downs in its first six possessions. "They almost packed it in, but then they got a spark," said Bob Ryan of NFL Films. On a first down for the Packers at the Green Bay 15 late in the second quarter, Starr fumbled when hit by Willie Townes, and Andrie scooped up the loose ball and ran seven yards for a touchdown.

Two minutes later, Willie Wood fumbled a punt deep in Packer territory and the Cowboys' Phil Clark recovered. Danny Villanueva kicked a 20-yard field goal just before halftime. Without generating a first down, the Cowboys had scored 10 points to get back into the game. The Packers had gained almost three times as many yards as the Cowboys in the first half, but they had a 14–10 lead.

Awakened by the Packers' largesse, the Cowboys began to dominate in the third quarter. Their defense hounded Starr and shut down the Packers' running game, and Meredith and the offense finally began to move. "I had been too cautious in the first half," Meredith told Blackie Sherrod in an interview before the next season. "I was very conscious of the cold. I tried to throw soft because the receivers' hands were too cold. I couldn't pop (the passes). Finally, at halftime, I just said the hell with it and threw the best I could."

Reeves, the crafty halfback, started the drive with sweeps around right end for gains of eight and 20 yards. Meredith passed to Clarke for 14 yards, and hit Rentzel for 11. On third-and-14 at the Green Bay 22, Meredith scrambled up the middle, veered to his left, and was hit by Packer linebacker Lee Roy Caffey; the ball popped free, and Adderley recovered. Green Bay's lead was preserved.

On the Cowboys' next series, Reeves gained 16 yards on two runs and a catch to move the ball to the Green Bay 30, but Meredith was sacked by Caffey and Villanueva missed a 47-yard field-goal attempt. Still, the Cowboys were optimistic. They had the momentum. The Packers' offense was stagnant.

When the third quarter ended, the Cowboys had the ball on the 50. The teams changed sides and waited out a television time-out. Meredith went to the sidelines to speak to Landry, who called for a halfback pass. Reeves would take a handoff from Meredith and begin running a sweep, then stop and throw a pass downfield if the secondary came up to stop the run. The play had generated four catches and two touchdowns during the season.

The play never worked better than it did that day. Reeves put his hands in his pants to warm them once he heard the call in the huddle, then took the handoff and headed to his left. The Packers' Willie Wood and Bob Jeter came up to stop the run, and Rentzel sprinted past them into the clear. "As soon as I pulled up (to throw) I heard Jeter curse," Reeves told NFL Films. "I was thinking, 'Just don't miss him, don't overthrow him.'"

He did not. Rentzel caught the pass and raced to the end zone. Just as they had in title game the year before, the Cowboys had come back from 14 points down against the Packers. But this rally was different: After seven quarters and eight seconds of championship play, the Cowboys finally had a lead.

"I think all of us thought that touchdown might win the game," Reeves told NFL Films. "The condition of the field was getting worse and worse. It was going to be hard for anyone to score."

The Packers punted on their next series, then got as far as the Dallas 33 on a drive before Chandler missed a 40-yard field goal attempt with less than 10 minutes to play. "We were all beginning to wonder, 'Oh, boy, is this it?'" Adderley said.

The Cowboys had the ball and the lead; the championship was theirs if they scored again or maintained possession long enough. The Packers gave them one first down with a penalty, and Meredith produced another with a pass to Clarke. Less than six minutes remained. But then the Packers' greatest ally—the frozen field—came through. On second-and-10, Cowboy halfback Craig Baynham slipped and fell after catching a pass.

Meredith also slipped and fell as he pulled away from center on third down. He scrambled to his feet and got off a rushed pass that fell incomplete. The Cowboys had to give the ball back.

"I think the offense just wanted to get off the field and get back to the heaters on the sidelines," one Cowboy defender, who asked not to be identified, said years later. "The last (offensive) series wasn't a great effort."

Villanueva's punt flew to the Packer 23. Willie Wood returned it nine yards. Starr and the Packer offense trotted onto the field with four minutes and 50 seconds left in the fourth quarter. Their end zone was 68 yards away. A fierce, frozen wind whipped into their faces.

A year earlier, it was the Cowboy offense that failed in the final moments. This time, the defense failed. Two factors were critical. One was that the Cowboys set up in man-to-man pass coverage. "If we had played a zone, it would have taken them longer to go downfield," Landry said years later. Also, the field was a sheet of ice now in the late afternoon shadows, and the Cowboys were unprepared. Several Packers had changed into tennis shoes, which provided better traction than cleats. The Cowboys had to stay in their cleats; having been told the field would be perfect, they packed only their cleats.

"Lilly packed some soccer shoes, but he was the only one," Jethro Pugh said. "We were told several times not to worry about the field. 'The field will be fine, a normal playing surface,' they told us. It was frozen hard. And it was real bad by the end of the game."

In the backfield with Starr were Chuck Mercein and Anderson. Mercein was a reserve fullback whom the Redskins and Giants had cast off; just five weeks earlier he was playing for a minor league team. The Packers had picked him up in desperation after Grabowski and Pitts were injured. He was destined for the roll call of Cowboy heartbreakers.

Starr began the drive with a pass to Anderson for six yards. Mercein, a bullish 230-pounder, charged across right tackle for seven yards and a first down. "Mercein wasn't quick or fast, but he was surefooted and as big as a lineman, and he was the only guy on the field who wasn't slipping," Mike Gaechter said.

Starr passed to Dowler for 13 yards, but then Anderson was cornered and dropped for a nine-yard loss by Townes as he looked to throw a half-back pass. Needing 19 yards for a first down, Starr calmly passed twice to Anderson for 12 and nine yards; Howley slipped as he tried to stop Anderson on both plays. On first down at the Dallas 30, Starr sent Mercein into the left flat and tossed him the ball. Cowboy linebacker Dave Edwards slipped as he approached Mercein, who escaped down the sideline and completed a 19-yard gain before diving out of bounds at the 11.

The Cowboys were slipping all over the field. "It was a lack of experience, not adjusting to the elements," Schramm said. "At the end of the game, the only thing you could do was run straight ahead. You couldn't make a cut because you would fall. The Packers adjusted and we didn't. They were the more seasoned team."

There were 71 seconds left. Starr again called Mercein's number, this time on a trap play. Packer guard Gale Gillingham pulled out of his position as though leading a sweep. Lilly took two steps to follow Gillingham and chase the play, leaving a hole in the defensive line. Mercein took the handoff from Starr and charged through Lilly's vacated position for an eight-yard gain.

"Bob took one step and saw the trap develop and started to react, and when he started to react, he slipped," Landry said. "It was over when they made it down to the goal line. They just had to push it across and we couldn't stop them because we had no traction."

From the three, Anderson bulled for two yards and a first down. For the second year in a row, the NFL championship game had come down to the one-yard line in the last minute. The Cowboys had failed to score the year before, and for a few moments it appeared the Packers might suffer the same fate. The Cowboy defense made a last stand. Anderson was stopped for no gain on the first down, then slipped on second down. The Packers called their final time-out with 16 seconds left. The ball was still on the one.

Starr went to the sidelines to talk to Lombardi. One of their options was to kick a field goal and try to win in overtime. Lombardi said later that he did not want to make the fans sit in the bitter cold any longer. He gambled, calling for a quarterback sneak with Starr carrying the ball behind Kramer. The call was dangerous; if Starr did not score, the Packers might not have time to line up and run another play. Their season would end on the one-yard line. "I heard the (sneak) call and went, 'What a stupid call,'" Packer receiver Max McGee told NFL Films. When Starr and Meredith went on *The Tonight Show* the following week, Johnny Carson asked Starr if the Packers would have had time for another play. "You wouldn't have," Meredith interrupted.

During the time-out, the Cowboys' defensive linemen tried to dig holes in the ice with their spikes to improve their traction. "I said to Lilly, 'Let's call a time-out and get an ice pick,'" Pugh said. "It was like we were standing in a pot of ice. My feet were numb from the cold. I tried scraping the ice, but I couldn't feel my feet."

The Packers broke their huddle and came to the line. Starr signaled for quiet, paused, and gave a "hut" signal. "I came off the ball as fast as I ever have in my life," Kramer wrote in *Instant Replay*. "I came off the ball as fast as anyone could. In fact, I wouldn't swear that I didn't beat the center's snap by a fraction of a second. I wouldn't swear that I wasn't actually off-sides on the play."

Pugh was set slightly too high, a habit the Cowboy coaches had tried to correct. "I slammed into Jethro hard," Kramer wrote. "All he had time to do was raise his left arm. His body was a little high . . . and with (Packer center Ken) Bowman's help I moved him outside."

Replays showed Pugh's feet sliding back on the ice, unable to grip the field. "Bowman and Kramer double-teamed me," Pugh said. "Kramer moved before the snap. He was offsides. Bowman threw an even better block from the other side. It was like a gunfight. Somebody pulls the trigger first and then it's too late."

Starr bulled into the end zone behind Kramer and Bowman and wound up nestled on top of the pile of linemen. The referee signaled a touchdown. The clock showed 13 seconds left. Lombardi's gamble had paid off. The crowd at Lambeau Field forgot about the cold and erupted in cheers.

The Cowboys had time for two plays—incomplete passes—and the game was over: Green Bay 21, Dallas 17. Thousands of fans poured onto the frozen field to celebrate and tear down the goal posts.

In the Packers' locker room, Bob Skoronski, an offensive guard, said, "This game was our mark of distinction." Indeed, it was. The earlier Packer teams that had won championships were superior to the '67 team, but this was their greatest moment. The victory summed up what they were about: mental and physical discipline, endurance, and performance under pressure.

Meredith was interviewed in the Cowboys' locker room by his friend, Frank Gifford. "I feel like I died," Meredith said, casting such a forlorn figure that hundreds of fans sent him supportive letters in the coming weeks.

Back in Dallas, I could not bear to watch on television. I felt as though I, too, had died. This was far more disappointing than the loss in the championship game the year before. It had been enough then to know that the Cowboys had come so far and so close after years of failing to make the playoffs. There was no redeeming value in this defeat; there was just heartbreak in knowing that the Cowboys had led in the fourth quarter and lost at the end.

I grabbed my basketball, went outside, and began shooting at the goal on the driveway. It was chilly, but I did not stop to put on a jacket. I took one shot, then another, then a third. After collecting the ball, I turned and slung it at the backboard. The ball caromed off the board and hurtled back toward me. I grabbed it and slung it back even harder. Never before had the result of a Cowboy game so touched me. I was no longer just a child looking up to the players and memorizing their statistics. I was an emotional investor, vulnerable to joy and disgust. The bitterness of defeat had matured me.

My mother heard me slamming the ball against the backboard and came outside.

"Are you all right?" she asked.

I grabbed the ball, stopped, exhaled deeply, and nodded.

He was 23 years old when shards of infamy rained down on him. Jethro Pugh was in his third season with the Cowboys, just 30 months removed from the obscurity of a tiny college in Elizabeth City, North Carolina, when he suddenly found himself at the center of the pro football world.

A cousin in New York City called him when he got back to his apartment in Dallas after the flight home from Green Bay following the Ice Bowl.

"Jethro, it's bad," she said.

"What do you mean?" Pugh asked.

"It's real bad," she said.

"What are you talking about?" Pugh asked.

"They're talking on TV like you're the one that lost the game," she said.

Pugh smiled. "Don't pay that any mind," he said.

He stopped smiling the next day when he saw the front pages of the Dallas papers, both of which ran large pictures of Kramer blocking him out of the way on Starr's touchdown.

"I said, 'My goodness,'" Pugh recalled years later. "I went over to Coach Landry's office. I said to him, 'You have to do something about this play.' He said, 'Jethro, you might as well get used to it, because that play is going to be part of pro football history. Nothing can be done about it now.' He was saying, 'Get used to it.' It was better than saying, 'Jethro, you screwed up.'"

Two days later, Pugh sat down to write a check and his hand started shaking. He could not grip the pen. Alarmed, he called Cowboy trainer Don Cochren. "There's something wrong with my hand," Pugh said.

"Get over here right now," Cochren said.

Pugh was one of a handful of Cowboys who contracted frostbite during the Ice Bowl. Renfro, Andrie, Townes, and Dick Daniels were the others. "I was really scared," Pugh said. "I was a health-education major in college. All I remembered about frostbite was that your fingers fell off."

His did not, but his case of frostbite guaranteed that the Ice Bowl would stay with him forever. "Whenever it gets below 40 degrees my feet start to sting and I have to wear gloves," Pugh said.

We spoke one day in 1996 at the Dallas-Fort Worth International Airport, where Pugh owned and operated six kiosks. We met at a shop in terminal 3-E. Pugh was behind the cash register, counting bills. He wore a blue shirt, a tie, dark slacks, and aviator-style wire-rimmed glasses. He was 52 years old, angular and trim, with close-cropped dark hair flecked with gray. His manner was affable.

He could have become another Boeke, a figure of dark legend. Much as the blame for the first championship loss to the Packers was pinned over the years on Boeke's penalty, the Ice Bowl was reduced to Kramer's block.

"The very next year we played the Bears in the Hall of Fame game in Canton, Ohio," Pugh said. "We practiced there the day before the game, and the field is set up on a hill and I saw the Hall of Fame building, and after practice I said to Ernie (Stautner), 'Let's go take a look at the Hall of Fame.' Ernie was walking ahead of me and he saw that there was a huge picture in the lobby of Kramer's block, and he came out and said, 'Jethro, I don't think you want to go in there.' I went on in and there was a picture of the play, all blown up. It was hard to get away from it. The play was pretty much everywhere for awhile. I was watching *Gentle Ben* on television one night and Bart Starr was in it and all of a sudden they showed the play again. I saw it quite a bit."

It did not help that Kramer's book came out that year and became a bestseller, turning Kramer into a national celebrity.

"The book bothered me," Pugh said. "We played the Packers in an exhibition game the next year and I was looking forward to it, but Kramer was injured, so I didn't get a chance to redeem myself."

As Landry predicted, the play became one of the most famous in pro football history. The weight could have shattered Pugh, but he never gave in to it. "He dealt with it, became reconciled to it," Pettis Norman said. It helped that his teammates never blamed him. They understood that the entire defense had allowed the Packers to drive 68 yards across a frozen field to the winning touchdown. They also understood that the odds had been against Pugh on the goal line; asking him to stand on a sheet of ice against a double-team and not yield a foot was asking the impossible.

"He actually held his place very well," Lilly said. "I know if they had run on me with two men blocking in those conditions, I would have slid back like Jethro. As it was, they didn't move him far."

Pugh outlasted the ignominy that clutched Boeke. Boeke left the Cowboys a year later, enabling the memory of his mistake to outgrow his performance, but Pugh remained a Cowboy and put together a fine career, starting for another decade after the Ice Bowl. He never made the Pro Bowl, but he became a fixture, a root of low-profile consistency with two Super Bowl rings. After retiring in '78 he remained in Dallas and established himself in business. He drove a luxury car. His children attended private schools. He was remembered as a Cowboy, just a Cowboy, not the Cowboy who lost the Ice Bowl.

The Ice Bowl was a frozen epic that sealed pro football's high place in the nation's sporting priorities. After almost a decade of rising attendance, higher television ratings, and larger headlines, pro football was no longer just challenging baseball; it was baseball's equal, if not its superior, in popularity. Baseball was a traditional game played by mortals. Pro football players seemed beyond mortality, enduring levels of violence and misery that fans could not fathom. The game was the sporting version of the space program, an alluring spectacle that stirred the imagination. The Ice Bowl, played in inhuman conditions, embodied all the elements of the NFL's rising popularity. It became a legendary game.

As the years passed it served as a bond connecting the Packers and Cowboys, turning them into brothers more than rivals. "Old Cowboys and Packers migrate to each other at alumni affairs," Ralph Neely said. "There'll be a bunch of old pros there, and you'll find the Packers and Cowboys at the same table. There is a shared respect."

Also a shared pain. Thirty years later, Neely feels a burning sensation in his lungs when he goes snow skiing; his doctor told him it probably dates to the Ice Bowl. Jordan feels stinging pain in his feet and hands in cold weather. The Ice Bowl left such scars on many players. "The first time my son saw me cry," Jordan said, "was when we were hunting in 10-degree weather. My feet and hands got to hurting so bad that I broke down. 'Son,' I told him, 'I got to go get in the truck.'"

Even though they lost, the Cowboys left an indelible mark on the public that day in Green Bay. Football teams still had personalities then, in the days before players began jumping teams and the league congealed into a homogeneous muddle. The Packers were the old guard, an assemblage of crewcuts left over from the '50s. The Cowboys were young, hip, and daring, a new breed symbolizing the '60s. They wore shiny uniforms, utilized multiple offensive sets, and relied on speed. Instead of running to daylight, they threw bombs to the World's Fastest Human. They had Meredith, the wisecracking quarterback. They had Rentzel, handsome enough for Hollywood. They had Hayes, the Olympic hero.

Put simply, the Cowboys were cool. They began hearing cheers in opponents' stadiums, the support of a growing national constituency. No team had more fans in other places. By '68 there was a Cowboy radio network encompassing almost 100 stations, with KLIF serving as the flagship providing the feed. On TV, the CBS affiliate in 28 cities, including four in Arizona, carried the Cowboy game every Sunday. "They became the glamour team, the pre-eminent team, maybe not always on the field, but in the eyes of the nation," said Bob Ryan of NFL Films. "They were always on television and they evolved into the glamour team."

Schramm said, "The Ice Bowl is what started the great popularity of the Cowboys nationwide. We were the underdog expansion team with the finger-snapping quarterback. We had a unique team. Cornell Green was a basketball player. Hayes was a track man. Reeves was a very unusual player. They were all very colorful, and they were going against the mighty legends, up there fighting in those horrible conditions. We lost the game, but I think we got more out of it than the Packers in terms of image and popularity."

A victory in Green Bay would have changed the team dramatically. Meredith would have heard fewer boos, if any, and probably not retired so prematurely. "Don felt the brunt of that defeat more than anyone, which was unfair," Jordan said. The team itself also never would have earned the reputation for being a star-crossed loser, the best team around that could not win "the big one."

"The Ice Bowl was our worst loss ever," Andrie said. "We were the better team and we were ahead, and to lose in those circumstances was just a crushing thing. We suffered for a year or two after that. I don't give a damn what anyone else says, it took us at least a year to get over it. There was a hangover. A bad hangover."

On the heels of their frustrating loss in the '66 championship game, the Cowboys were devastated by the Ice Bowl. The defeat sent a wrecking ball through their confidence and sowed a deadly seed in their minds: the fear that they could not win big games. "It hurt us badly, left a terrible taste in our mouths, just killed our motivation or something for the next year or two," Lilly said.

"The Cowboys were the better team, but if you lose the game, you're still the loser," Bob Ryan said. "The Packers drove 68 yards on an icy field, and they drove a stake into the Cowboys' hearts. That game ended a phase of the Cowboys' history. They weren't the same after that for a few years."

Chapter Ten

Had I remained 11 years old forever, I would have had only one deity; my other interests could not compete with the Cowboys in the aftermath of the '67 season and two straight trips to the NFL championship game. My knowledge of the players was so honed that I could tell them without a scorecard; I knew them by their silhouettes, their running styles, the slopes of their shoulders. I knew the players on other teams better than I would when it was my job to know them 20 years later. That spring I discovered Strat-O-Matic football, ordered a set of teams through the mail, and planned a season to run concurrently with the real NFL season that fall. My obsession with football and the Cowboys was at a zenith.

Of course, I did not remain 11 forever. Inevitably, other interests came along to compete with the Cowboys for my attention. Music and girls chipped away ever so slowly at my single-mindedness, teaching me the astounding lesson that there was more to life than football. Imagine that!

Music began to intrigue me one Sunday afternoon in '64 when my sister came running down the hall shrieking, "The Beatles are coming! The Beatles are coming!"

I had no idea what she was talking about. "Why are you so excited about a bunch of bugs?" I asked.

"The Beatles play music, stupid," she said. "And Paul is gorgeous."

Having an older sister ensured that I would grow up ahead of schedule. She let me borrow a few of her Beatles 45s to play on my plastic record player. I said farewell to "The Ballad of Davy Crockett."

John, Paul, George, and Ringo carried my interest for a few years, but then my sister discovered other groups such as The Rolling Stones, The Who, The Dave Clark Five, and The Monkees. I followed her lead. When I was 10, I upgraded to a real record player and began listening to albums. Much as I had memorized the Cowboys' uniform numbers and statistics, I memorized the words to the songs on my albums. The lyrics spoke of love, and not the kind I had for my parents. There was a forbidden quality to the music that stirred a tingling in my stomach I had never felt before.

On Saturday afternoons my mother dropped me off at a record store in Preston Center. I wandered the aisles with my money clenched in my hands, and always came home with a new album or two. Much as I had spent hours playing imaginary football games in the backyard, I spent hours in front of the mirror in my room strumming an "air guitar"—a tennis racket held upside down—and listening to music with the volume turned up. I knew I wasn't going to be a Cowboy after my devastating fourth-grade football experience; now I was going to be a rock star.

Then I fell in with a new classmate named Paul, who had moved down from New York and listened to rowdy rockers such as the MC5 and Joe Cocker. Paul was defiantly unathletic; the Cowboys did not interest him, exposing him to mild ridicule that he dismissed with a shrug. He had long hair and dressed in flowery clothes. My balls and bats remained in the closet when he came to play on Saturdays. We sat in my room and listened to records.

Paul left after two years, but not before he raised my music awareness. In the late '60s, as I reached my teens, I became a regular concert-goer at Memorial Auditorium. My father would drop me and a friend off by the front door on Friday nights, then pick us up at a prearranged time after the show. I saw The Who perform *Tommy,* the rock opera. I saw Led Zeppelin touring the United States for the first time. I saw Jimi Hendrix play the national anthem for 30 minutes in an arena that was two-thirds empty.

As I listened to songs of love, I watched my sister move through high school as one of the prettiest and most popular girls. She had a stream of football players banging on the front door and tiptoeing past my room on the way to her room down the hall. I knew I was supposed to listen and learn. My music had educated me.

I was painfully shy around girls myself. Several of my friends could strike up conversations with them, flirt, and make dates. I was desperately envious. In sixth grade I had my eyes on a girl in the class below me, a little angel with a long brush of blond hair and a broad, bright smile. I closed my eyes and envisioned laughing with her and taking her to a movie, but I could not even summon the nerve to speak to her. I kept my distance and my silence, and kept my dreams to myself.

In the summer of '68, as I neared my 12th birthday, I went to Camp Indian Acres, in Fryeburg, Maine. It was a traditional experience in our family; my mother and sister had spent summers at the sister camp, Forest Acres, and my Uncle Milton and cousin Jack had gone to Indian Acres before me. I swam in the Saco River, played baseball and basketball, and moved up and down a tennis ladder. Once a week, there were dances with the Forest Acres girls. Finding myself far from home and surrounded by new friends and a convivial spirit, I found the courage I had lacked at home.

At the first dance, I approached a pretty, blond slip of a girl. Her name was Lisa. I asked her to dance and moved awkwardly onto the floor. Steppenwolf's "Born to Be Wild" came roaring onto the sound system. Terrified at what we had done, we flailed our arms and legs for a couple of minutes without saying a word. When the song ended I hurriedly retreated to the safety of the boys' side of the dance hall.

A few minutes later I went back to her. She was sitting in a chatty cluster of friends that fell silent as I approached. Suddenly, I was the boy with the knack around girls; far from home, I had reinvented myself. She smiled and followed me onto the floor. We lingered for an extra song.

My college-age counselors teased and encouraged me throughout the next week. Inspired by the attention, I went back to Lisa at the start of the next dance. She had heard similar reassurances from her counselors, no doubt; they all loved playing matchmaker. We danced through two songs and then actually spoke. We discussed where we were from, what we liked to do at camp, who our friends were. We skipped one song to hunt down a soda. My heart was hammering, but talking to her was easier than I had expected.

After we drank our soda, we headed back to the dance floor. A counselor with a mischievous grin slid a slow song onto the turntable. It was a horrifying moment. Finding the nerve to dance and speak with Lisa had been difficult enough; now I had to find the nerve to reach out and hug her. I was 11 years old and in way over my head. I had no choice. I never could have faced my counselors had I turned and walked away. I would have heard about that for the rest of the summer and probably for as long as I attended that camp. I was trapped. With my insides bubbling up in my throat, I put my arms out in invitation. Lisa, no less trapped than I, came forward and nestled inside them.

Feeling our way as we groped, we began to shuffle our feet and lean back and forth as we listened to the music. She put her head on my shoulder, sending a jolt of electricity through me. I smelled her scrubbed, fresh scent, and felt her soft hair on my cheek, her delicate arms wrapped lightly around my back. My panic subsided, replaced by the tingle of victory. I had done it. I had dared to speak to a girl, and discovered, to my amazement and joy, that she liked me. The Cowboys, as momentous as they were in my life, could not compete with that.

Every morning at camp, a counselor read the previous night's major league baseball scores before breakfast. My friends from New York and Boston spent the first half of the meal debating the Red Sox, Yankees, and Orioles. I was from a different world, the pro football world; I hoped the counselor would include NFL exhibition scores in his morning report, but he ignored them, as if football did not exist. I scrambled to find out how the Cowboys had done, borrowing *Boston Globe* sports sections from my counselors. My parents clipped out the game stories from the Dallas papers and mailed them to me. One year they gave me a two-month subscription to the *Times Herald.*

I was still at camp when the Cowboys played the Packers in the Salesmanship Club game in August of '68. I had not missed a Cowboy home game in four years; I was homesick that night. Discovering later that the Packers had beaten the Cowboys again made it easier to have missed the game. The Packers were doing their best to ruin my life.

The Cowboys beat the Oilers in Houston and then lost to the Colts in Dallas to finish with a 3–3 exhibition record. I was home for the game with the Colts. Meredith was brilliant in the first half, completing 15 of 22 passes, but he threw four interceptions in the second half and the fans turned on him.

"We want Morton!" they chanted.

The boos turned to cheers when Meredith gave one of his best performances in the Cowboys' regular-season opener the next week at the Cotton Bowl. He completed 16 of 19 passes in a 59–13 defeat of the Lions. When Morton took over late in the game, the crowd chanted, "We want Meredith!" The Cowboy huddle broke up laughing. After the game, Dave Edwards tossed a game ball to Meredith in the locker room. "This goes to a guy who has been under a lot of pressure, but not from us," Edwards said. Meredith, normally glib with reporters, was terse. It was as if the booing and criticism had pushed him beyond the limits of his emotional endurance. He was retreating.

The Cowboys shut down the Browns the next week, 28–7, then won four more in a row by a combined score of 126–43. Dan Reeves went down for the season with a knee injury—he would never be the same—but the Cowboys barely flinched. They had a 6–0 record and a two-game lead in the Capitol Division. Once again the Cowboys had a free pass to the playoffs. "We played all season just to get to the big games," Andrie said. "It was like, 'Let's just get through the season.'"

The Packers came to the Cotton Bowl to play the undefeated Cowboys in a nationally televised Monday night game. The Packers were a fading champion, having won just two of their first six games in the wake of Lombardi's retirement. Cowboy fans felt that the last obstacle blocking the Cowboys from a championship had been removed—but the Packers whipped the Cowboys that night, 28–17. The Cowboys blew a 10–0 lead, Starr tore up the Cowboy secondary, and Meredith left the game in the second half when Willie Davis slammed him to the ground and broke his nose. Lombardi, now the Packers' general manager, fretted in the press box when Morton entered the game. "Meredith doesn't worry me, but this guy is trouble," Lombardi said. The Packers handled him easily.

The Cowboys lost at home to the Giants two weeks later, cutting their division lead to one game. The Giants were a one-dimensional team—Fran Tarkenton throwing to Homer Jones—but they had a 6–3 record after their 27–21 win in the Cotton Bowl. The Cowboys were 7–2.

Meredith tore knee cartilage the next week in Washington, and Morton played well in relief in the Cowboys' 44–24 victory; the Giants kept pace with a 7–6 win over the Eagles. Morton started and played well again in a 34–3 defeat of the Bears in Chicago, and the Giants lost in Los Angeles, giving the Cowboys breathing room in the standings.

Meredith was booed when he returned and struggled against the Redskins the next week at the Cotton Bowl. The Cowboys needed a late touchdown from the defense to win, and, even though they clinched the division title when the Giants lost in Cleveland, Meredith confessed dejectedly to reporters that he was "sick and tired" of the boos.

The Cowboys beat the Steelers and Giants to finish the regular season with a 12–2 record. Only the Colts, at 13–1, had a better record. The Cowboys led the league in scoring, averaging 31 points a game, and set an NFL record for first downs in a season. Meredith had one of his best seasons despite his numerous injuries. He completed 55 percent of his passes, a career high, and threw for 2,500 yards and 21 touchdowns; a poor performance in the meaningless last game had cost him the league passing title. Rentzel and Hayes combined for more than 100 receptions worth almost 2,000 yards. The defense was first in the league against the run for the third straight season. Perkins again made the Pro Bowl, and Craig Baynham filled in ably for Reeves with almost 500 yards rushing and 29 pass receptions.

The Cowboys' opponent in the Eastern Conference championship game was the Browns, who had won the Century Division with a 10–4 record. The game was in Cleveland, but there was every reason to believe the Cowboys would have little trouble. They had won four games in a row against the Browns, including a 28–7 victory earlier in the season and that 52–14 destruction in the conference title game the year before. Fans in Dallas already were anticipating an NFL championship game against the Colts at the Cotton Bowl the next week. Forty-four thousand tickets had been sold for the game, and the Cowboys had made arrangements to sell the remaining 30,000 at Fair Park on the Monday after the Cleveland game.

The Browns could not match the Cowboys' flashy statistics and records, but they had improved since losing to the Cowboys in September. Bill Nelsen replaced Frank Ryan at quarterback after two early losses, and the offense came alive. With Nelsen throwing to Paul Warfield, and Leroy Kelly leading the league in rushing, the Browns averaged almost 40 points a game during an eight-game winning streak that ended with a meaning-less loss to the Cardinals on the last Sunday of the season. They were more dangerous than they appeared.

A Cleveland sportswriter stirred the Cowboys' emotions early in the week with a critical column pointing to their two championship losses as the mark of a team that would not know greatness. "Such losses are the kind that separate great teams from good ones," wrote Chuck Heaton in the *Cleveland Plain Dealer.* A copy of the column wound up on the bulletin board in the Cowboy locker room, as such criticism often does. The Cowboys scoffed, but many players admitted years later that Heaton was right: The losses to the Packers had hurt them. "I don't think we had confidence going into that game, despite our record," Lee Roy Jordan said. "We had lost our confidence in the Ice Bowl and never got it back. I don't think the coaches believed in the team, and they didn't make us believe."

The weather for the game was gray and misty, and the Cowboys played as though they were depressed. Meredith's first pass was intercepted. He did not attempt another for 20 minutes. The offense was stymied in the first half. "We were very flat," Landry said. "It was one of our worst games."

The defense came through when Howley returned a fumble for a touchdown, and a field goal gave the Cowboys a 10–3 lead. The defense was playing well, but then, suddenly, there was a breakdown just before halftime: Kelly was wide open behind the secondary and Nelsen hit him with a pass for a 46-yard touchdown. "That was the shocker that we never came back from," Landry said after the game.

On the first play of the second half, Meredith lobbed a pass into the left flat. Browns linebacker Dale Lindsey read a key and anticipated the play; he leaped and tipped the ball, caught it as it came down, and sprinted 27 yards to the end zone for a stunning touchdown. The Browns were ahead, 17–10. Their 80,000 fans were roaring.

After the kickoff, Meredith hit Rentzel with a pass over the middle, but the ball bounced off Rentzel's hands into those of cornerback Ben Davis. It was another interception. Two plays later Kelly raced 35 yards for a touchdown off right tackle. The stadium was shaking as Don Cockcroft kicked the extra point to put the Browns up, 24–10.

Landry then made a fateful decision: He pulled Meredith. The Cowboy players were stunned to see Morton trotting onto the field, but Meredith was 3-of-9 with three interceptions. "I hated to pull Don, but I was trying to give the team a spark," Landry said after the game. "I just went over to Don (on the sidelines) and said, 'I think I oughta go with Morton.' He agreed."

The Cowboy offense drove for a field goal, but the Browns came back with a long touchdown drive that sealed the victory. The celebration began in the old stadium by Lake Erie. A late Cowboy touchdown put the final score at 31–20. There would be no championship this year, not even a championship game. The Cowboys had been blown out of the playoffs.

As the clock wound down, Tex Schramm made his way to the sidelines. When he came upon the forlorn Meredith, he buried his head in Meredith's chest and wept. Meredith wrapped his arms around Schramm. The two men hugged in the chilling mist, a portrait of disappointment. Reporters watching the scene later disagreed about its significance; some wrote that Schramm simply was grieving, others suggested that Schramm was saying farewell to Meredith, that both men knew that this was the end, that it was clear that Dandy Don could take the team no farther.

"I remember the moment very well," Schramm said 28 years later. "I was standing by the bench and he came off the field. We had tried so hard and come so far, and to see him come out of the game like that, for some reason, it just struck me as enormously sad. I don't think I thought it was his last game. I just knew how badly he felt about not being able to do it that day. It just struck me and I broke up. I still break up when I think about it. There was something very, very sad about it."

After the game, the players showered, dressed, and took the team bus to their chartered plane waiting at the Cleveland airport. Meredith, who had not spoken to reporters after the game, claiming he had "nothing to say," boarded the plane, ate a hamburger, and sat back. "We were sitting across the aisle from each other," Pete Gent said. "He looked at me and said, 'Let's get out of here.' I did whatever he said, so I followed him off. We got back into the airport, found a flight to New York and went there. We stayed at Frank Gifford's house for a few days. It was an interesting experience. Kind of fun."

Landry said Meredith would not be disciplined for missing the flight because the season was over. That was not literally true; the Cowboys now had to play in the Playoff Bowl, the game for the conference runners-up, played at the Orange Bowl in Miami. The Cowboys had been thrilled to qualify for the game three years earlier, but it was a bitter letdown now. The players called it the Sewer Bowl.

Meredith returned to Dallas and flew with the team to Miami, resuming his role as a leader. "We need to win to get in the right frame of mind for next season," he said. The Cowboys beat the Vikings, 17–13. Meredith played solidly. No one, not even Meredith himself, knew it was the last game of his life.

His career represented the beginning of pro sports in Dallas. The maddening swirl that exists today—the four major pro teams and dozens of prominent personalities, the endless controversies and overlapping seasons, the shouting on the radio and bluster in the newspapers, the money and opinions flying everywhere—all traces back to one Joseph Donald Meredith.

Before him, only one other athlete had so captured the city's attention: Doak Walker, Dallas' first superstar. Walker's celebrity was upbeat, almost sweet; he turned the city into one big pep squad when he ran with the ball for SMU on Saturday afternoons in the late '40s. Dallas was still an adolescent sports town then, a college sports town. Meredith had the same renown in the '60s, but his stemmed from controversy, cynicism, and failure as much as accomplishment, adulation, and success. Unintentionally, and to his great dismay, he carried Dallas into its sports adulthood. He was the first Dallas athlete to hear venomous criticism, the first whose salary was an issue, the first whose personality became as relevant to fans as his performance. Those attitudes and priorities are the staples of the tabloid-style hype that would become so endemic to pro sports in the '90s. Meredith was years ahead of his time.

Fans in Dallas had never booed when Meredith began his Cowboy career. "I had never even really heard the sound," he said in an interview with *Sports Illustrated* late in his career. By the time he retired, the fans at the Cotton Bowl routinely booed, criticized, and stood in judgment without fully informed opinions. Someone had to serve as the laboratory rat as the city developed the harder edge that came with the pros. That someone was Meredith. He was in the wrong place at the wrong time. It was his destiny to become the sacrificial figure on whom Dallas lost its innocence as a sports town.

He was well-suited to the purpose, a character of infinite ironies and complexities, witty and brooding, whimsical and introspective. "He was kind of an enigma," said Jerry Tubbs, who played with him and coached him. Nothing about him was as it seemed. Raised in the country, he possessed a sophisticate's guile and charm. Reputedly frail, he played through unspeakable pain. Seemingly nonchalant, he was fiercely competitive. A comic figure in playing days, he became a tragic figure in Cowboy annals: the underappreciated, misunderstood quarterback who never won a championship.

That so many Cotton Bowl fans turned on him was a surprise; Texans are provincial and he was one of their own, raised in the hills and pines of East Texas. His father owned a dry-goods store in Mount Vernon and served on the local school board. Meredith played basketball and football, sang in the church choir, belonged to the Future Farmers of America, starred in one-act plays, and constructed a legend. He was always the quarterback, in any endeavor. "I have been a star since I was six," he said in a 1983 interview with *Parkway Magazine,* a Dallas publication. "I was the youngest kid on the school team. Whenever we chose up sides to play commandos, I was the one who always chose. Then everyone wanted to be on my side."

Dallas was an hour's drive away, and Meredith made his first splash there as a basketball player. He led the Tigers of Mount Vernon High School to the championship of the Dr Pepper Holiday Classic in December of '54, averaging 33 points and beating the best Dallas teams. Described in the *Morning News* as "a basket-cramming junior," he set a tournament record with 52 points in one game.

Still, football was his sport. He honed his passing skills by throwing balls through a tire in his backyard, and made all-state playing quarterback and middle linebacker. "Can you imagine Don Meredith playing middle linebacker?" said Robert Draper, a Dallas businessman who grew up in Mount Vernon and married one of Meredith's classmates. "Most people consider him frail, but he was a tough mother at linebacker. If you came over the middle he busted your ass. He was a tough kid."

He said his Methodist faith was an important factor in his decision to attend SMU instead of the University of Texas or any of the numerous other schools that recruited him. SMU's football program was in decline by then, relegating Meredith to a career as the best player on mediocre teams. The Mustangs went 6–4 in his junior year and 5–4–1 in his senior year. Tall and nimble, with a quick delivery and a strong arm, he was the best passer in the Southwest Conference as a senior with 105 completions and 11 touchdowns in 181 attempts. Though not a consensus All-America, he was regarded as one of the country's best college quarterbacks.

The expansion Cowboys signed him to a five-year, six-figure contract. "We're putting all our eggs in his basket," Schramm said. It seemed a blessing that he would play professionally so close to home, but coming to the Cowboys meant he would spend his career struggling to co-exist with Landry, a yin to his yang, and also take a terrible physical beating playing behind poor offensive lines on losing teams until late in his career. His timing was terrible; had he entered the NFL a year earlier, he would have played for another team far from home, felt less pressure to produce, and possibly never experienced such infamy. Had he come to the Cowboys several years later, he would not have had to sacrifice his body for so long. "He was unlucky enough to be born at the wrong time," Walt Garrison said.

"If he had come to us later on, his career would have turned out totally differently," Lilly said. "He wouldn't have had to become such a character and overcome so much physically. As it was, he had to overcome so much physically when we were losing that I think it affected him mentally. It's just a shame he came when he did. He still carried us a long way."

His contract was an indication of his important place in the Cowboys' plans, but Landry wanted him to learn the pro game from the sidelines as Eddie LeBaron played. Meredith pouted at being benched. "I was really immature," Meredith told a Los Angeles reporter in a '66 interview. "I got that five-year contract and I thought I was something. When Landry put me on the bench, I thought I would hurt him by not working. I just hurt myself."

The fans' disenchantment with him began in those early years. He was a well-paid native son from whom bigger and better things were expected. The fans began to view him as an underachiever. His contract and his status as a home-grown star created a level of high expectations against which he was judged throughout his career.

"In my opinion, he was lionized beyond his capabilities," said Harry Sebel, a stockbroker and Cotton Bowl season-ticket holder. "Plus, he gave off the impression that football wasn't number one on his list of priorities. His nickname was 'Dandy Don.' Whatever the reality was, he seemed not to take it that seriously. And the fans resented it."

The reality was more complicated than it appeared. Meredith badly wanted to win, particularly after he matured and became the starter, but he also was young, spirited, and determined to enjoy himself. Landry said later that he "always liked" Meredith but "we didn't see eye to eye on everything." That is an understatement. Landry wanted Meredith to study more and work harder. Meredith had fun. "He didn't take it real serious; it was just a game to him," Tony Liscio said. He sang in the huddle, played pranks, and joked at tense moments. He injured his shoulder before the '65 season in a late-night water fight with Buddy Dial at training camp. He seemed to view himself as a natural heir to Bobby Layne, a Texan who flourished at quarterback in the '40s and '50s as a hard-drinking tough who played hurt and hung over. "Layne played drunk, and we drank a lot," Pete Gent said. Meredith did not play drunk, but "he might go out the night before a game and just generally do some things you might not like if you were from the school of training hard," Jerry Tubbs said.

"Meredith just wasn't that serious," said Sam Huff, who played against Meredith as a linebacker with the Giants and Redskins. "He talked the entire game. He would be singing and talking so much over there, I don't know how he was able to concentrate. And he was so damn funny, just as crazy on the field as he was in the broadcast booth later on. He would come out of the huddle and say, 'Hey, Sam, you're lined up in the wrong spot.'"

In '67 Meredith played against the Redskins with broken ribs protected by a pad filled with red fluid. Huff delivered a blow that exploded the pad, drenching Meredith with fluid. "Huff thought it was blood and I think he thought he had killed Don," Jim Boeke recalled. "Don played it up. He lay there for a minute with his eyes closed. Then he smiled and got up and went back to the huddle."

Not all the fans were critical of him; many, such as my father, were enamored of his personality and style. He was a natural comedian with a quick wit and droll delivery. His teammates never knew what was coming next. He once drew three Giants offsides on one play by coming to the line and shouting, "Hey! I just forgot the play!" Before another game, he filled his socks with padding and trotted out for televised pregame introductions with his calves cartoonishly bulging, as though he were a circus clown.

"You laughed all the time, and we needed that because Landry was always so serious," Jethro Pugh recalled.

Yet he was not just a frustrated comic fishing for laughs and attention. His comedy was calculated. "He was trying to keep us loose," Lilly said. "We struggled for so long, and it got frustrating. I never did know what Don was doing, but he was keeping us together. He seemed very nonchalant on the outside, but you knew he cared a lot because he had ulcers all the time. He really wanted to win."

He had a flip side that few of his teammates saw. He was sensitive to criticism and brooded after losses. Until late in his career he claimed that the fans' booing never upset him, but it was clear that the accusation that he was a loser upset him profoundly. Flying home from a loss in Washington in '65, his eyes welled up with tears as he said to Gent, "I'm not a loser, Pete, I'm really not."

His desire was evident in his remarkable willingness to play through pain. "Of all the quarterbacks or even all the players I ever had, he was tougher than anyone," Landry said years later. "He had a tough time back there for a long time. He didn't have any protection. He played hurt, which earned him the respect of his teammates. That's the mark of a good quarterback."

"So many times I went to sleep when I was supposed to block a linebacker, and Dandy wouldn't see the guy coming and get his head snapped back," Frank Clarke said. "I'd go up to him after the game and say, 'Dandy, about those linebackers, I'm so sorry.' My God, if he'd had the kind of protection [Troy] Aikman gets, it'd been fun to watch him."

The Cowboys did not give him adequate protection until late in his career. He paid in a withering currency of blood and broken bones. "For a while, it was like feeding him to the wolves back there," Jim Boeke said. "We were young and not blocking as well as we could. Don got hit left and right. Aikman gets hit a few times a game; Don got hit all the time. He got killed back there."

His toughness and spirit earned him the unyielding support of his teammates. "He is still one of the most amazing guys I have ever seen on any field or floor or anywhere," Gent said. "He wasn't physically endowed like Aikman and he didn't have an exceptional arm and he was erratic, but he had the amazing ability to coalesce everyone around him. Everyone loved him and wanted to win for him."

Boeke said, "If Meredith had led us over a cliff, I would have been the first one to follow. He was that great as a leader. All the guys liked him and wanted to play for him. He didn't just hang out with the receivers and running backs. He hung out with the linemen. He made everyone feel important. He just had an incredible way of motivating people."

Meredith was in a no-win situation for much of his career: The Cowboys were not a strong team until '66, and yet, as a well-paid, prominent player, he was expected to win and produce. The pieces finally fell into in place for him in '66: His offensive line was capable, the team was talented and motivated, and he was comfortable with Landry's multiple-set offense. Suddenly, after failing to live up to expectations, he fulfilled his potential. He won the Bert Bell Memorial Trophy as the most valuable player in the NFL.

"As far as reading defenses and knowing the game plan and what was going on, he was the best quarterback the Cowboys ever had," Garrison said. "He could pick a defense apart. He'd call a play in the huddle and you'd think it was the stupidest play ever, and it was the smartest. Because he set defenses up. He'd say, 'Hey, guys, we're going to run this and it's not going to work now, but we're setting it up to use again later in the game and it'll work then.' He was on another level from the rest of us as far as that kind of stuff."

He was a pocket quarterback with a quick wrist and an uncanny flair. Though not a scrambler, he could gain important yards on the run; in '66, his finest year, he rushed for 242 yards and five touchdowns. "Don was probably the finest natural athlete I ever played with," Manders said. "If he'd had even a semblance of an offensive line for all those years, there is no telling how well he would have done."

Garrison said, "People never realized what a great athlete Meredith was. He was a single-digit handicap golfer. He'd kick your ass playing ping-pong or pool. He could do a lot of stuff. People didn't realize it because they just saw him with his feet all torn up and his ankles broken. He looked like he could barely get around out there sometimes, barely walk, but he was a great athlete."

Meredith called the majority of the plays in '66. "His refusal to let Landry control the team on the field was the key to that first winning season," Gent said. "Everything changed the next year. Don told me he had decided that Tom was right about a lot of things, and Tom was right about a lot of things, but calling the plays from the sidelines wasn't one of them. We were never the same after Don gave that up."

Nor was Meredith's reputation the same after the Cowboys lost to the Packers in the '66 championship game. He played well, but he threw an interception at the end and the fans never forgave him, even though a missed blocking assignment ruined the play. The loss in the Ice Bowl the next year only intensified the fans' displeasure. "Things got tough, and it was tougher on Meredith than anyone else," Bob Ryan of NFL Films said. "He was blamed, which wasn't necessarily fair."

He contemplated retirement after the Ice Bowl. "I sat behind him on the flight home that day and he was absolutely devastated, crying and saying it was all his fault," Bill Mercer said. He huddled with Landry on the plane and later told the *Times Herald*'s Steve Perkins that he was quitting. He later backed off the decision and signed a new three-year contract, reported to training camp a week early, and was the cover boy for *Sports Illustrated*'s pro football issue. He went to the Pro Bowl for the second time that season. "He could have gone on for several more years," Landry said later.

It appeared he would. After the playoff loss in Cleveland, he attended a quarterback camp in May of '69 with Morton and Roger Staubach. He made several promotional appearances for the team. By July the Cowboys were preparing to open training camp; Landry had said Meredith and Morton would compete for the starting job. Meredith was 31 years old and coming off one of his best seasons, with two years left on his contract, when he suddenly announced his retirement at a press conference in Dallas. "It's been on my mind very heavy since late January or early February," he said. "I just don't want to play with the mental attitude I have toward the game right now. It would be like going to play a round of golf and not taking all the clubs with me on the course. I was hoping, sincerely, that this feeling would change. I did feel a little lift at quarterback school in May, but it wasn't enough and I don't want to compete this way."

He had flown back to Dallas from a promotional appearance in early July and met with Landry the next morning. "Don came by my house after the meeting," Gent said later, "and he told me, 'I told Tom that I was retiring and he didn't try to talk me out of it or anything.' I think the thing was, with Tom and Don, that Tom had just decided that he was through with Don."

Landry denied that at the press conference two days later.

"Did you try to talk him out of this?" a reporter asked.

"Very definitely," Landry said. "We want him as part of our team because we think he's an important part of the team. I tried to talk him out of it, but his reasons were good as far as I'm concerned. If you lose the desire to play, you really shouldn't play."

It was easy to discern that Landry was not crushed by the news. "There will be a readjustment period with Morton," Landry said. "How long that period lasts, I'm not really sure. But I think when the season is over we'll be back on the right track and strong as ever."

Landry added that the Cowboys, who had recently traded backup quarterback Jerry Rhome, would go with just Morton and Staubach. "No discredit to Don," Landry said, "but Craig is a little bigger and stronger" and probably could withstand more punishment. Landry had moved on emotionally and strategically. He had no choice with the start of training camp so close, but his passionless response was startling.

The true story went mostly untold at the press conference. Many of the reasons underlying Meredith's decision were not mentioned. He was beaten up physically and mentally after nine years of injuries and boos. He also was under an enormous personal strain. "It came down to a family thing that finally ended his career," Landry said years later. "He had problems with a child (born with a birth defect) and at that time his marriage wasn't going well. I think he was just frustrated." Added Gent, "He was going through so much personal turmoil that it was amazing he could go out there and play that last season."

Perhaps most important, he was tired of playing for Landry. They were opposites who failed to attract. Landry was the solemn perfectionist, Meredith the carefree court jester. "Tom and Don had different outlooks on life, pure and simple," Eddie LeBaron said. Landry wanted Meredith to care more, but Meredith wanted Landry to accept some of the blame for the Cowboys' failings, for which Meredith had taken hard falls. Landry's take on the playoff loss in Cleveland drove Meredith over the edge, according to teammates years later.

"Don was really down on Tom after that game," Jerry Tubbs said, "because he felt like he'd had to take all the blame. He'd thrown those interceptions, but he'd had keys telling him to throw to certain places when certain (Browns) did certain things. He was just following his keys that the

coaches had given him. Well, on that first play of the second half they had
a pick on and Tom had said not to worry about it, and Don threw it and the
guy intercepted the pass and ran it in for a touchdown, and Tom never did
defend Don in the papers. There'd always been a little friction between
them, but that one really hurt Don."

Landry had, in fact, attempted to deflect some of the blame from
Meredith after the game. "Those interceptions were not all Meredith's
fault," he told reporters. But the inference was that the receivers, not the
coaches, had made mistakes. "Don was blamed for the Cleveland loss by
the media and by the coaches," Lilly said. "I never thought that was fair.
The whole team played terribly."

The loss sent Meredith careening toward retirement again, and this time
there was no change of heart, no renewal of his enthusiasm during the offseason.

"He left way too soon," Schramm said. "He was 31 years old, which, by
today's standards, means he was just getting to his prime. He had many
good years left. But he didn't want to play any more. When I tried to talk
him out of it, he said, 'All of a sudden, I just felt this was it.' And he meant
it. He didn't want to come back. He didn't want to endure any more of the
controversy about him and Morton, or the booing, or the stuff with the
press and public. He didn't like that. And that was that. We went with
Craig after that, and we certainly weren't better off without Don. He was a
hell of a leader and a competitor. A special player."

The Cowboys had to endure two more playoff defeats and another quarterback change—Staubach for Morton in '71—before finally winning a
Super Bowl. Staubach went on to become a Hall of Famer now remembered for having given the Cowboys the leadership they lacked. There are
those who wonder if the Cowboys ever would have won a Super Bowl had
Meredith stayed on and played.

"He was in his prime when he walked away, but you know what? We
may never have done as well if he had stayed," Tubbs said. "We might
have, you never know, but we might not have (done as well) because if you
get close to winning and you don't, and your coach and quarterback are
strong personalities that don't mesh well, it's not good. Roger was just the
ideal person for Tom. It was an ideal matchup."

Staubach never denied that his timing was as fortunate as Meredith's
was poor. Staubach became a starter only after the team was fully devel-

oped and carried by veterans. He was the last ingredient of a championship team—a team that Meredith had led throughout its construction.

"It just isn't fair to Meredith to say that the Cowboys had to get to Staubach before they could win a title," Bob Ryan said. "They were unlucky in the '66 title game, and Meredith played great that day. They could have won the Ice Bowl. There is no doubt that Meredith could have won a championship."

"Roger was probably the best winner the Cowboys ever had as a quarterback," Garrison said, "but I really hate to say that because Meredith probably would have been the best winner if he'd had the help that Roger had. Don didn't have a lot of help for a long time. That's why I wish he had stayed and played another year or two. It's just a shame that a guy went through all that and didn't get a chance to play in a Super Bowl. It's just a damn shame."

The Cowboys would not give me his telephone number.

I gave their publicity office a list of 20 players from the Cotton Bowl days whom I wished to contact. They gave me 19 phone numbers.

"Don Meredith does not want to be contacted," said Rich Dalrymple, the team's chief publicist.

I was not surprised. Several former colleagues in the newspaper business had sought to interview Meredith at length for books—one about Landry, the other about *Monday Night Football*—and he had politely but firmly declined, offering only a few wry observations. "Don basically just doesn't do this kind of stuff anymore," Steve Sabol of NFL Films told me. Sabol said he had talked Meredith into sitting down to tape a lengthy interview several years earlier, but only because Meredith owed him for several small favors.

"You won't get him," Sabol said.

That Meredith did not wish to undertake a lengthy review of his football career was hardly surprising. It did not have a happy ending. The boos that rained down on him in the Cotton Bowl were loud enough to reverberate for a lifetime. "I'm not speaking for him, but he's bitter about Dallas," said Ralph Neely, his good friend. Added Schramm, "I'm sure he wished he had stayed to play in a Super Bowl."

Meredith was more universally popular after football, in his reincarnation as a *Monday Night Football* analyst and actor. He twice joined and left *Monday Night Football,* a show that made him a major star. He was a popular television figure in the '70s and '80s, appearing in *Police Story,* numerous commercials, talk shows, and movies-of-the-week. Younger viewers probably had no idea that he had even played pro football; he was just a funny guy with a country schtick.

Now, he wanted no part of the limelight. "It's surprising to me," Jethro Pugh said. "He is the last guy I would have picked to withdraw. He was the life of the team. Always talking to reporters, saying funny things."

You could only contact him by fax at his home in Santa Fe, New Mexico. His teammates, many of whom had not spoken to him in years, helped him maintain the privacy he sought. I asked several for his fax number, which was printed in a Cowboy alumni directory they all had, but they declined. That was Meredith's business, they said.

He was still an enigma as a 58-year-old former player. Not that he was a recluse; he made occasional appearances in Dallas and elsewhere, often at charity golf functions. I spoke to a longtime Cowboy fan, Robert Draper, a fellow native of Mount Vernon, whose wife was Meredith's classmate from first grade through their high school graduation. He had just seen Meredith at a high school reunion. "He's just Don Meredith when he goes home, the same as he ever was," Draper said.

A friend of Clint Murchison's had introduced Meredith to Santa Fe years ago, while Meredith was still playing for the Cowboys. He bought a townhouse there in the '70s as a change of pace from Hollywood and Los Angeles, and bought a house in 1982. He lives there now with Susan, his third wife, a former high-school basketball star. His older brother, Billy Jack, also lives in Santa Fe. "I asked Billy Jack what they did out there," Robert Draper said. "He said the sunrises were spectacular and the sunsets were even better, and in between there wasn't a darn thing to do."

My best chance to speak to Meredith came as a result of sheer serendipity. Meredith's wife was from Baltimore, where I live. His brother-in-law ran a tennis center not far from my home. The brother-in-law and I had mutual friends, and he knew me from my columns in the *Baltimore Sun.* He agreed to speak to Meredith on my behalf. A week later, in November of 1996, he called back with bad news. "I mentioned it to Don and I gave him your phone number, and he said he was interested in the book, but I don't think he wants to participate," his brother-in-law said.

Soon after that, a reporter for the *New York Times* stumbled into Meredith at a rare promotional appearance in New York City. Meredith spent two hours signing photos, football cards, helmets, and magazine covers at a Kmart store, as a favor to a friend, the chairman of Kmart.

"I don't miss the limelight, not at all," Meredith told the reporter. "I'm just more comfortable out of it."

He said he played a lot of golf, no longer acted, and did not need to work. "I piddle around," he said. And he did not want to be called "Dandy Don" anymore.

"Dandy is somebody else," he said. "He wasn't a bad guy."

The reporter wrote that Meredith was "charming, but guarded." I knew then that he was not going to call. I had a long list of questions ready for him—What was the main reason for his premature retirement? Did he regret not sticking around to play in a Super Bowl? What was his relationship with Landry? How would his career have been different if he had joined the Cowboys in '65? How did the booing affect him? The Ice Bowl?—but I never had the chance to ask them.

I could have pushed harder, gotten obnoxious, and flown to New Mexico without an appointment, but what was the point? After a lifetime in the spotlight, Meredith obviously just wanted his privacy now. I would have relished the chance to pick the brain of the brightest star of my favorite childhood teams, but he did not want to rehash old controversies, and I respected his wishes. It was fitting, in a way, that he was not available to clear up any of these decades-old mysteries. He was never fully understood when he was playing. No one ever knew for sure why he retired. He was never an easy mark, always tough to figure out. Why should that change now?

Chapter Eleven

A decade before the Cowboys became known as "America's Team," they had a less flattering nickname: Next Year's Champions. It was the title of a book written by the *Times Herald*'s Steve Perkins, a diary-style account of the '68 season that ended so suddenly in Cleveland. That defeat, along with the championship losses to the Packers, forged the Cowboys' reputation as a starlit team that always lost the big game, a team that promised more than it delivered.

Many in the Cowboy family were displeased with Perkins' book, which they felt revealed too many secrets, and their displeasure was doubled when the book's cynical title caught on with the public as an appropriate nickname. "That book came out, the nickname stuck, and it was a tough deal," Bob Lilly said. "Once something like that gets stuck, it's hard to get rid of it."

The euphoria that the city had experienced when the Cowboys became a championship contender gave way to an edgy skepticism; neither the players nor the fans knew if the Cowboys had what it took to go all the way. "We were reeling after that loss to the Browns," Lee Roy Jordan said. "A lot of people were saying to themselves, 'Maybe we aren't as good as we thought we were.'"

A team in such a precarious emotional state could have come undone with the loss of its starting quarterback and leading rusher, but the retirements of Meredith and Perkins in July of '69 did not stagger the Cowboys. "They were always good at turning the page and having new guys ready," said Calvin Hill, who joined the team as a first-round draft choice from Yale in '69.

Morton replaced Meredith, to the delight of many fans; Staubach also joined the team as a 27-year-old rookie after completing his four-year Navy service commitment. Perkins was replaced by Walt Garrison, whom Perkins had tutored for four years. "They were almost the same player," Lilly said. Hill emerged as an exhilarating halfback. Blaine Nye and Rayfield Wright moved into the offensive line. Mike Ditka, a former All-Pro tight end with the Bears who had languished for two seasons in Philadelphia, was obtained in a trade.

The defense was mostly unchanged, but the remaking of the offense gave the team a new appearance that defused much of the discontent from the playoff loss to the Browns. "There is a freshness, a different feeling," Landry said early in the season. "There is something underneath this club. They're more determined."

He was obviously delighted to have a starting quarterback who was not only less controversial, but also a strong-armed passer. Even though the Meredith-led offense had registered the fourth-highest point total in NFL history in '68, "the potential (of the Morton-led '69 version) is greater," Landry said, because of Morton's arm. "He can throw that sideline pass sharply, like Jurgensen or [John] Brodie. Don could throw the sideline pass, but he didn't like to."

The potential also was greater because of Hill. The Cowboys had raised eyebrows around the league by drafting an Ivy Leaguer in the first round, but Hill made an immediate impact. He rushed for 70 yards and threw a touchdown pass in his first regular season game, rushed for 138 yards in his second game, and totaled 206 rushing, receiving, and passing yards in his third game.

The Cowboys had drafted him because of his size, speed, and intelligence; he was six-foot-four and 225 pounds, ran the 40-yard dash in 4.6 seconds; he enrolled in SMU's Perkins School of Theology as a rookie. They had first tried him at tight end and linebacker in Thousand Oaks. "I think I would have ended up at tight end had Danny Reeves and Craig Baynham not gotten injured," Hill said. "Danny had suffered his first serious knee injury the year before, and Craig was his backup and hurt a rib in camp. If they had been able to perform, my sense is that I would have shuttled between tight end and linebacker."

Hill ended the debate about his position by rushing for 106 yards in the second exhibition game against the 49ers. "I had been away from camp for two weeks at the college All-Star game, and I was completely confused when I got back," Hill said. "I was playing strictly on instinct that night. My whole rookie year was instinct. I didn't understand the blocking. I didn't know if the ball was being handed to me or tossed to me. Morton improvised all the time because of my lack of knowledge."

No one could tell. Hill was a wonder as a rookie. Perkins had carried the rushing game for years, but Hill was bigger, stronger, and faster. "He was our first breakaway back," Tony Liscio said. "We ran a sweep up at Franklin Field and I made a block and looked up and Calvin was already halfway down the field. I went, 'Damn this is different.'"

Cowboy fans had never seen such a runner. Hill slashed into the line at hard angles, hurtled through the air, and crashed into linebackers and defensive backs. By November he had almost 200 more rushing yards than any other back in the league. "Everything I did was right," Hill said. "It was a magical season. An amazing year."

Morton was just as brilliant until he suffered a separated shoulder in the fourth game at Atlanta. The injury bothered him for the rest of the season. He still threw for five touchdowns in a 49–14 victory over the Eagles the next week, then guided the offense in a 25–3 victory over the Giants.

Three straight playoff losses had backed the team up against a harsh standard—Super Bowl or bust—but the Cowboys had renewed the fans' optimism by winning their first six games by a combined score of 181–61. "That's the best I've ever seen the Cowboys," Giants quarterback Fran Tarkenton said.

Then they traveled to Cleveland, site of their playoff calamity, and were dealt a brutal dose of reality by the Browns. Garrison fumbled on the first series, setting up a Cleveland touchdown. Baynham fumbled the ensuing kickoff, setting up another Cleveland touchdown. The Browns led 28–3 at halftime and went on to win, 42–10. The *Fort Worth Press* ran a "Choke

Chart" listing eight Cowboy losses in big games. Once again, they were "Next Year's Champions."

They recovered with wins against the Saints and Redskins. Hill rushed for 109 yards against the Saints and was brilliant against the Redskins with 150 yards rushing, two pass receptions, and three kickoff returns worth 100 yards. The victory in Washington was Landry's first against Vince Lombardi, now coaching the Redskins. With a 9–1 record and a three-game lead in the Capitol Division, the Cowboys were on the verge of their fourth straight division title despite having played only two opponents with winning records.

Yet the Washington game also marked the beginning of the Cowboys' downfall. Hill jammed the big toe on his right foot in the fourth quarter, and Sonny Jurgensen passed for 338 yards and four touchdowns; both developments were deemed minor at the time, but they were indicator lights for the rest of the season.

Hill was never the same after injuring his toe. He sat out one game and most of another, then returned and played through persistent pain that limited his ability to plant, cut, and run. His injury baffled doctors at first; there was no swelling, and X-rays revealed no broken bones. Only later was it determined that he had fractured the sesamoid bone in the ball of the foot. In any case, his effectiveness was diminished. After rushing for 809 yards in the first nine games, he gained only 143 in the last five.

At the same time, the secondary, which Jurgensen had exposed, became a concern. The Cowboys lost to the undefeated Rams in Los Angeles, 24–23, with Rams quarterback Roman Gabriel passing for 224 yards and two touchdowns. Four days later, the 49ers' John Brodie passed for 255 yards and a touchdown in a 24–24 tie on Thanksgiving at the Cotton Bowl. The Cowboy secondary had allowed 827 passing yards and eight touchdowns in three games. Strong safety Mike Gaechter had a sore tendon, and Phil Clark, the latest "answer" at right cornerback, was struggling.

A rookie, Otto Brown, replaced Gaechter in a 10–7 victory in snowy Pittsburgh that clinched the division title. Impressed, Landry tried Brown at right cornerback the next two weeks, and Brown played well in wins over the Colts and Redskins. One month after shredding the secondary, Jurgensen was held without a touchdown pass. The crisis in the secondary appeared over.

The Cowboys finished the regular season with an 11–2–1 record, having led the league in 16 statistical categories. They were favored by six points over the Browns in the Eastern Conference championship game at the Cotton Bowl, even though the Browns had beaten them by 32 points earlier in the season. The Browns had won the Century Division with a 10–3–1 record. They had plenty of offense with Nelsen, Leroy Kelly, and Paul Warfield, but they were aging on defense. The talk in the Dallas papers was about Otto Brown starting at cornerback, and the possibility of Ice Bowl II: playing in Minnesota for the NFL title.

The Eastern Conference championship game was played in Dallas on December 28th—ten years to the day after Landry signed his original Cowboy contract. It was a miserable anniversary. A steady rain fell all day. Three thousand seats were empty. The pregame mood was somber. The Cowboys showed up in body only.

The drenched crowd mustered a roar when the Cowboy defense held on the first series and the Browns' Don Cockroft lofted a short punt. Bob Hayes signaled for a fair catch and scrambled out of the way. On the Cowboy bench, Morton and the offensive starters shed their rain jackets and started for the field. They never made it. Cockroft's punt landed on Rayfield Wright, who was oblivious to the ball as he retreated to block for Hayes. The ball hit Wright's leg and bounced away. Bob Matheson recovered the fumble for the Browns at the Dallas 34. The crowd fell silent. The Cowboy defense trotted back onto the field and the Browns drove to a touchdown in eight plays.

"I didn't see the ball until it was right on me," Wright said after the game. "I saw Hayes throw up his hand. I had no idea that (the punt) was that short or even close to me."

It was a freak play that summoned the memories of prior playoff defeats. "I looked down the sidelines (after the turnover) and I thought I could see a letdown on a lot of faces," Morton said after the game. It was the mark of a team that still did not believe in itself despite its many accomplishments, a team shaken by prior playoff failures.

The Cowboys had scored more points than all but one other team in the league during the regular season, but their offense was pathetic against the Browns. It did not help that Morton's sore shoulder restricted his passing and Hill's sore toe rendered him all but useless. They were unable to run the ball effectively, leaving them in third-and-long situations that Morton failed to convert. Morton missed his first six pass attempts; after the game, he apologized for playing so poorly.

The Browns kept the ball for 23 of 29 snaps in the first quarter, and continued their dominance in the second quarter. Nelsen was as sharp as Morton was dull, repeatedly hitting Warfield on slant patterns for first down yardage. The Browns scored another touchdown in the second quarter and added a field goal before halftime for a 17–0 lead. The crowd booed the Cowboys as they left the field having managed just three first downs and 39 yards of offense.

Warfield's success was particularly depressing. Landry had devised a special defensive scheme, with Renfro and Brown switching between cornerback and free safety depending on where Warfield lined up, with the goal of having Renfro on Warfield as often as possible. It was a sound plan in theory, but it was not working. "That was a killer," Hill said. "When you're doing everything you could to stop a guy, and you still couldn't stop him, it was like it took our heart away or something."

Renfro had not known the scheme would be used until the morning of the game. "We worked on it all week, but I didn't know we were going to use it (in the game)," Renfro said after the game. "The switch didn't work too well. There was a lot of confusion back there. I'm not sure we always knew what defense we were supposed to be in."

The Browns made it 24–0 early in the third quarter on a short touchdown drive set up by an interception. The Cowboy offense finally stirred, driving 72 yards to a touchdown, but the Browns came right back with another touchdown drive, and then cornerback Walt Sumner returned an interception 88 yards for a touchdown and a 38–7 lead. The Cotton Bowl emptied. Steve Perkins' book had prophesied the ending of yet another Cowboy season: For the fourth year in a row, they were "Next Year's Champions."

Staubach replaced Morton and led the offense to a touchdown. The Cowboys had no chance, but Landry called for an onsides kick. Cowboy kicker Mike Clark advanced on the ball planning to dribble it forward with a tap, but he slipped and whiffed. The ball toppled off the tee and went nowhere. It was the perfect metaphor for the end of the Cowboys' first decade.

•   •   •

The Browns were ahead by two touchdowns when a man in the row in front of us leaned back against my father's legs. My father flinched his legs, but the man, wearing an overcoat and brim hat, slumped back more forcefully. My father started to speak, then saw the man's head roll to one side and knew instantly there was a problem. The man's wife glanced at her husband, saw his eyes roll into his head, and gasped.

It had been years since my father worked in an emergency room, but suddenly, late in the second quarter on a rainy afternoon at the Cotton Bowl, his services were needed. The man was having a heart attack. My father told us to make room. We left our seats and stood in the aisle as fans in nearby sections stood to see what was causing the commotion. The man in the hat was slumped against our row, his face a horrifying whitish blue.

An emergency medical crew carted the man to a nurse's station located on the concourse. My father went along. The nurse's station was not equipped to handle a grave emergency. A paramedic had to borrow oxygen from the ambulance parked outside the stadium. The man was loaded into the ambulance and taken to Baylor Hospital. My father rode in the ambulance, but he knew there was little hope. The man was dead on arrival.

The ambulance driver gave my father a ride back to the game. He arrived in the third quarter, with the Browns ahead, 24–0. Thousands of fans were leaving. Rain was falling and so were the Cowboys. "I was better off where I was," my father grumbled as he sat back down. Pop asked about the man and my father gave us the news. We all sat back in horror. I had never seen anyone die. My stomach turned. We left early and went home, and I climbed into bed and covered myself with extra blankets to fight a lingering chill. My mother brought me a bowl of soup. She was worried about my reaction to what I had seen. I was fine, if a bit shaken, but I told her it had been my worst day ever at the Cotton Bowl.

Some good did come out of it. My father wrote a letter to Clint Murchison explaining how ill-equipped the Cotton Bowl had been to handle a serious emergency, and Murchison made sure a better medical facility was installed at Texas Stadium. He wrote a letter thanking my father for alerting him to the situation. Maybe someone else's life was saved because the man in the row in front of us died that day at the Cotton Bowl.

•   •   •

What was wrong with the Cowboys in the late '60s? Their record between '66 and '69 was 42–12–2 in the regular season and 1–4 in the playoffs, with their only victory in the '67 Eastern Conference championship game against the Browns. Years later, NFL Films included them in a video essay on the best teams never to win a championship. Were they just unlucky, or did they have a fatal flaw? Was there a thread connecting their playoff defeats?

Obviously, they were a fine team of championship quality. They won more games, had more All-Pros, scored more points, and set more NFL records than any other team in those four seasons. They had two Hall of Fame players, Lilly and Renfro, and a Hall of Fame coach, Landry. Yet something was wrong. They failed in the final minutes against the Packers in '66 and '67, and played far below their capabilities against the Browns in '68 and '69.

To suggest that there was an "umbrella" explanation for all four defeats, that the Cowboys had fatal flaws that doomed them, is something of a reach. They were just a yard away from overtime in '66, and one play away from victory in '67. If they could come that close, within one twist of fate, they were capable of winning. Their shortcomings were not inherently fatal.

"The Packers were legendary, but the Cowboys were as good, if not better," said Herb Adderley, who played for those Packer teams and joined the Cowboys in '70. "The talent level was the same. Both teams were great. The difference in the championship games, each of them, was one play at the end. Dave Robinson forced the interception in '66 and Jerry Kramer made the block in '67. Otherwise, there was no difference between the teams."

That was not entirely true. Experience was a difference that cost the Cowboys in '66. The Packers, playing in their fifth NFL championship game, kept their cool when the Cowboys reached the two-yard line with a chance to tie the score late in the game. The Cowboys, playing in their first championship game, committed a series of mistakes on that final series.

Losing that game did not damage the Cowboys' confidence, but losing the Ice Bowl did. It was after that game that the Cowboys developed fatal and unseen flaws. They became frightened of their reputation as a runner-up, and fearful of losing again. Failing in the playoffs became, for them, a self-fulfilling prophecy. Their shortcomings became relevant. They had never had a strong right cornerback. They were not overly tough or physical, and neither emotional nor close. Mixed with the bitter taste of recurring defeat, those deficiencies became meaningful.

"Failure, like success, has a carryover effect," Landry said after the '69 season. "After we lost (the Ice Bowl) our chances of winning (in Cleveland in '68) were much worse. And after that loss we were at a big psychological disadvantage in the ('69) playoffs and lost again. Football is a mental game and a cycle like that is hard to break."

Landry had effectively created the Cowboys, painting them into history with the brush strokes of his tactical genius. He revolutionized defense with his 4-3 and Flex concepts. He revolutionized offense with his wide-open, multiple-set design. "It will go down in history that Landry changed football," Mike Gaechter said. "Before him, football was pretty straightforward. You just tried to beat the guy in front of you. Landry created the scheme defense and wide-open offense everyone adopted."

The Cotton Bowl Cowboys were his masterpiece, the product of his singular vision. "It was his system, more than the players, that made us great," Gaechter said. "We had some great players, but also some average players that Landry took and plugged in and made great. It was his coaching that made the difference. We got good when we started to believe in his concepts and play them well."

Yet no coach is perfect, and Landry came with drawbacks as well as assets. The most important was his distant management style. He saw the game as a chess match more than a physical contest, and that was reflected in the Cowboys in many ways. One was their lack of emotion. Landry was ineffectual as a motivator. "I played for Lombardi, who was a master motivator and could get people to overachieve," Adderley said. "He knew which guys he had to yell at, which guys he had to pat on the back, which guys he had to bring into his office. He got them all to play. Landry didn't do that. It was a big difference between them. Landry said, 'Look, I'm not being paid to motivate you. You're a professional. You need to motivate yourself.' I think one of the reasons the Cowboys got to big games and lost was that they didn't know how to motivate themselves. Some guys did, but not enough."

Lee Roy Jordan said, "I don't know that we took the emotional side of the game sufficiently into account. Our practice preparation lacked the intensity level it took to win a championship. We said, 'We're professionals; if we practice too hard, our legs will get tired.' A lot of times we had to hold up on defense because they didn't want us to mess up the play. The right intensity is a must, and sometimes we didn't have it. That came from Tom and his staff."

Sometimes the Cowboys almost resembled a stable of pampered thoroughbreds more than a pro football team. As brilliant as Landry was, he underestimated the importance of playing physical football in the Cowboys' first decade. The Flex was a defense built on denying emotion and intensity in favor of recognition and discipline, and the multiple-set offense was a thinking man's attack. That left the Cowboys vulnerable to more physical teams such as the Browns and Packers.

"The Cowboys were a real smart team and always tough to beat, but they were a finesse team, and that's why the real aggressive, physical teams could beat them," Sam Huff said. "The Packers got their nature from Lombardi and the Cowboys took their lead from Landry. He wasn't a mean coach. He was a great coach and he had a system, but he was a dapper guy and the team reflected him."

The Cowboys also lacked the Packers' cohesive spirit. The players admired Landry's football intelligence, believed in his system, and respected him personally, but his studied emotional distance translated into a coolness on the field.

"We weren't a close team," Calvin Hill said. "Tom was a superior coach and I really appreciated the opportunity to play for him from a football standpoint, but you always felt a distance. Teams tend to reflect the coach's personality. Tom is almost a shy man in some respects. There was frustration about the losses, but there wasn't a warmness. I always thought we could be close. Maybe it reflected the corporate nature of the team. The computer thing. The fact that the owner treated it like a business. Things were just very corporate. It wasn't a family affair. I've often wondered, if we'd been closer, whether that would have translated into better teams. As it was, you always felt you were replaceable. It was almost a totalitarian thing. There wasn't a lot of joy. Playing football should be joyful. It was difficult to feel warm and fuzzy playing for the Cowboys."

Lilly described the players' consensus view of Landry in an interview with the *Times Herald*'s Frank Luksa in '72: "We sort of look at him as a powerful figure, kind of like a dictator in a way. He's not a fatherly figure.

He can't be. There's contracts, trades, and cuts he is involved in. Most of us look at him as being very fair. He runs a tight ship. You can't use one word to sum him up. He's aloof, yet fair. We respect his intelligence and coaching, but we don't know him. He feels we get paid to do a job and it's not his job to get us 'up' for the game, and he's right."

The divide between the players and coaches widened with each playoff loss in the late '60s. Thirty years later, Jordan sat in his office near Love Field and addressed the issue.

"I'm 55 years old and I better start speaking my mind before it's too late," he said. "I'm very fond of coach Landry, but I believe that had he accepted some responsibility for the losses, we would have had a much better rapport. I don't think I ever heard him say, 'I called a bad play,' or 'I had a bad game plan,' or 'the other coach just prepared them better.' That would have brought us closer together and prolonged the careers of players such as Meredith and Perkins. We would have been a much better team if the coaches had shared some responsibility for the losses. But it was the opposite: We all shared in the winning, but no one shared in the losing. That prevented our development as far as unity and confidence."

But again, the losses to the Packers precipitated the shattering emotional divide. Landry's tactical brilliance and aloof management style brought the Cowboys so close to two championships that their hearts broke when they failed to win. Only then did genuine discontent arise.

"We played with great emotion as the underdogs in '66 and '67, but after that we were the team that was expected to win, and I'm not sure we were mature enough to handle that," Schramm said. "We had a talented team, but it was a strange team in some ways, with basketball players and track stars and unusual talents, and all sorts of makeshift people plugged in. We were somewhat immature, lacking in experience, and, in my mind, lacking the talent to be a dominating team. We could almost get there, but we weren't good enough to take that final step. And then we got in that mentality. Those were tough days."

Four years after agreeing to merge, the NFL and AFL completed their consolidation and integrated in 1970. Unable to agree on conference and divisional alignments, the 26 owners put five combinations in a hat and used the one that Commissioner Pete Rozelle's secretary pulled out.

The league was divided into the National Football Conference and American Football Conference, each of which was composed of East, Central, and West divisions. The NFC consisted of the premerger NFL teams minus the Colts, Browns, and Steelers, who were switched to the AFC to give each conference 13 teams. The Cowboys landed in the NFC East with the Cardinals, Redskins, Eagles, and Giants.

The merger brought a new scheduling formula. In '70 the Cowboys had to play road games early in the season against the Chiefs and Vikings, the Super Bowl teams from the prior season. They also had to play the Packers and Browns, their playoff nemeses. The improving Cardinals and Redskins figured to make the NFC East race interesting. For the first time since '66, the Cowboys would begin a season not knowing that their place in the playoffs was almost assured.

The players considered this a positive development. Their playoff failures had left them wary of their easy road to the postseason. As skillful, well-coached, and successful as the Cowboys were, they had built their glowing records and statistics against soft schedules composed mostly of losing teams. The strength in the premerger NFL was in the Western Conference, where the Packers, Rams, Colts, and Vikings played. Unlike those teams, the Cowboys never had to sweat out a division title. That was not the proper conditioning for the playoffs.

"I remember Dave Edwards talking about that after we lost to Cleveland in '69," Calvin Hill said. "He said that our easy schedule hurt us in the playoffs."

A month after the Cleveland loss, the front office sent out questionnaires to the players regarding all aspects of the Cowboys' operation. The rest of the league snickered, but the Cowboys were desperate. The players answered anonymously and sent their responses to Jordan, who destroyed the postmarked envelopes and gave the questionnaires to Landry. The idea was to give the players a forum for appraising and criticizing without fear of reprisal.

"We were trying to communicate better with the players," Landry said later. "They didn't have to sign the questionnaires. They could say what they felt we needed. I think it helped. They became much more a part of the team than they had been before, and that made a big difference."

Landry discerned from the questionnaires that the players felt the team relied too much on finesse, trickery, and big plays, and not enough on traditional physical football. When the next season began, it was clear Landry had taken the suggestion seriously.

Not that the incorporation of the players' opinions quelled their discontent; after a decade of low-profile dissatisfaction with their pay, they went public with demands for more money. Bob Hayes started it with a "pay me or trade me" shocker two weeks before training camp was scheduled to open. "This is why we don't win the title," Hayes said. "Not one guy on the club is happy with what he is being paid. I'm very unhappy."

Renfro then confessed his displeasure with his $20,000 salary and pledged that he would be "on the move regarding my contract." The players' union struck for the first time that summer over the issue of preseason pay, delaying the start of training camp by two weeks; when a settlement was reached, George Andrie balked at reporting to camp and Calvin Hill grumbled about the team's reluctance to renegotiate his contract.

The summer of '70 was not a summer of love in Dallas. The frustrated Cowboys were beginning to resemble a dysfunctional family. They went 1–5 in the preseason, ending with losses to the Chiefs and Jets at the Cotton Bowl. The 13–0 loss to the Chiefs was galling; eight years after leaving Dallas for Kansas City, the Chiefs returned to their original home as the reigning Super Bowl champions and won easily.

Near the end of the preseason there was a positive development that would prove critical in the coming seasons: the acquisition of Herb Adderley. He had balked at reporting to the Packers' training camp because he was angry that the coaches had not recommended him for the Pro Bowl the year before. The Packers packed him off for two linemen, Malcolm Walker and Clarence Williams. The Cowboys would never make a more important trade; Adderley had lost some of the speed that made him a feared defender, but he was experienced, guileful, and still quick. Finally, the Cowboys had a right cornerback.

"Having two cornerbacks made a world of difference for that team," Adderley said, "because we just shut down the flanks and forced everything inside. I shut down my side and Mel shut down his side. I think I gave up one touchdown in my first season there."

Jerry Tubbs said, "Herb wasn't very good any more physically, to be honest, but he was smart and a competitor and knew what it took to win. He was near the end of his career and he'd guess and get beat, but he had some ability and he really helped our team through sheer want-to and mental toughness and determination. He almost had a sixth sense that came from experience. And he really added leadership qualities. He was a good worker and gave his all and people would say, 'Hey, that's a guy who played on those championship teams.' "

Mike Ditka, obtained the year before, also had won a championship with the Bears in '63. Ditka and Adderley toughened the Cowboys. "Herb walked into his first meeting and held up his finger with a championship ring on it and said, 'I'll help you get one of these,'" Jethro Pugh said. "He brought a real swagger that was missing after the Cleveland games."

The Cowboys began their second decade in the wake of the publication of another doubting book: *Dallas Cowboys: Pro or Con?* written by *Morning News* columnist Sam Blair. The book was an anecdotal look at the Cowboys' first decade. Wrote Blair in summation, "By now the public had to wonder if (the Cowboys) were truly a professional football club or just an extraordinary collection of con artists. Perhaps too many people, including the press, had become too impressed with the Cowboy organization with all its super-smooth executive and coaching talent, its promotional flair, its fast, glamorous players, and its fancy scouting system full of keen-eyed guys and uncanny computers. Maybe all that just meant that the Cowboys, perhaps without even realizing it, had been putting them on for 10 years."

It became clear when the season began that Landry was trying a new tactical approach. In their first two games, the Cowboys relied on rushing plays rather than long passes and trick plays. With Ditka and Pettis Norman shuttling in plays called by Landry on the sideline, the Cowboys attempted twice as many rushes as passes in wins over the Eagles and Giants. After a loss to the Cardinals in the third week, Craig Morton attempted only 10 passes in a 13–0 win over the Falcons. The Cowboys rushed for 218 yards and passed for 39.

With a 3–1 record, the Cowboys flew to Minnesota to play the defending NFL champions and experienced a replay of their playoff catastrophes. The Vikings gave them their worst beating ever, 54–13. With their "Purple People Eaters" defense and a simple, sound offense, the Vikings had surpassed their expansion brothers from the early '60s. Bob St. John wrote in Monday's *Morning News* that "this was probably the worst Dallas team since 1965."

Galled, the Cowboys traveled to Kansas City the next week and beat the defending Super Bowl champions, 27–16, trampling the notion that they were fodder for strong teams. The victory included the birth of a new star: Duane Thomas, a rookie running back. He was a Dallas native from West Texas State whom the Cowboys had drafted in the first round that year. At the time it was regarded as a curious pick because the Cowboys seemed set in the backfield with Hill and Garrison, but their scouts had seen potential in Thomas's strong, gliding running style. Everyone realized why in Kansas City: Thomas broke a 47-yard touchdown run and gained 134 yards on 20 carries.

The football mavens at NFL Films were stunned when they saw Thomas on film. "We thought he was the closest thing to Jim Brown that we had ever seen," Bob Ryan said. "He blocked, he caught the ball. He was awesome. His speed and moves for a guy that big were unbelievable. You can't extrapolate a career, but he was one of the most fantastic talents ever to come into the NFL."

The Cowboys beat the Eagles the next week, then lost to the Giants and fell out of first place. The Cardinals came to town for a division showdown at the Cotton Bowl, the Cowboys' first appearance on *Monday Night Football,* the new ABC telecast creating a sensation. Millions of viewers tuned in every week to watch a game and listen to Howard Cosell and Don Meredith discuss football and life. Meredith, who had said when he retired that he did not want to become a broadcaster, suddenly was a TV star. The show in the broadcast booth was as interesting as the games; the debates between the bombastic Cosell and chicken-fried Meredith made for lively viewing.

The Cardinals presented a formidable challenge. They had a 6–2 record, and their last two games had been spectacular: a 44–0 win over the Oilers and a 31–0 win over the Patriots. Jim Hart was the quarterback, surrounded by fine players such as fullback MacArthur Lane, receiver John Gilliam, and defensive backs Larry Wilson and Roger Wehrli. "On film they looked like one of the best teams we had ever seen," Lilly said. "They were just killing people."

Knowing that the game was on *Monday Night Football* brought an air of anticipation to the Cotton Bowl, which was sold out. The Cowboys used the occasion to give yet another infamous performance. The Cardinals'

Johnny Roland returned a punt 74 yards for a touchdown, and Gilliam scored on a 48-yard end-around to give the Cardinals a 14–0 lead in the second quarter. The Cowboy offense was inept; Morton completed just eight of 28 pass attempts and was intercepted three times. The Cardinals poured it on in the second half. The final score, incredibly, was 38–0.

I had gone to the game with a school friend instead of with my family. His older cousin drove and we sat on the other side of the stadium. Somehow my friend and I got separated from his cousin, who took off before the game was over. I had to call my father at home at midnight, and he had to drive all the way back down to Fair Park to pick us up. It was a disastrous night all the way around.

It appeared that the Cowboys had hit bottom under the weight of their playoff failures. They were a pale imitation of the team that had challenged the Packers for the NFL championship four years earlier. "This is not the team I used to know," a visibly upset Meredith told the national TV audience. In the second half the fans began chanting for Meredith, the quarterback they had scorned. "We want Meredith!" they shouted, knowing he was in the press box. Meredith laughed and shook his head. "There's no way I'm going down there," he said. Who could blame him?

The headline in Monday's *Morning News* read, "Redbirds Chirp Bye, Bye Cowboys." The Cardinals had a two-game lead in the NFC East. The Cowboys had a 5–4 record, a two-game losing streak, and little hope of making the playoffs. They were in decline. Landry met with the team before practice on Tuesday. "We felt like the coaches quit on us," Dave Manders said. "They basically said we were going to start playing for next year. Looking back, I guess it's possible it was a motivational ploy, but I don't think so. I think they thought the season was over."

After meeting with Landry, the players met by themselves. "The press had written us off, the wives and girlfriends had written us off, and the coaches had written us off," Ralph Neely said. "We were way out of first and we all got up and spilled our guts out. We just decided 'to hell with the coaches, to hell with the wives, to hell with the press.' We were all alone now and we were going to go out, have fun, and play for ourselves. The pressure was off."

After four years of playing in must-win circumstances, the Cowboys no longer were expected to win. Since '67 they had been afraid to lose for fear of not living up to expectations, but now, amid the rubble of the loss to the Cardinals, they stopped caring. "That game changed the mentality of the team," Pugh said. "We developed a harder edge."

"We created something called the Thickskin Club," Neely said. "We even had our own secret handshake. The purpose of the club was to remind everyone that we were playing just for fun now. Let's say you were in practice and the coach jumped on your butt, normally it got to you and you swelled up like a toad, but now someone would tap you on the shoulder and say, 'We're just having fun now, remember? They can't get to you now.' And you would tell yourself, 'Yeah, I'm not loafing, I'm OK here.' We never told the coaches. Never told anyone."

Bob Lilly said, "That's when we finally got tough. After the St. Louis game we would go into restaurants where people normally would have brought us dinner, and now they were laughing at us or didn't even want to talk to us. That was the point where we finally stopped caring what other people thought. We just started playing for ourselves, sort of a 'to heck with everyone else' attitude. The defense got together and said, 'We may give up some yards, but we're not going to let anyone into the end zone.' And we started playing better."

Landry tossed out his planned practice on the Tuesday after the St. Louis game; the players played touch football, setting the tone for a relaxed week. The carefree approach resulted in a 45–21 defeat of the Redskins in Washington. Hill was out with an injured shoulder, but Thomas rushed for 104 yards and three touchdowns. After the game the players learned that the Cardinals had tied the Chiefs, 6–6. Maybe the Cardinals were not so invincible after all.

Four days later, the Cowboys played the Packers on Thanksgiving at the Cotton Bowl. The Packers had a 5–5 record, but they still had many players from their championship teams and the Cowboys had never beaten them. The Cotton Bowl was not sold out, a reflection of the skepticism that had arisen around town. The Cowboys' defense provided the foundation of a 16–3 victory. The Packers managed just 154 yards of offense.

On the Monday after the holiday weekend the team was stunned by the news that Lance Rentzel had been charged with indecent exposure in an incident involving a 10-year-old girl in University Park. According to the police report, Rentzel stopped his car in front of the girl's house, rolled down his window and asked for directions, then asked the girl to step closer to the car to look at a map, and exposed himself. A neighbor took down the license plate, which was traced to a courtesy car loaned to Rentzel.

The incident had occurred before the Packer game, but the Cowboys kept it quiet until after Thanksgiving. When the papers finally picked it up, Rentzel suspended himself. Only then was it reported that the "personal problems" Rentzel had experienced while playing for the Vikings had included another incident of indecent exposure to small children, according to a police report and the residents of the neighborhood in which he had lived. Rentzel would never play again for the Cowboys; he later pleaded guilty to a five-year probated sentence requiring continued psychiatric treatment.

The players were upset about Rentzel, but they maintained their focus. The Redskins came to town that Sunday with a team shredded by injuries to halfback Larry Brown, fullback Charlie Harraway, and split end Charlie Taylor. The Cowboys pounded them, 34–0. It was a happy day: The Cardinals lost to the Lions in Detroit, 16–3, leaving the Cowboys a half-game out of first place and tied for second with the Giants. They were back in the running for the playoffs.

With two games left in the season, the Cowboys now confronted a colossal emotional hurdle: They had to go to Cleveland and play the Browns, the team that had shamed them into the period of self-doubt that had culminated with their 38–0 loss to the Cardinals. The Browns were struggling with a 6–6 record in the AFC Central, but the prospect of playing them sent a shudder through the city. "I'm a little bit afraid of going up there," Renfro said during the week, "but I'm also ready. Beating them would mean a lot."

The team that traveled to Cleveland was ready for the Browns. Adderley and rookie Charlie Waters had fortified the secondary; the pass defense had allowed just 10 touchdown passes, as opposed to 23 at the same point in the '69 season. The loss to the Cardinals had hardened the team's emotional edge. Landry had changed the emphasis from finesse and big plays to defense and the rushing game. In the 11 months since their playoff loss, the Cowboys had corrected the problems that had doomed them against the Browns. They were tougher, harder, and not as vulnerable to the pass.

A driving rain fell before and during the game, turning the field into a sea of mud. That was a reminder of past playoff failures. Then Hayes fumbled a punt and had to retreat into the end zone to fall on the ball, giving the Browns a safety and a 2–0 lead that lasted until halftime. That was another reminder of past failures.

The stage was set for the Browns to ruin the Cowboys' season again, but these Cowboys responded to distress. They made plays. Richmond Flowers blocked a punt to set up a 39-yard field goal by Mike Clark, giving the Cowboys the lead, 3–2. Clark then added a 31-yarder after two passes from Morton to Hayes. The Cowboys had a 6–2 lead early in the fourth quarter.

Bill Nelsen drove the Browns into scoring territory and hit Gary Collins on a slant pattern at the Dallas eight, but Collins fumbled when hit by Waters and Adderley, and Howley recovered. Back came Nelsen one more time late in the game, driving the Browns to a first down at the Dallas 17. An offensive pass interference penalty pushed the Browns back, and Dave Edwards dove into the mud to intercept a pass and seal a huge victory.

"That was probably the biggest game we ever played," Jerry Tubbs said. "That was the game that got us over the hump. To beat them up there in the mud and cold, after the way they had annihilated us, was a watershed moment. We started to believe again."

The Cowboys celebrated in the locker room. "I guess this proves we can't lose 'em all," Clint Murchison said.

The Cardinals lost at home to the Giants the next day. They were 1–2–1 since beating the Cowboys on *Monday Night Football*. The Cowboys were 4–0 and now tied with the Giants for first. "I saw (Cardinal quarterback) Jim Hart at the Super Bowl that year," Lilly said, "and I asked him, 'What happened to you guys? You were as good as any team I ever saw for three or four games.' He told me, 'Attitude. We just couldn't handle success.'"

The Cowboys still were not assured of making the playoffs as they prepared for their last game of the regular season, against the Oilers at the Cotton Bowl. The four-team NFC playoff field would consist of the three division winners and the second-place team with the best record, known as the wild-card team. The Giants held the advantage; they would win the East if they beat the Rams at Yankee Stadium, relegating the Cowboys to the wild-card race. So many teams were competing for the wild card that it might come down to a coin flip.

The situation was resolved without such complications. The Giants fell apart and lost to the Rams, 31–3, opening the door for the Cowboys to win the division. The Cowboys stepped through the door by crushing the Oilers, 52–10. Morton threw five touchdown passes and the defense did not allow a touchdown for the fourth straight game.

Out of the ashes of a 38–0 defeat, the Cowboys had won five games in a row and a fifth straight division title. "It all started with 38–0," Walt Garrison said. "When you lose like that, your teammates are your only friends. Everyone else hates you. The players got together and said, 'Hey, this is just a game, it's supposed to be fun.' That worked for us."

The Cardinals lost again on that final Sunday and failed to make the playoffs. The Giants were out, too. The NFC playoff field consisted of the Vikings, winners of 12 of 14 games and the Central Division title; the 49ers, who had won the West by a game over the Rams; the Lions, winners of the wild card race; and the Cowboys, who would enter the playoffs with a 10–4 record, their poorest regular-season record since '67.

The Vikings, with the best record and a crushing defense, were favored to advance to the Super Bowl. The Cowboys had ceded the role of the glamorous favorite. They would play the Lions in a first-round game at the Cotton Bowl, and oddsmakers favored the Lions, also winners of five games in a row, by three points. The Cowboy defense had not allowed a touchdown in 17 quarters, and Thomas had rushed for 803 yards replacing the oft-injured Hill, but the offense was a car without a driver. Morton's passing had been erratic throughout the season. He had 60 fewer completions, 800 fewer yards, and six fewer touchdowns than the year before.

"Craig played with a bad shoulder in '69 and underwent an operation after the season, but he didn't take time to rehabilitate himself," Roger Staubach wrote in his autobiography *Time Enough to Win*. "That was his problem. I think if he had it to do again he would have come back in better shape for the '70 season. He just wasn't back all the way. He had the whole offseason to get ready and didn't do it. He came to training camp and had some trouble with his arm, which led to bone chips in his elbow."

Yet Morton had completed 60 percent of his passes in the Cowboys' five-game winning streak. He was a capable veteran. A greater threat to the Cowboys' chances was their own fragile confidence; the first round of the playoffs, their downfall in the past two seasons, was a huge psychological barrier. Losing again in the first round would be ruinous. "If we had lost that [Detroit] game, we may never have come back," Renfro said. "I don't think we ever played a bigger game."

The Cotton Bowl was sold out when the Cowboys and Lions kicked off on a sunny Saturday afternoon, but the air was thick with tension. It was as if the city could not bear to watch. The Lions were dangerous, ranked second in the NFC in scoring. They had come together after coach Joe Schmidt benched veteran quarterback Bill Munson in favor of Greg Landry. Their offense included playmakers such as backs Mel Farr and Altie Taylor, receivers Earl McCullough and Larry Walton, and a Pro Bowl tight end, Charlie Sanders.

The crowd shivered when one of Morton's first passes was tipped and intercepted, giving the Lions the early break that the Browns had always forced, but then Pugh belted Greg Landry on a scramble, the ball popped free, and Charlie Waters recovered. A pass to Garrison and two runs by Thomas set up a 26-yard field goal by Mike Clark.

The Lions threatened in the second quarter, but Altie Taylor fumbled at the Dallas 29. The Cowboys' 3–0 lead held up through halftime and the third quarter. The Cowboys' offense was stymied, more by Morton's poor passing than the Detroit defense—Morton would complete only four of 18 attempts in the game—but the defense was strong.

Early in the fourth quarter, the Cowboys began a series at their 23. Landry gave up on the passing game. Thomas carried for five, six, and 13 yards, Garrison for six and three, Thomas for 16 around right end, Garrison inside for seven. With the backs charging through holes and the crowd cheering as the sun dropped behind the upper deck, the Cowboys drove to a first-and-goal at the Detroit five. Thomas carried twice to the one. Garrison moved the ball to within a foot of the goal line on third down. Landry elected to go for the touchdown. He called his 14th straight rushing play, but Thomas tripped on Garrison's foot and lost two yards. The Cowboys had driven 77 yards and failed to score.

The Lions took over. Greg Landry faded to pass on third down and was trapped in the end zone by Pugh and Andrie for a safety worth two big points. The Lions now had to score a touchdown. There were five minutes left in the game. The Cowboys could not make a first down and punted the ball back to the Lions, who took over on their 20 with 2:18 left. In a dramatic move, Schmidt pulled his young quarterback, Landry, in favor of Bill Munson, the veteran whom Landry had supplanted earlier in the season. It was a desperate move, and it almost worked. Munson completed a pass for a first down at the 32, and then, after three incompletions, hit Mc-

Cullough on a 39-yarder down the left sideline to give the Lions a first down at the Dallas 29 with 47 seconds left.

The crowd fell silent, anticipating the worst, then raised a roar in support of the defense. Were the players worried? "Hell, no, we had it going," Andrie said later. They did. Munson found no open receivers on first down and sailed a pass out of bounds, then threw so hard on second down that the ball went through Farr's hands. On third down, Munson aimed a pass over the middle at Charlie Sanders, but the ball was deflected by Renfro and popped into the air. Renfro leapt and came down with the biggest interception in Cowboy history.

"Munson laid the ball high and I went for it," Renfro said after the game. "I juggled it for awhile. I didn't realize what had happened until I heard the crowd."

The Cotton Bowl vibrated with noise as it rarely had before. The Cowboy offense trotted onto the field, Morton fell on the ball, and the clock ran out on a 5–0 victory. The Cowboys had beaten two opponents—their past and the Lions. The defense had carried them. After averaging 25 points a game during the season, the Lions had failed to score.

"That stretch of games was the best our defense ever played," Lee Roy Jordan said. "We weren't covering up for anyone in the secondary anymore. We had the mentality that no one was going to score. All we needed was a field goal to win. We told the offense, 'Just get us three.'"

The Cowboys were back in the championship game, one step from the Super Bowl for the first time since '67. They had expected to play the Vikings, but the 49ers upset the Vikings, 17–14, in the other first-round playoff game. The NFC championship game would be played at Kezar Stadium in San Francisco, against a 49ers team coached by Dick Nolan, an assistant to Landry from 1962 to 1967. Nolan had turned around the 49ers in three years. They had 35-year-old quarterback John Brodie, All-Pro receiver Gene Washington, an offensive line that had allowed only eight sacks all season, and a defense that was the mirror image of the Cowboys' 4-3 Flex.

Kezar Stadium was packed on a sunny afternoon; Jimmy "The Greek" Snyder had favored the 49ers by four points ("two for the quarterback and two for the home field") and Bay Area fans could almost smell a trip to the Super Bowl. The first half was tentative. The 49ers relied on Brodie's passes and the Cowboys relied on their running game, with Morton's elbow still sore. The 49ers took a 3–0 lead in the first quarter. Mike Clark kicked a 21-yarder in the second quarter. The score was tied at halftime, 3–3.

The game turned on the 49ers' second possession of the third quarter. On first down at his 21, Brodie was sacked by Dave Edwards on a blitz. Attempting to make up the lost yardage, Brodie faded to pass, found no open receivers, and, under pressure from Cowboy defensive end Larry Cole, dumped the ball off to his fullback, Ken Willard. Jordan sniffed out the play, dove for the pass, and intercepted it at the San Francisco 13.

"I was just trying to dump the ball," Brodie said after the game. "I threw it at the ground and Jordan made a hell of a play."

Landry called a "45 slant" on first down: Thomas carrying off right guard. The rookie took the handoff, saw no daylight, veered back across the field, broke two tackles, and headed for the end zone. He bowled over a safety and crossed the goal line. The Cowboys had the lead for the first time.

Brodie threw another interception on the next series; Renfro caught a long pass intended for Washington and returned it to the Dallas 38. A holding penalty moved the offense back, but Garrison caught a screen pass and ran for 23 yards and a first down. A pass interference penalty was worth another 24 yards and a first down at the San Francisco five. Morton, who would complete only seven of 22 passes, then beat a blitz and found Garrison open for a short touchdown pass and a 17–3 lead midway through the third quarter.

The 49ers came right back against the Cowboy defense, which eased up momentarily. Brodie moved the offense 73 yards to a touchdown in eight plays, with the touchdown coming on a 26-yard pass to Dick Witcher, who beat Adderley with an inside fake. The touchdown was the first the Cowboy defense had allowed in 24 quarters.

The 49ers forced a third-and-long on the next series, but Morton completed a 21-yard pass to Reggie Rucker to maintain possession and blunt the 49ers' momentum. "That was a huge play," Landry said. The Cowboys controlled the ball with their running game in the fourth quarter; Brodie never had a chance to complete his comeback. The 49ers ran out of chances on a fourth-and-six at their 39 late in the game, when Willard dropped a pass. When the final gun sounded, the Cowboys were champions of the National Football Conference. They were going to the Super Bowl.

"The San Francisco game was the greatest I ever played in," Walt Garrison said. "After we got our momentum going after the 38–0 game, we started saying, 'We got to get to the Super Bowl, we got to get to the Super Bowl.' And we did. The Super Bowl itself was kind of anticlimactic, even though it was the Super Bowl, because at last we had proven we could get there. That was the goal we had been setting. That was the mountain we had been climbing. And we had climbed it."

After two straight wins by AFL teams in the Super Bowl, the Baltimore Colts struck a blow for the old-guard NFL in the first year of the merger by beating the Oakland Raiders in the inaugural AFC championship game. The Colts were not as menacing as the Colt team that took a 15–1 record into Super Bowl III and lost to the Jets, but it was a veteran team with a strong defense led by Bubba Smith, Mike Curtis, and Ted Hendricks, and a capable offense built around golden-oldie quarterbacks Johnny Unitas and Earl Morrall. Don McCafferty was the head coach now instead of Don Shula, and the team reflected McCafferty's unassuming personality.

The Colts had won 13 of 16 regular season and playoff games, but the Cowboys had more speed, a better offense, and superior personnel. "The Cowboys were the better team, without question," said Bob Ryan of NFL Films. After a week of practice in Dallas, the Cowboys flew to Florida and checked into the Galt Ocean Mile Inn in Fort Lauderdale. A long week of media hype began on Monday with interviews at the New York Yankees' spring training stadium. The players were surrounded by reporters from newspapers around the country.

"In the first part of the season I couldn't feel the togetherness we had in Green Bay, nor could I see the togetherness even among the older guys," said Adderley, playing in his third Super Bowl. "To win you have to have that kind of togetherness. I felt it after the loss to St. Louis. Guys weren't saying 'me' anymore, they were saying 'we.'"

Duane Thomas' session was the highlight of the day. Thomas came off as a mystic in cleats.

"Does the Super Bowl represent the ultimate in big-game experience?" he was asked.

"If the Super Bowl was the ultimate, they wouldn't have it again next year," Thomas said.

The game was played in sunny, warm weather, classic South Florida conditions. Both teams wore their road uniforms; the Cowboys had on blue tops and silver pants, the Colts all white. The Cowboys were never comfortable wearing blue—some fans considered it bad luck—but the players were confident as the opening kickoff neared and the Orange Bowl filled with 80,055 fans. "There was no doubt in our minds," Jordan said, "that we were the better team."

They began to exert their perceived superiority as soon as the game began. A fumbled punt set up a short field goal by Mike Clark, and then Morton drove the offense deep into Colt territory with a 41-yard pass to Hayes in between two defenders. The Colts were stacking their linebackers against the run and daring Morton to beat them with passes, a predictable tactic considering Morton's sore-armed ineffectiveness (11 completions in 40 attempts) against the Lions and 49ers, but Landry had anticipated such a defense and weighted his game plan with passes to the running backs. The plan was working.

A stand by the Colt defense forced a second field goal by Clark, giving the Cowboys a 6–0 lead. Unitas was struggling to make any gains against the powerful Cowboy defense. On the next series, Unitas was pressured on a play at the Baltimore 24 and sailed a high ball over the middle toward his split end, Eddie Hinton. The ball bounced off Hinton's hands and flew high into the air, not unlike a long rebound coming off the backboard in basketball. Renfro just missed a leaping interception, and the ball flew on to Colt tight end John Mackey, who caught it near midfield, turned, and raced to the end zone for a stunning 75-yard touchdown.

The Cowboys argued that the score should be disallowed because two offensive players had touched the ball consecutively, which was against the rules, but the back judge, Hugh Gamber, ruled that a Cowboy defender had touched the ball in between Hinton and Mackey. Which defender?

"Not me," Charlie Waters said after the game.

"I was 10 yards away," Cornell Green said.

"I never felt it," Renfro said. "It went over my head. If I got a fingernail on it, then it was a great call."

The league's supervisor of officials, Mark Duncan, watched a televised replay in the press box and suggested to the *Times Herald*'s Steve Perkins that Green had touched the ball.

"I will bet Mr. Duncan $5,000 that I didn't touch the ball," Green said after the game.

The Cowboys would feel cheated by the call until they saw films of the play taken from different angles by NFL Films cameramen. The ball's spiral did subtly change between Hinton and Mackey, indicating a touch. Green clearly was not the culprit; Mark Duncan was wise not to have accepted Green's wager. If there was a defender who touched the ball, it was Renfro.

"I don't know if people will ever get it straight," Renfro said years later. "I told everyone I had no sensation of touching the ball. I never denied touching it. I said I had no sensation, that's all, and that's where I left it. People still ask me if I touched it. What did I say from day one? The final result was inconclusive. It happened, it's over. The play had no bearing in the end. We threw two interceptions in the fourth quarter. That had a bearing."

In any case, the call stood and the score was tied, 6–6, after Cowboy rookie Mark Washington blocked the extra point. The Colts then committed another turnover on their next series when Andrie crunched Unitas and forced a fumble that the Cowboys recovered at the Baltimore 29. The play was the last of the day for Unitas, who left with bruised ribs after completing just three of nine passes. The Cowboy offense turned the fumble into points on a seven-yard touchdown pass from Morton to Thomas. The 13–6 score stood at halftime.

Another Colt fumble on the second half kickoff threatened to turn the game into a rout. Richmond Flowers recovered the fumble at the Baltimore 31, and the Cowboy offense moved to a first-and-goal at the two. On first down, Thomas took a handoff and slanted toward the end zone, but the Colts' Mike Curtis hooked the ball loose as Thomas stretched it toward the goal line.

"The ball was free, it came right to me, and I grabbed it," Dave Manders said years later. "There wasn't even another hand on it. No question whatsoever. As plain as it could be. Loose ball, I have it. But I get up and hand the ball to the referee and he's signaling Baltimore ball. Incredible. I started complaining and the referee said, 'One more word and you're outta here.'"

The referee, Jack Fette, was pointing in the Colts' direction when Manders handed him the ball. After the game, two Colts, Jim Duncan and Billy Ray Smith, would claim they had recovered the fumble. The truth was that neither had recovered it. "Manders was on the ball, but Billy Ray was screaming, 'Our ball! Our ball!' and it worked," the Colts' Bubba Smith told reporter Bob West of the *Beaumont (Tex.) Journal* several weeks later. "I couldn't believe it when the official started pointing toward our goal."

Said Ralph Neely, "What happened there was that Billy Ray was a better salesman than Dave Manders."

A touchdown would have given the Cowboys a 20–6 lead early in the third quarter—enough cushion for a Cowboy defense that had allowed just one touchdown in 27 quarters. "If they had scored there, I don't believe we could have come back," Bubba Smith told Bob West.

Manders agreed. "We get that call, we win the game, it's simple," he said. "The Colts didn't have any offense."

But the Cowboys did not get the call. They still had a seven-point lead, the game was still in doubt, and Jack Fette would join Jim Boeke and Chuck Mercein as a lasting symbol of Cowboy frustration.

The defenses dominated after that; neither offense could sustain a drive in the next 20 minutes. The Colts would commit seven turnovers during the game, but the Cowboys were unable to convert any into points in the second half. The Colts' run-oriented defense limited the Cowboys' rushing game—Thomas would average just two yards a carry—and Morton's passing was ineffectual. The Cowboy offense would produce just one touchdown in the game even though the defense gave it the ball five times in Colt territory.

"If Morton was a pitcher in baseball he would have been knocked out in the first inning," Adderley said. "He overthrew Duane on one wide-open touchdown and missed a lot of passes. Landry wouldn't put Staubach in. Morton played worse that day than any quarterback I'd ever seen in a big game, but Landry was set in his ways and stubborn enough not to make a change."

Midway through the fourth quarter, the Colts, growing desperate, attempted a flea-flicker. Reserve halfback Sam Havrilak took a handoff, swept wide, stopped, and looked back across the field for Earl Morrall, who had come into the game after Unitas was shaken up in the second quarter. Pugh was in the way, so Havrilak looked downfield and completed a pass to Hinton, who raced for the end zone but fumbled when hit by Renfro and Green. The ball bounced crazily into the end zone, skipping and twisting away from a half-dozen players. The ball finally rolled out of the end zone, and the Cowboys were awarded possession on a touchback.

The Cowboys had the ball and the lead with eight minutes to play, but they gave the Colts life. Morton aimed a pass at Garrison, but the ball bounced off Garrison's fingers and the Colts' Rick Volk intercepted and returned the ball 31 yards to the Dallas three. Tom Nowatzke bulled over the goal line for a touchdown with 7:35 to play. Jim O'Brien, the Colts' rookie kicker, converted the extra point to tie the score at 13–13.

The Cowboys drove the ball to midfield on the next series before punting. Cliff Harris, a rookie who had played for the team on weekends during an Army stint, sprinted downfield and batted the ball down just before it bounced into the end zone. Operating deep in their own territory, the Colts took no chances and punted after three plays. The Cowboys took over at the Baltimore 48 with two minutes to play. It appeared the Cowboys would have the last chance to win the game.

Once again, they gave the Colts life. Duane Thomas lost a yard on a running play and Neely was called for holding behind the line, resulting in a 24-yard loss. The Cowboys were moved back to their 27 and wound up facing third-and-34. Landry had called almost all of the plays in the game, as he had throughout the seven-game winning streak, but Morton called the third-down play because the clock was running and there was no time to run messengers in and out of the game. Morton called "13 takeoff," a pass to Dan Reeves, who would either run a post or go into a hole in the Colts' zone. A handoff would have been more prudent considering how much yardage was needed for a first down; the Cowboys would have been wise to run the clock out and try to win in overtime. Yet Landry would not second-guess Morton's call after the game. "We were not thinking about running out the clock," Landry said. "We were going for the win."

Scrambling to avoid a rush, Morton threw a high, wobbly pass that went off Reeves' hands and flew right to the Colts' Mike Curtis. The pass was high, but Reeves took the blame for the interception. "There is no way I should have missed that ball," Reeves said after the game. "You just don't miss them like that when you get your hands on them."

Curtis returned the ball to the Dallas 27. There were 69 seconds left on the clock. The Colts ran two running plays, called a time-out with five seconds left, and brought on O'Brien, their long-haired rookie kicker from the

University of Cincinnati. He had missed an extra point and a field goal attempt earlier in the game, but he was perfect on the kick of his lifetime. It split the uprights as the final gun sounded in the late-afternoon shadows.

Colts 16, Cowboys 13.

The Cowboys had forced seven turnovers, come within one missed call of blowing the game open in the third quarter, never trailed for 59 minutes and 55 seconds—and lost. They were still "Next Year's Champions" after all.

It was too much for Lilly to bear. He had been a Cowboy for 10 seasons, experienced the lows of the early '60s, the rise to prominence, the frustration of the Cleveland games. "We had finally put it all together and put ourselves in position to win," Lilly said. As O'Brien's kick sailed through the uprights, Lilly ripped off his helmet and flung it downfield. It bounced on the artificial turf, rolled toward the Cowboy end zone, and stopped 50 yards downfield. Lilly stood among the jubilant Colts, his hands on his hips, his head bared, abject despair lining his face. It was the face of the Cowboys.

"To lose that game like we did, that was the lowest point of my career," Lilly said. "The Ice Bowl, the Cleveland games, they were bad. But the Baltimore game was the worst I ever felt. Baltimore still doesn't impress me that much. I still feel like we had a better team. I think we kind of got screwed. I don't take anything away from the Colts. But we should have won. When we didn't, after we had blown so many chances, we just didn't know if we would ever get another chance."

A year later, Dave Manders found himself in Billy Ray Smith's living room. Smith was a native Texan who lived in Plano, a Dallas suburb, in the offseason. Manders was looking at real estate in a development where Smith lived. Smith showed him around and invited him in for a visit.

"He had that big ol' Super Bowl ring on," Manders said. "I told him, 'I recovered that fumble, you know.' He smiled real big, and he said, 'Well, you must not have recovered that fumble because I got this on,' and he held up that ring. Man, did it hurt for him to hold up that ring. It hurt bad."

Chapter Twelve

The clutter and commotion of the city gave way to the sparse ease of the country as I drove west from Fort Worth on a sunny morning in January of 1996. The traffic thinned and I turned off the interstate at Weatherford. Billboards advertising chain restaurants and expensive condominiums gave way to signs for auto parts stores and home-cooking joints. The flattened landscape seemed a pale yellow, almost white, the color of Texas in winter, and the road curved between sharp hills after I passed through Mineral Wells and turned onto a two-lane road pointing north toward Wichita Falls. The plains of West Texas were colliding with the northern brink of the hill country. Pretty soon it was just me and the highway and the big, blue sky.

I was on my way to visit Bob Lilly, the greatest Cowboy of all. He lived now in Graham, a small town west of Fort Worth. The radio was full of talk of the Cowboys' Super Bowl chances, but my mind was drifting back, not ahead. The country drive summoned memories of my first years in the newspaper business, when, fresh from the University of Pennsylvania, I covered high-school football for the *Times Herald.*

It was a splendid job, maybe the best beat I ever had; I drove back and forth across the state dipping from a well of small-town glories. I went to Pilot Point, north of Denton, where the fan club met at 5 A.M. I went to

Archer City, where *The Last Picture Show* was filmed and life was imitating art in the form of a miserable football team. I went to Temple, where the coach had lacquered fingernails, a plush office, and a mob boss's carriage. I met the women who planted a Victory Turnip Patch, and I covered a game between teams coached by identical twins named Donnie and Ronnie. (Ronnie won.) I had a white coach tell me he needed more black players, and a black coach tell me he needed more white players. I covered a playoff game that drew 50,000 fans to Texas Stadium, and I sat in a living room and listened to a college recruiter offer illegal enticements. I interviewed a quarterback who admitted he was having sex with a cheerleader, and I sat at the knee of a coach from Odessa Permian, who, upon upsetting Highland Park in the playoffs, winked and told me, "We didn't come in to the big city on a load of matchsticks."

The high school beat was more than just a job for me; it was an education, a lesson in what it meant to come from Texas. I was a third-generation Texan, but my North Dallas upbringing had screened me from the Texas that I saw on the job for the *Times Herald*. My lack of a twang and my expensive education had always left me feeling inadequate as a Texan, somehow less than authentic, but three years under the Friday night lights changed that. I grew comfortable on the farm-to-market roads and learned the secrets and traditions lurking in the tall grass behind the Dairy Queens. Only later did I understand that the experience had made me whole.

It all came back to me as I sped along an empty two-lane road toward Graham. The high-school beat had pulled me in this direction a couple of times, into the fringes of the spare, windy flatlands that began here and stretched all the way to California. Lilly had grown up out here, in Throckmorton, a small farming community 30 miles west of Graham. Now, after living for years in Fort Worth, Dallas, Waco, and New Mexico, he had come home with his wife and youngest son to complete the circle of his life. He was 56 years old and 25 pounds under his playing weight, a living legend with five grandchildren and a natural humility that came charging through the long-distance telephone line as we were arranging to meet.

"When you get to town, pull into the McDonald's and give me a call," he told me. "I'll give you directions from there."

After I stopped at the McDonald's and spoke to him, I got back in the car, drove up a hill, and eased onto a street lined with unpretentious ranch-style homes, a street plucked straight out of the Dallas suburbs. Lilly was standing at the end of his driveway, smiling and motioning. His hair was graying and his face was thinner than in his playing days, but his high hips, broad torso, and thin, pointed nose were the same. His voice was gentle, almost soothing.

"Good to see you," he said as I climbed out of the car, as if we were old friends. "Let's talk inside."

As we settled on the couch, I told him of the memories that the drive from Dallas had brought back, of my time on the high-school beat, navigating a world of small towns, farming, and football. Lilly nodded. It was the world from which he had come, and the world he had sought when he returned to Texas in '89 after spending nine years in Las Cruces, New Mexico, where he owned a photography studio and gallery.

"We came back for a couple of reasons, but a big one was that I wanted my son, Mark, to have the opportunity to live the small-town life where you could participate in sports," Lilly said. "He really enjoyed his time here. Plus, my mother was getting up in years, and I wanted to be close enough to her to where she would have some peace of mind. And my daughters were starting to have kids. We were just starting to feel kind of remote in New Mexico."

Lilly's mother, now 88 years old, still lived in Throckmorton; she had worked as the county treasurer in her last job before retiring. Her brother also still lived in Throckmorton, where he had run a jewelry store for years. Lilly's daughters and grandchildren lived in Sherman and Waco. I asked him if his grandchildren knew that their grandfather was famous. He smiled. "They love me because I take 'em to Wal-mart," he said. "Actually, the oldest boy is eight years old and just starting to play football and realizing that everyone knows his granddad."

Lilly started playing football at a similar point in his life, as a six-year-old in Throckmorton. His father encouraged him. "My father loved football," Lilly said. "He never played himself because he was a cripple in one leg. A drunk driver hit him when he was 17 and riding on a motorcycle. Crushed his leg. But he was a great fan. He went to all the SMU and TCU games in the '30s. He drove out to the Rose Bowl to see SMU, and he drove to New Orleans to see TCU in the Sugar Bowl. He started taking me along to the games when I was a kid. There was a fullback (from Throckmorton) who played for TCU, which was why I decided to go to TCU. That was the only place I knew. I was from a small town."

Lilly's family lived in Throckmorton before the Civil War. When Lilly was a boy, his father worked first as a mechanic and then operated a bulldozer and other heavy machinery. Farmers paid him to clear land and bale hay.

"I worked right alongside my father, uncles, and kinfolks," Lilly said. "That's the way it was in rural Texas. We worked together 12 hours a day sometimes, hauling hay, plowing, working cattle, whatever. Nobody had much money, but people were honest and weren't interested in having the biggest house in town. I lived on a rent farm part of the time growing up. We finally built a home when I was in eighth grade. It was 800 square feet, maybe a thousand. I thought it was wonderful."

I told Lilly that my grandfather, like his father, had been a native Texan and a great football fan who supported SMU and TCU.

"What business was your granddad in?" Lilly asked.

"Cotton," I said. "He worked at the Cotton Exchange in Dallas for 50 years."

We were both of Texas stock, from football-crazed families.

"I went to the games when I was little, just like your dad and you," I said. "I wanted to play, too. You grew a little more than I did."

Lilly's father had admired Sammy Baugh and attempted to groom Bob as a quarterback, but he grew too tall to take snaps and became an end. He started slowly in organized play, he claimed: "I was underweight and uncoordinated, and I got beat up pretty good," but soon developed into a standout.

"I always had a tremendous desire to play," he said. "I just enjoyed it. You were in high school and you got a letter jacket and that meant you would have a girlfriend. And then you found out you got silver football patches for making all-district and you could put them on your jacket and they looked good. The town would throw a banquet if you won district. There weren't a lot of people in town but they were all involved with the team. I loved it."

The family abruptly moved to Oregon when Lilly was a senior in high school. "There was a drought in the early '50s that lasted seven years and wiped everyone out, including my dad," Lilly said. "I have very fond memories of growing up out here, but it was very different the last two or three years because of the drought. We were barely eating. Finally we just sold everything and moved up to Oregon. We had family there. Things were better. We lived in Pendleton, in the foothills. The wheat was waist deep. I had never seen wheat like that. We went trout fishing. I went elk hunting for the first time, pheasant hunting. We sledded in the snow. People were great. They had that small-town hospitality. But I never really wanted to stay. My roots were here."

He was recruited by many colleges coming out of Pendleton High School, where he was all-state in football and basketball and won the state javelin championship. Oregon and Oregon State pursued him, as did Washington and Washington State. Southern Cal and UCLA wanted him to visit. Texas and Texas A&M sent letters. Bear Bryant called.

TCU's recruitment consisted of a one-cent postcard sent by an assistant coach who had seen Lilly play as a sophomore in Throckmorton. That was all it took. "They asked me if I was interested and I sent 'em back a ten-cent postcard saying I was," he said. "They told me they'd pay my way down for a visit."

Lilly and a friend hopped into a '47 Studebaker with a sack full of sandwiches and drove straight from Oregon to Throckmorton. "One slept, one drove," Lilly said. "We spent the night at my grandmother's and went on into Fort Worth. They showed me around, fed us real good, paid me a couple hundred dollars for expenses. I signed and went back and told my mom and dad."

Lilly's father had a mild heart attack that August, just before Lilly enrolled at TCU, and his parents returned to Throckmorton. His father recovered and got a job hauling mail from Fort Worth to Throckmorton. "That was what he did the last few years of his life," Lilly said.

As a freshman at TCU, Lilly was involved in a celebrated incident. Finding a Volkswagen parked in his spot one day, he supposedly picked up the small, foreign car and deposited it on the sidewalk. He obviously was not lacking for strength. His muscles were the dividend from years of hauling hay. A TCU teammate named Harry Moreland watched him wreaking havoc on the practice field one day and said, "Man, if I was as big and strong as Lilly, I would charge folks just to live."

He was powerful, but also quick for a player so large. As a sophomore he started at defensive tackle on a TCU team that won the Southwest Conference title and played a scoreless tie with Air Force in the '57 Cotton Bowl Classic. He made the all-SWC team as a junior averaging eight tackles a game, and was named to every major All-America team as a six-foot-five, 250-pound senior, even though he asked the sports information office not to promote him for national honors. His nickname, which he hated, was "The Purple Cloud." TCU coach Abe Martin claimed never to have coached a better defensive lineman.

The Dallas Texans selected him in the first round of the AFL draft, and Lilly used that as leverage to chart his course in the NFL. The Cleveland Browns were going to draft him, but he told them he wanted to live in Texas and would sign with the AFL's Texans if the Browns chose him. "I was just a naive country boy and I was going to stay home and play in Dallas one way or another," he said. The Browns traded the pick to the Cowboys for an offensive tackle named Paul Dickson and a first-round pick the following year.

The Cowboys signed Lilly to a contract before the draft, at the East-West Shrine Game in California, then made him the first draft choice in Cowboy history. "It was pretty close between the Cowboys and Texans as far as money," Lilly said. "I think I got a $5,000 bonus and my salary was maybe $11,500."

That summer, Cowboy personnel director Gil Brandt put Lilly on a plane to the college All-Star Game in Chicago. "As he was waving goodbye I looked down and noticed that he didn't have any socks on," Brandt said years later. "He was just a big ol' country boy."

His quickness convinced Landry to try him at defensive end, a position he had never played. He was an end for his first two-and-a-half seasons with the Cowboys, a time he does not remember fondly. Even though he made the Pro Bowl in '62, his play was not exceptional and he was not happy.

"He matured in his later years, but (in his early days) he would say some things," Tubbs said. "We would be having a rough day on the practice field and he'd just say, 'I hate it, I hate it, the only reason I ever played football was my daddy made me.' His wife at the time was kind of goofy and he was having trouble at home and he was a little frustrated. Later on he became a solid guy, and he was always a good, good guy. But he was something else in those early years."

Lilly said, "I bitched a lot, like a lot of people do, but I loved football. I just got frustrated because I hated to lose and we were losing. I hated the position, too. I liked to make things happen, but you could only do that rushing the passer as an end. Otherwise you were just out there. Half the time you never even got blocked. It was just too slow for me. I thought a lot faster than that and played a lot faster than that. People would run screens and stuff at me and they'd be going around me. I almost got (linebacker) Jerry Tubbs killed. Every time I see him I still apologize to him. It was tough. I was at a position I hated, and I was frustrated."

He was moved to tackle halfway through the '63 season and immediately became a force. His combination of quickness and strength was better utilized in the middle of the line. "He was quick and well-coordinated, like a 150-pounder as far as body control," Tubbs said. "He could escape just about any block. You just don't see 265-pound guys that agile. He wasn't fast like Randy White, but he was quicker and he had good strength. It was just hard to block him. It was hard for two people to block him."

Lilly made All-Pro in his first season at tackle in '64, as Landry installed the 4-3 Flex, the schematic defense that asked players to read keys instead of chase the ball. Lilly excelled in the Flex, but it confined him.

"The one bad thing about the Flex," Lilly said, "was when you think a lot you're not as physical because you can't just go in there and knock your man around. You had responsibilities. You couldn't just take off. You had to stay where you were and hold your block and cover your lane. Landry gave me a little more freedom because I had the ability to get back into the play (if he made a mistake), but I always enjoyed going to the Pro Bowl where we didn't have the Flex and you could just tee off. That was my kind of football."

Tubbs said, "In the early years Lilly would get frustrated because he knew what he could do and he'd take a chance and Tom would call him on it. He would get so frustrated because he had to stay in there and do a certain thing, and if he tried a loop or something Tom would say, 'You just can't do that,' and gosh, Lilly would get so mad. The system in some ways helped him, but in some ways it held him back. In some places they just let people go, but Lilly couldn't go all the time and he was the best defensive lineman I ever saw."

As frustrated as he got, he never rebelled. He came to believe in the

Flex. "Our goal was to stop the run and force teams into passing situations," he said. "It worked pretty well. Someone would run on us maybe one game in a season. We held a lot of teams under 100 yards [rushing in a game] and we won a lot. And I would rather win than play like I wanted. Guys like Merlin [Olson] and Deacon [Jones] were great players who got to play with more abandon, but they never did get to a Super Bowl."

He was slowed in '65 by an injury, then became a perennial All-Pro beginning in '66. He played in between George Andrie at end and Jethro Pugh at the other tackle. His job was to stop the run and pressure the passer. He was so strong that opponents rarely directed plays at him, yet he was so quick that he often made tackles on plays directed elsewhere.

"A guy like Lilly comes along once in a generation," Landry said. "You just don't find people that big and strong with such quickness. He really had the knack of escape in the middle of our 4-3. He was always in the middle of everything the offense was trying to do."

The era's most famous defenders were Dick Butkus and Sam Huff, linebackers renowned for their fury. After NFL Films put microphones on them during a game and gave us a glimpse of their violent world, fans assumed that all defensive players were the same. Lilly was naturally suited to such a stereotype as a big-armed Texan who steamrolled linemen and crushed quarterbacks, but he was not that way. "He was a hustler and a competitor, but he wasn't one of those crazy types," Tubbs said. "Butkus would stand there and growl at you. Lilly wasn't a growler."

As Cowboy assistant coach Ernie Stautner told the *Fort Worth Star-Telegram* when Lilly was inducted into the Pro Football Hall of Fame in 1980, "Being mean wasn't Bob's style. He tried it, but being roughhouse didn't work for him. He just couldn't do it."

He did not play to intimidate or dominate, and seldom took the game personally. He played for one reason only: to win. "I never played to kill anybody or anything like that," he said. "Personalities never played into it. The competition was what I loved. That was what made me intense."

Off the field, he also had little in common with the Butkus/Huff stereotype. He had a droll sense of humor and a natural aversion to the spotlight. He was the classic old-school pro, unconcerned with self-promotion. "I preferred to be anonymous," he said. "I never tried to win honors and they never made any difference to me one way or another. You knew when you were playing well, and that was what mattered."

The only time he was not his customary, unassuming self was in the wake of Jim O'Brien's game-winning field goal in Super Bowl V, when he threw his helmet halfway down the field. He was in such a state that he did not even know he had thrown his helmet until one of the Colts brought it back to him on the field. "I was standing there and this young guy came up to me and said, 'Here's your helmet, Mr. Lilly.' He called me Mr. Lilly. I didn't know who he was. I was totally embarrassed. I said, 'Oh, no, I'm so sorry. I hope it didn't hit you or anything.'"

Lilly erased that despair with joy when the Cowboys made it back to the Super Bowl the next year. He made the most famous play of his career, a 29-yard sack of Dolphins quarterback Bob Griese that set the tone for the Cowboys' lopsided victory. Lilly slipped away from his blocker and chased down a scrambling Griese with help from Larry Cole.

"I ran into Griese on an airplane three years ago," Lilly said, "and he said, 'Oh, no, not you. We went 17–0 the next year and the only thing people ever asked me is, "Why did you let Lilly catch you?"'" I told him, 'Don't worry, I won the Super Bowl but all anyone ever asks me is, 'How far'd you throw your helmet?'"

The 29-yard sack was a symbolic play, a defiant gesture that stated that the Cowboys finally had overcome their postseason demons and were headed for the pinnacle of pro football. It was only fitting that Lilly make the statement; he was the franchise's first draft pick and greatest player, the ultimate Dallas Cowboy.

"I savored the feeling of being in that (winning Super Bowl) locker room for a year," Lilly said. "All that frustration of being runner-up finally was lifted off our backs. It was one of the highlights of my life, that game and that feeling."

He made All-Pro for the seventh and last time in '71. That year he made 12 tackles in a game against the Bears, a performance close to perfection. He made the Pro Bowl the next year, but then his health and performance declined. He tore a hamstring in '73, played with a sore neck, and retired after the '74 season.

"I quit just right," he said. "I played hurt for a year and a half. My last year they had to inject my spine at every practice and game. I knew it was

time to get out. They wanted me to play another year. They didn't understand. I never slept that last year. In fact, I have missed many a night's
sleep since. It's my neck. It's not as bad as it was. The more the muscle de-
teriorates, the better it gets. Isn't that something?"

Ralph Neely's salary was $20,000 when he joined the Cowboys in '65 as
a bonus-baby rookie. Lilly, who had played four years with the Cowboys
and made two trips to the Pro Bowl, earned $16,000 that year. His salary
rose with his stature, but he never made the big money that saturated the
game shortly after his retirement. He earned $45,000 in 1970 and $75,000
in his last season. "I was probably four years too early to get in on the big
money," he said. "Not that I was ashamed of what I made. But I never
made a whole lot off the Cowboys."

He began preparing for life after football in the early '70s when he took
on a partner and began investing his money. He turned a profit on motels,
computers, and real estate, and lost on restaurants and perfume, but he
came out ahead and sank his earnings into a beer distributorship covering
four counties around Waco. Lilly moved his family to Waco after he retired
and managed the distributorship for six years. He also did commercials for
Black and Decker tools and several other companies, raising his national
profile. He was on an economic roll.

"I knew just a little bit about business after I got out of football," he
said. "I was 14 years behind and I basically started at the bottom. But I had
two partners and they treated me very well and we made some money."

His life changed after he witnessed a devastating car crash involving a
driver drunk on the brand of beer sold at his distributorship. He sold the
business and became a born-again Christian, following his wife's example.
"I thought it was money that made everyone happy and I was making more
than I ever made playing pro football, but . . . I wasn't fulfilled," he told a
Fellowship of Christian Athletes newsletter in 1988. "I'd noticed changes
in [his wife] Ann and I told her, 'I don't know what it is you've got, but I
want it.' I started going with her to Christian events, reading the Bible and
watching the 700 Club. I began to have tremendous peace and joy."

In '84 he moved with Ann and Mark to Las Cruces, where he had
owned land and businesses for more than a decade. He bought a rundown

building, fixed it up, and opened a photography studio and gallery in Old Mesilla, an adobe-style historic district. He had an artistic side that few fans knew existed. Given a camera and 200 rolls of film for making the Kodak All-America team as a college senior, he became interested in photography, bought more expensive equipment, and took hundreds of pictures of teammates, friends, and family over the years. "I always had a camera around my neck," he said.

In 1983 he published a book of his favorite Cowboy-related photographs, titled *Bob Lilly: Reflections.* In New Mexico he fell in love with the spare, dramatic countryside and became a landscape photographer. Even after he moved back to Graham in '89 he still scheduled trips to the Southwest to take pictures of the dramatic vistas. The joy that these trips gave him was obvious as he sat in his living room telling me about them.

"I plan everything," he said. "I have a few friends I do this with. We'll meet, get on Southwest Airlines, go somewhere, rent a car, and stay in a $30 hotel. We know exactly where we want to be, and when we want to be there. We make an outing of it. We get there before daylight. It's great. We have done it all sorts of ways, but we have the most fun at the cheap hotels."

He had a fine reputation as a photographer; his large, colorful, signed works now sold at a gallery in Weatherford. There were two prints hanging in his living room, the most striking a cross-lit view from the top of a steep canyon, looking down into the shadows and a group of wild horses. "The horses weren't planned," Lilly said as we stared at the photograph. "I was set to take the picture and the horses came running through. It was breathtaking."

There also was a landscape of sorts hung over the fireplace in his den, but it was a football landscape: a black-and-white shot of Lilly and the Cowboy defense waiting for the Cleveland Browns' offense to reach the line of scrimmage in the famous mud game in Cleveland in '70. The sky is gray, the field and the players are covered with mud, and the players are waiting defiantly, with their hands on their hips. The picture evoked not just a moment, but an era.

"That's the way football used to be," I said.

"Isn't that the truth," Lilly said.

On his mantel was a trophy celebrating his place on the NFL's All-Time team, selected on the occasion of the league's 75th anniversary. Lilly was the only Cowboy to make the team.

"That was a pretty neat deal," he said casually.

Otherwise, there were few reminders from his football days on display in the house. He had moved on. He did not mind talking about the old days, but he was not stuck in the past. His post-football life was full. "I have an electronic imaging business that I do on a computer, out of my home," he said. "I do some outdoor shows on cable television. I represent a couple of companies in the outdoor business and I go to trade shows. And I take a lot of pictures."

We were standing on his driveway; I had my car keys in hand, preparing to leave.

"I haven't changed that much," he said. "I don't have the motivation to be the richest guy in town. I never did have any money when I grew up. Money wasn't a motivating factor for me. Competitiveness was. To win, to be a champion, that was a factor. I had to have enough money to live, but it's never meant a whole lot to me. I don't care one way or the other. I don't care if someone is rich or poor. People will tell you that if you ask them. I have as many friends who are poor as have money. In fact, I probably have a lot more who are poor. I live in a relatively modest home. We could afford a bigger, better one, but I'm very comfortable. This is five times as nice as what I grew up in. I really think I would feel kind of out of place in a $200,000 home or a $400,000 home."

He was back where he belonged, in the Texas countryside that had produced thousands of football-crazed boys over the years. None played the game better than Robert John Lilly.

"Gosh, I loved it," he said. "I loved the competitiveness, the family feeling, everything. I loved football when I was terrible and getting beat up in ninth grade. I loved football when I started to get good at TCU. I loved the competition and having teammates. That's what made the game. Every time I see my old teammates, we have a blast. I don't think you'll see it again, a guy playing with the same group of players, same organization, same owner, same city, same coach for 14 years. It was the golden years of football."

We looked down a hill to the schoolyard that his property overlooked. A light wind was blowing.

"I still dream about playing football," he said. "I have a recurring dream. It's me as I am today, about 25 pounds under my playing weight, and I'm standing on the sidelines at Texas Stadium with gray hair coming out from under my helmet. Coach Landry is saying, 'We gotta have you, Bob.' And I say, 'Look at 'em, coach, they'll kill me.' And he says, 'No they're not. They're not going to kill you, Bob.' Then I wake up."

I looked at him. "That's bizarre," I said.

He smiled. "Isn't it? Coach Landry is saying, 'We gotta have you, Bob.' I dream that all the time."

Chapter Thirteen

The Cowboys spent their adolescence at the Cotton Bowl. So did I. When they matured into one of pro football's best and most popular teams, they left the Cotton Bowl in the fall of '71 and moved into Texas Stadium. I was 15 years old, no longer a child myself.

The move to Texas Stadium was a labored process. Clint Murchison had explored the idea of a new home for the Cowboys beginning in '65. He and his front office loathed the Cotton Bowl almost as much as I loved it. "Not enough bathrooms, not enough parking, just an increasingly old facility all the way around," Gil Brandt said. "People were running around the press box that we didn't know. It was a bad scene."

Murchison wanted a new downtown stadium. He envisioned it as part of an arts district including a new music hall and art museum. Dallas mayor Erik Jonsson conferred with architects and urban planners who discouraged the idea, citing traffic problems and the six days a week that the stadium would sit idle. Jonsson proposed that the Cowboys renovate the Cotton Bowl, an idea Murchison dismissed as "pouring money into a hopeless situation."

In December of '67, Murchison announced that the Cowboys would leave the Cotton Bowl for a new $35 million stadium in Irving, a suburban municipality located northwest of downtown. The city fired back by announcing a renovation of the Cotton Bowl including artificial turf and chair-back seats replacing the wooden benches, but it was too late. The Cowboys were leaving for the 'burbs.

The new stadium was financed by construction bonds that season-ticket holders purchased giving them the right to buy tickets. The bonds, priced at $1,000 for choice seats and $250 for the rest, went on sale early in '68. Even though the opening of the stadium was still years away, loyal fans schemed to get the seats they wanted. Pop stood in a line almost all night with hundreds of other fans.

"My business partner and I were the third or fourth people in line," said Harry Sebel, a season-ticket holder starting in '62. "My partner had a rental house in town, and, in lieu of one month's rent, the tenant stood in line for us for two days. We got seats on the 50."

Over the next three years, the newspapers ran a steady trickle of stories about the new stadium under construction at a confluence of three highways. Fans knew the Cowboys' days at the Cotton Bowl were numbered. I was not sad about it, fond as I was of the old place. The Cotton Bowl and most other stadiums around the country suddenly seemed outdated in the wake of the opening of the Astrodome in '65. I wanted a stadium like that. The Astrodome was nicknamed "The Eighth Wonder of the World," and not just because it was an indoor stadium with plastic grass called Astroturf. It also bowed deeply to the fans' comfort and convenience. There were thousands of parking spaces ringing the stadium, wider seats, escalators, numerous bathrooms, fancy food, and luxury suites. There was an enormous scoreboard displaying statistics and scores from other games, and an electronic fireworks display that went off when a Houston player hit a home run or scored a touchdown.

A stadium with such amenities had been a futuristic dream when the Cowboys began playing in the early '60s; the Cotton Bowl's spartan character was typical of an era in which most pro football teams played in old major league ballparks, bland college stadiums, or austere Depression-era hulks. Then the Astrodome opened, and within 10 years there were new, fan-friendlier stadiums opened or planned in New York, Philadelphia, San Francisco, Detroit, Cincinnati, Kansas City, Pittsburgh, Atlanta, and New Orleans. The Cowboys were at the forefront of the revolution.

They played their last full season at the Cotton Bowl in 1970. The wooden benches were gone, replaced by blue and silver metallic seats. The grass field also was gone, replaced by a bright green carpet. The changes were welcome, yet dismissed with a shrug by most fans. The future was under construction in Irving: a stadium with luxury suites and televisions and big scoreboards and clean bathrooms. I could hardly wait.

By the beginning of the '71 season, the Cowboys had all the pieces of a championship team, with one exception.

Their defense finally was complete; it had carried the team to the Super Bowl the year before. Their offensive line was one of the best. Calvin Hill, Duane Thomas, and Walt Garrison were an enviable set of running backs. The team was built around a core of veterans and had a toughened attitude bred by the bitterness of near-misses and the imported leadership of Herb Adderley and Mike Ditka. There were seven future Hall of Famers, including Lance Alworth, a flanker acquired in an offseason trade with the Chargers, and Forrest Gregg, the Packers' former guard, whom Landry had coaxed out of retirement.

There was just one problem, one area of uncertainty that had cost the Cowboys against the Colts in Super Bowl V and threatened to undermine them again in '71: the quarterback.

At 28 years old, Craig Morton was entering his seventh season with the Cowboys and his third as the starter. He was supposed to be at the peak of his career, but the Pro Bowler the Cowboys had envisioned had failed to materialize. Morton was capable, but injuries had diminished his skills, criticism from the fans and the press had diminished his self-confidence, and poor playoff performances had diminished his teammates' belief in him. He had completed just 31 of 90 pass attempts in his four playoff starts, with three times as many interceptions as touchdowns.

Morton was not a natural leader in the mold of a Meredith or Bart Starr. "He was stoic," Mel Renfro said. He also was a bachelor who enjoyed the Dallas nightlife and "was not really settled into a lifestyle of dedicating himself to football, (which) he couldn't get away with," wrote Roger Staubach in his 1980 autobiography, *Time Enough to Win*. Morton did not help his standing when a policeman caught him urinating in public behind a service station on Central Expressway at 3:30 A.M. two months after Super Bowl V, and when he later admitted to reporters that he had experimented with hypnosis as a cure for his passing woes.

"Craig was a good guy and a good quarterback, but you almost felt sorry for him that he couldn't fill the role," Landry said.

Staubach had backed up Morton during the '69 and '70 seasons, getting an occasional start when Morton was injured. Staubach was tired of sitting on the bench. He was older than Morton at 29, but he had little game experience and was worried about getting a chance before it was too late. He was contemplating asking for a trade when Landry visited with him on the team plane as it flew home from Super Bowl V. "I want you to work extra hard this offseason," Landry said. "I think you can make your move this coming year."

Landry put the starting job up for grabs, to be decided during the '71 exhibition season. Staubach and Morton were given equal playing time as the Cowboys won five of six games. Staubach outplayed Morton, throwing for more yardage, more touchdowns, and fewer interceptions, but Morton also played reasonably well. Landry named Staubach the starter for the regular-season opener in Buffalo, but added that both quarterbacks would play. He had not made up his mind.

Morton wound up starting in Buffalo—Staubach had a broken blood vessel in his leg—and completed 10 of 14 passes for 221 yards in the Cowboys' 49–37 victory. Staubach was back in the lineup the next Sunday in Philadelphia, but he was knocked out early when the Eagles' Mel Tom whacked him on the head after a play. Morton came off the bench and completed 15 of 22 passes in a 42–7 victory, earning the start in the home opener against the Redskins the next week. When Morton struggled in the rain, Staubach came on in relief in the second half and led a rally that fell short.

Staubach was back in the lineup the next week against the Giants in a *Monday Night Football* game at home. It was an emotional occasion, the Cowboys' last home game at the Cotton Bowl. Texas Stadium finally was ready after three years of planning and construction; the Cowboys would christen it against the Patriots two weeks later.

The last game at the Cotton Bowl was chilly and unspectacular. Landry benched Staubach at halftime even though the Cowboys were ahead. The Cowboys won, 20–13, giving them a final record of 43–31–4 in regular season games at the Cotton Bowl. Staubach was furious in the locker room after the game. "Coach Landry is going by feel, and he obviously has a feel for Craig," Staubach said. Landry's explanation: "Roger was rusty."

Morton started the next week in New Orleans, but Staubach came on in relief when the Cowboys fell behind by 17 points. Staubach threw two touchdown passes, but the Saints hung on to win when a fumbled punt late in the game denied Staubach a chance to complete the rally. The loss dropped the Cowboys' record to 3–2. The Redskins, reinvigorated by head coach George Allen and a core of veterans nicknamed "The Over the Hill Gang," were 5–0. Just as they had in '70, the Cowboys were digging a hole in the NFC East standings.

The first game at Texas Stadium was a bizarre and unforgettable day for those of us weaned on the Cotton Bowl. Instead of driving the back roads of East Dallas, we took Northwest Highway and wound up on State Highway 183. A traffic jam caused us to miss the opening kickoff; Pop fumed as we listened to Duane Thomas break a 56-yard touchdown run on the game's fourth play. Instead of parking by the railroad tracks, we parked on a broad concrete plain in the shadows of the stadium. The nearest building was a half-mile away. We entered the stadium through a new gate, bought a program from a new vendor, and sat next to new neighbors. We had a strange new view of the field, from 20 yards to the left of the 50-yard line instead of from 20 yards to the right.

The Cowboys won easily, 44–21, with Staubach throwing for 197 yards and two touchdowns, but the change from the earthy Cotton Bowl was so monumental that it was hard to concentrate on the game. I spent the day staring in wonderment at the new surroundings. Texas Stadium was everything the Cotton Bowl was not: It was clean, comfortable, and organized, with wide aisles, wide seats, broad concourses, convenient bathrooms, and cold sodas. It was a space-age creation, a "half-dome" with a 90,000 square foot rectangular hole in the middle of a 22-gauge steel canopy roof; sunlight shining through the hole created artful geometric patterns of shade and light that moved back and forth across the field during the game. It was luxurious, with two rows of $50,000 luxury suites between the upper and lower decks, and a stadium club behind the west end zone in which fans drank and ate as they watched the game through a wall of dark glass.

The Cowboys had sold more than 30,000 bonds; only nine seats were unsold between the 30-yard lines. Many buyers had utilized a payment plan in which they put 20 percent down and paid $8 a month over 30 months. It seemed to me, as a 15-year-old, that the money had been used wisely. The stadium was a football palace. It had a $1.2 million, 140-foot-long scoreboard that reacted to big hits and plays with cartoon-style exclamations: "Crunch!" "Whatta Boot!" "Gotcha!" "Touchdown!" It had 105 restrooms and 36 concession stands featuring pizza, barbecue, Mexican food, and fried chicken. It had escalators that carried fans to the upper deck. It had uniformed hostesses at every section; they were called Texettes. It had those luxury suites, each of which had three color televisions, two couches, a wet bar, and two rows of leather swivel chairs facing the field. It had 130 acres of parking surrounding the stadium. It had the canopy roof that would keep the fans dry if it rained. The Cotton Bowl seemed worlds away.

The move changed the Cowboys' fundamental personality. The players and coaches were the same, but the reflection that the franchise gave off to the rest of the football world was different. The Cowboys had always cultivated a mildly snobby character with their multiple-set offense, reliance on computers, and Landry's unemotional approach, but moving to Texas Stadium pushed their elitist reputation to a new zenith. The joke was that the architects of the new stadium had left a hole in the roof so God could watch His favorite team play.

At the Cotton Bowl, the Cowboys had been a workingman's team on rollicking, emotional, and slightly naughty Sundays. At Texas Stadium, they took on a regal bearing as the showpiece of what amounted to a private club. Suddenly, they were no longer Dallas's team. They were North Dallas's team, a toy for the wealthy. Many loyal fans from the Cotton Bowl could not afford the price of a bond and a season ticket. A wave of new fans replaced them, a money crowd, a herd of "haves."

"The change was dramatic," disc jockey Ron Chapman said. "The people who had gone to the Cotton Bowl were people who could afford a ticket or two, or maybe a season of two tickets. They were pretty much the average guy. But once the team moved and you had to be well off to buy good seats, it disqualified a lot of those people and qualified a lot of corporations and wealthy individuals who hadn't gotten in on the ground floor the first time. They were the well-to-do, which meant they were more controlled, more serene, better dressed, more refined, and not half as much fun. They were harder to impress and they were always 'Doing nicely, thank you very much, and you will win, won't you?' "

Thousands of fans who had supported the team at the Cotton Bowl had to learn to cheer from home. Bob Lilly later estimated that no more than 10,000 fans followed the team to Irving.

"The bonds made it too expensive," said Vernell King, a Braniff reservations supervisor and Cotton Bowl season-ticket holder.

"I had three season tickets in the first row of the upper deck at the Cotton Bowl, great seats that cost me a total of $210 a year," said Johnny Minx, who was working on the *Times Herald*'s loading dock in those days. "Texas Stadium would have cost me four or five times as much, including the price of the bonds. There was just no way."

Jack Anthony, a Dallas attorney, was one of the season-ticket holders who moved with the team to Texas Stadium. "I would go up to the stadium club, eat lunch and watch the game," he said. "It wasn't football. It was an event. The football was almost an afterthought. It was a fashion show up there. You had every kind of person, from John Connally to Priscilla Davis to millionaires. You name it. Just a weird, strange mix of people. It was like a society ball. You couldn't believe you were at a football game. It was totally different from the Cotton Bowl."

Texas Stadium was a king's lair, with fans who belonged in a king's court. Home games were no longer emotional outpourings; they were social occasions marked by reserved, "tasteful" cheering from a crowd that felt it was above traditional football rabble-rousing. Cowboy management was so concerned with fostering a stylish appearance that fans were not allowed to put up signs or banners on the stadium walls. The Cowboys assumed an air of bloodless glamour, a postmodern coolness that topped off their computerized image.

To opponents, the hole in the roof perpetuated the notion that the Cowboys felt they were superior. The Dallas Cowboy Cheerleaders, wiggling on the sidelines, perpetuated the notion that Texans believed everything was bigger and better in the Lone Star State. The players felt like Roman gladiators on a field sunk below ground level, with Dallas's elite staring down at them. As Blaine Nye said to Ralph Neely as they stood in the tunnel before one game, "You know why they sunk the field? So the gladiators can't get out."

Andrie said, "Personally, I think we lost something when we moved to Texas Stadium. The players could see it. It was a different clientele that didn't really care if we won or lost. They wanted to drink their cocktails and go to their parties. The Cotton Bowl crowd lived and died with us. Ask any player. Everyone hated Texas Stadium. It was a nice facility and everything, but we hated the turf, hated the way the people acted. I think that kind of made the Cowboys suffer. It took the game away from the real fans and gave it to people who had money. They had to do it, but it got to where we wanted to play on the road. We'd go to Philly and New York and the fans were after our throats, like always. But we didn't have that intimidating crowd at home. Our fans had changed. It was like the team didn't want them to yell too loud."

Our family quickly grew accustomed to life at the new stadium. Our routine changed, but not that much. Instead of making Pop's house our last stop on the way to the game, Uncle Milton drove across town and fetched Pop during the morning while I was in Sunday school, and then they collected my father, picked me up, and we set off for the game. We still arrived early, even though the walk from the car was shorter now for Pop. For 80 years he had arrived early to everything from piano lessons to operas to football games; he was not about to stop now. We ate sandwiches picked up at Wall's Delicatessen on Preston Road. Pop still sat in the seat by the aisle, planted his cane in front of him, and plugged in to the radio broadcast. I still sat beside him.

I loved Texas Stadium when it opened. It was modern and exciting; sitting in it was like sitting in the cockpit of a jet. Yet I, too, sensed a vague uneasiness. It was so quiet in there. There were so many people who seemed so uninterested in the game. It was bizarre.

"We gave up the shoeshine guy for the lawyer when we moved," Jethro Pugh said. "We lost a lot of our real fans. Lilly couldn't get his relatives in because the seats were tied up in bonds. It was weird, a strange place all the way around. When we were shaking hands with teams after games they'd say, 'Boy, this is a weird place.' "

The bond between the fans and players was abruptly severed. Players no longer mingled and signed autographs after games, as at the Cotton Bowl. "The team bus went down into a tunnel and we got out at the dressing room and never saw anybody," Lilly said. "When we left, we rode with friends or took the bus and never saw anyone. You could sneak out. It wasn't the same. You might sign a few autographs, but the bus was waiting and police were blocking everyone."

Lilly played nine seasons in the Cotton Bowl and four in Texas Stadium. There was no comparison. "Texas Stadium was kind of a cold place to play in," he said. "We still had good crowds, but playing inside that thing was never the same as playing in the sunshine. The turf was the worst turf in the world. It was a killer. And the contrast of the harsh sunlight coming down, and the shadows, it was just weird. We got to like it OK; it was one of those things you accepted. But I thoroughly enjoyed the Cotton Bowl. Those people were all for us. They weren't interested in being part of a style show."

The Cowboys' new home was a classy, quality stadium that would hold up far better than most other stadiums in its generation—it was still comfortable and functional on its 25th birthday in 1996, unlike stadiums of a similar age in San Francisco, Cincinnati, Atlanta, and Pittsburgh, which had been deemed outdated—but it engendered a subdued atmosphere. Early on, the Cowboys tried to elicit cheers with a Godlike voice slowly booming "Go! Go! Go!" on the public address system; that was frightening, not inspiring. The crowds remained restrained until the sale of beer was legalized in the '90s and it became fashionable for players to run around waving their arms and asking for noise. The crowd was younger and tipsier, but still not emotional. Cowboy coach Barry Switzer implored the fans to cheer louder than usual before an important game against the Packers in '96. He lamented the longstanding lack of an inspiring home crowd at Texas Stadium.

"They have to beg for cheers at Texas Stadium," Walt Garrison said. "No one ever had to beg for cheers at the Cotton Bowl."

Staubach's sharp performance against the Patriots figured to earn him a start against the Bears the next week in Chicago, but Landry surprised the fans, media, and players by announcing that both quarterbacks would play. Reviving a tactic he had used with Meredith and LeBaron, and again with Morton and Jerry Rhome, Landry would have Morton and Staubach alternate plays as part of a "quarterback shuttle." One would replace the other on every down, bringing in plays Landry had called.

Landry said he was using the tactic because the Bears had a complicated defense. Morton and Staubach looked at each other and rolled their eyes when Landry announced the plan at a team meeting. The press was critical. "Does Landry crave this chiefly for himself? Could it be that Tom is on an ego trip?" wrote Sam Blair in the *Morning News*.

Yet the shuttle worked for the most part on a cool, sunny day in Chicago. The Cowboys generated 481 yards of offense, including 342 yards passing. Staubach completed seven of 11 passes and Morton completed 20 of 36 in between dashes on and off the field. "You guys looked like two ships passing in the night," a teammate told Staubach after the game. Landry alternated them throughout the game, except for the last two minutes of the first half and the last part of the fourth quarter, when the offense was in a "hurry-up" mode and the shuttle was not prudent. Morton took over then.

"The shuttle seemed to work," Landry said after the game. "We moved the ball."

They did, but they did not beat the Bears. Three fumbles, three interceptions, and three missed field goals by Mike Clark offset the shuttle's success and condemned the Cowboys to a 23–19 defeat. They now had a 4–3 record and trailed the Redskins by two games. Their season was in jeopardy.

The players desperately wanted Landry to pick a starting quarterback and stick by his decision, but the choice was difficult. Morton was experienced, competent, and ran the offense as Landry wanted, but he was shaky in the clutch and lacking as a leader. Staubach was a classic leader, the antithesis of Morton: a dependable family man, a tireless worker, devoted to his craft, but he was not as experienced as Morton and tended to stray from Landry's system and improvise with his scrambling.

"I think Landry preferred that Morton win the job because he ran the offense and knew where the ball was supposed to go," said Bob Ryan of NFL Films. "I don't think he was ever really comfortable with Roger because of Roger's style of play. But obviously Staubach was the man for the job."

Landry called Staubach at home on Tuesday, a day off. "I've got good news and bad news," Landry said, according to Steve Perkins' account in the *Times Herald*. "The good news is that I've abandoned the two-quarterback system."

"What's the bad news?" Staubach asked.

"You're number one," Landry said.

Landry announced his decision to the press at his luncheon the next day: "I think a change in this team is necessary. I didn't last year (after the 38–0 loss to the Cardinals), so I didn't make a change, but this year is different. Don't ask me if we'll go seven games this way. Who knows? When you make a choice you expect it to go seven games. And I'm not going to explain one way or another why the choice was made. It's just Roger's time to make his move, if he's going to make it."

Morton accepted the decision gracefully: "I'm behind Roger and I'll do everything I can to help him. I'm not bitter."

Staubach was the starting quarterback. The players were pleased. "I think we knew the year before that Roger was the guy," Lilly said. "Craig was a good quarterback and would have been an outstanding quarterback had he had good knees, but he wasn't the leader Roger was. If Roger needed an inch for a first down, he'd use a quarterback sneak or roll out and hit the linebacker right in the head to get that one inch. We had great respect for him."

Said Adderley, "Roger was the best man for the job and everyone knew it. We went, 'What took the man [Landry] so long?' "

Landry's two-quarterback system was a source of constant controversy in the first half of the '71 season, but it was not Topic A in the locker room or among the press and fans. The hottest Cowboy topic in the fall of '71 was Duane Thomas, the reluctant, recalcitrant, rebellious halfback.

"It all started toward the end of the previous season," Calvin Hill said. "Me and Duane and Margene Adkins and Bob Asher were driving to lunch at a Dairy Queen. This was in the day when athletes did not share what they earned. Margene said to me, 'I know you're going to treat us because you were the Rookie of the Year last year.' I said, 'I ain't even playing now.' Duane said, 'I'm just making 20 grand.' We all fessed up, and it turned out Duane was making less than Asher and Margene. That got him upset. He was the number-one draft pick and starting, but he was making less than guys drafted behind him."

Thomas pledged to ask for a renegotiated contract after the season. "And he did," Hill said. "I went with him that day when he went up to see Tex. He went rushing out of the meeting and he changed. He went from this guy who was gregarious to a guy who realized he thought he was getting screwed. He decided then that when the Cowboys asked, 'How are you doing? I hope you're fine,' they weren't really serious."

Four months after Super Bowl V, Thomas announced his retirement from pro football. He said he was upset that his contract called for him to earn $500 less in his second year than he did as a rookie. "Nobody cares what happens to the players," Thomas said. "It's all business, the dotted line. Then, when you get into the season, you're supposed to be a big family."

Fans had grown accustomed to reading about the players' salary gripes in the paper, but no one was prepared for what happened next. Thomas relented on his decision to retire, but then, when training camp opened in July, Thomas refused to report and held a press conference in Dallas at which he said Landry was "plastic, just not a man at all," Schramm was "completely dishonest," and Brandt was "a liar." He also said the Cowboys exploited black players and treated them "like stupid animals."

One week later, Thomas said he would report to camp after all. "The only reason I'm coming back is for my people—the black people," Thomas said. He met with Landry upon arriving at Thousand Oaks. "He kept telling me I'm at a threshold, just one more good year," Thomas said after the meeting. "I told him, 'Hey, man, go to hell. You are not God. You go play halfback.'"

Schramm and Landry were stunned. They had never experienced such resentment and anger from a player. Many black Cowboys had quietly seethed about their second-class status off the field throughout the '60s, but they were from a different generation and not as comfortable confronting authority. Thomas was the first prominent Cowboy from the militant element that developed in the black community during the decade of Malcolm X and Bobby Seale. "Duane," Renfro said later, "was an angry young man."

Recognizing a major problem, Schramm and Landry reluctantly traded Thomas to the Patriots along with two young players, Halvor Hagen and Honor Jackson, receiving in return a running back, Carl Garrett, and a number-one draft choice. Thomas reported to the Patriots and argued with the head coach, John Mazur, at his first practice. A United Press International reporter recounted the conversation that occurred as Thomas was lining up for a play:

"We want our running backs in three-point stances with their other hand on the ground," Mazur said.

"In Dallas they told us to get down in a stance with our hands on our knees, so we could see the linebackers better," Thomas said.

"Well, here we do it my way," Mazur said. "In a three-point stance."

"Maybe so," Thomas said, "but I'm doing it my way."

"No, you're not," Mazur said. "You're going to get out of here right now. Get the hell in the locker room."

The trade was voided when Thomas refused to take a physical. Thomas was returned to the Cowboys, and Garrett and the number-one pick were returned to the Patriots. Hagen and Jackson remained with the Patriots in exchange for two other draft picks.

Thomas returned to Thousand Oaks and embarked on a new approach to life as a Cowboy: silence. He stopped talking to reporters, coaches, even his teammates. He practiced hard, played hard, and returned to the starting lineup once he was back in playing shape, but he refused to communicate beyond what was necessary on the field.

"It was amazing," Jethro Pugh said. "We were best friends, but you could ask him something and he was just silent. One time I was sitting in front of my locker and he came and went into my pants, got my car keys and some money, went and got some lunch, came back, put the change and keys back in my pocket and walked away. Without saying a word. I said, 'At least you could say thanks.'"

Thomas's locker was next to Renfro's. "He never talked to me," Renfro said years later. "Once every two or three weeks he would lean over and say, 'How are the kids?' I would say, 'Fine, Duane.' And then he wouldn't say anything again for another two or three weeks."

The players were amazed at Thomas's audacity, and his success in intimidating the front office. "Here was a guy who was challenging the establishment, and the establishment was blinking," Calvin Hill said. "None of the rest of us knew how to get a reaction. Nothing you could do would faze Tom, and if you threatened to hold out, Tex would say, 'Go ahead.' Duane scared them. You never knew what was going to happen from day to day. It was wonderful theater. I used to look forward to going to practice to see how people would react, to see what he would do. It made it different. It wasn't boring. We had to wear jackets and ties on away trips, but one time Duane came in a T-shirt and a clip-on tie, and they didn't touch him."

•   •   •

After calling Staubach with the news about the starting quarterback job, Landry dialed Tony Liscio, the offensive lineman who had retired after playing for the Cowboys since '63. Landry was desperate for tackles. Neely had broken his leg while riding a motorcycle; he was out for the year. Forrest Gregg had a pulled groin muscle. Don Talbert had a broken bone in his foot.

"I had gotten into real estate, and I was sitting in my office and the phone rang and it was coach Landry," Liscio said. "He said, 'Well, we don't have any tackles. Do you think you can come out and see if you can still play?' I said to him, 'How much time do I have to think about it?' Thinking maybe he would give me a couple of days. He said, 'I can give you 30 minutes.' "

The Cowboys had traded Liscio to the Chargers as part of the package that brought Lance Alworth to Dallas, but he had retired when the Chargers tried to trade him to the Dolphins. He had a sore back and a sore knee, and he was weary of the grind.

"I called my wife after I hung up from Landry," Liscio recalled, "and she said, 'It's up to you.' I figured I might as well go out there and try. I knew if I could hang on for three games I could add another year to my pension. So I met [offensive line coach Jim] Myers on the field that day. They wanted to see if I could run. Luckily, my weight was down. That was Monday. I got on the plane on Friday and flew to the game. I had a bad hamstring, a sore shoulder. I thought I'd never be able to play. But I got out on the field, the adrenaline started flowing and I didn't feel any g. I think I came out of one play."

Staubach made his first start as the number-one quarterback st the Cardinals that Sunday in St. Louis. "We went to mass that r g, me, Roger, Lilly, and Andrie," Dave Manders said, "and we we ing in a coffee shop afterwards having breakfast, and Lilly was sitt re bitching. You know, 'God, what a lousy day outside, I don't w y today.' That was just Lilly's way of blowing off steam. Roger w there with wide eyes, looking at him, like, 'What kind of a team i way?' "

It was a team that needed a strong leader at quarte time, 10–3, them that against the Cardinals. The Cowboys tra ey controlled and still trailed by four points late in the third qu the ball for 16 of the last 18 minutes and Staubach completed two third-down passes on a winning drive late in the fourth quarter. Toni Fritsch, an Austrian soccer star who had replaced the slumping Mike Clark, kicked a 26-yard field goal with 1:43 left to give the Cowboys a 16–13 victory.

St. Louis safety Larry Stallings tried to intimidate Fritsch before the winning kick. "You're going to choke!" Stallings shouted as the teams lined up.

Dave Edwards laughed. "You might as well shut up," Edwards said. "He doesn't understand you anyway."

That was not true, it turned out. Fritsch said to reporters after the game, "I no choke-a."

The happiest man in the locker room was Staubach. He had completed 20 of 31 passes and brought the team from behind to win. Four weeks after being yanked at halftime against the Giants, he was given the chance to win. "Coach Landry came to me at halftime and told me it was my game win or lose, and that felt good," Staubach said.

The Cowboys beat the Eagles at Texas Stadium the following Sunday. Staubach's performance in the 20–7 victory was unorthodox, to say the least. Repeatedly scrambling when he found his receivers covered, he gained 76 yards rushing in the first half. "He wasn't reading defenses that well yet, which was why he was scrambling," Walt Garrison said. "If he looked at the receiver he was supposed to throw to and the guy was covered, man, Roger was gone."

The Redskins lost to the Bears that day to drop their record to 6–2–1. The Cowboys were at 6–3, within a half-game of the lead in NFC East. The next game on the schedule? Cowboys at Redskins. The Redskins had upset the Cowboys at the Cotton Bowl earlier in the season, but the Cowboys were a different team now with Staubach entrenched at quarterback.

"He had a hell of an impact," Adderley said. "He was tough and committed he could make plays in and out of the pocket. He wasn't a real leader. He was 29 years old and just starting to play. But he was incredibly competitive. We knew he would do what it took to win."

He was way running the ball against the Redskins in Washington. At the end of a 36-yard drive in the first quarter, Staubach faded to pass, found no receivers open, and took off scrambling. The field opened up and Staubach ran 29 yards to the end zone. It was the game's only touchdown. The Cowboys won, 13–0. They were back in first place.

The Redskins won their next three games to keep the pressure on the Cowboys, but the Cowboys were on a roll. Staubach led a late drive that delivered a 28–21 victory over the Rams on Thanksgiving; when Staubach was injured on a scramble near the end of the drive, Morton came in and handed off to Thomas on the game-winning touchdown run. Ten days later, with Thomas and Hill starting in the same backfield for the first time—Garrison was injured and Hill was coming back from an injury—the offense was awesome in a 52–10 defeat of the Jets at Texas Stadium. Thomas rushed for 112 yards; Hill rushed for 62, caught four passes for 80 yards, and scored three touchdowns. The Cowboys then shattered New York's other team, the Giants, at Yankee Stadium. Thomas rushed for 94 yards, Hill for 89, and Staubach completed 10 of 14 passes for 232 yards and three touchdowns.

With the playoffs looming, the Cowboys suddenly were so dominant that it almost seemed unfair. Yet the players did not relish their success. Regular-season accomplishments meant little now after so many playoff failures. "The whole focus was on getting back to the Super Bowl and winning it before our time was up," Lilly said. "It was not a real fun year. We didn't really enjoy it. And we had the thing going with Duane, who wouldn't speak to the white guys, or the black guys, either. That created a little tension, which might have been a good thing. We were constantly kind of mad at each other. We had that kind of an attitude. It was a very tense year."

Thomas maintained his silence as the team coalesced around Staubach and drove for the playoffs. "I think he got caught up in the situation and didn't know how to get out of it," Hill said. "When we were in Hawaii together (as World Football League teammates in '75) he told me, 'I had built this image and I didn't know how to break it back down.' His silence became such a powerful thing that he was seduced by it. Just knowing him and how much he liked to talk and learn, it had to be a very tough thing for him to do. It was amazing that he was able to do it. Duane has a tremendous willpower. He is a very gregarious guy. A great teammate. But he went from one extreme to the other, and then he didn't know how to get back."

It had no effect on the field. The Cowboys ended the regular season by beating the Cardinals at Texas Stadium, 31–12. The victory gave them seven straight wins and six straight division titles. The other teams in the

NFC playoffs were the Vikings, winners of the Central Division with an 11–3 record; the 49ers, winners of the West at 9–5; and the Redskins, who earned the wild card berth with a 9–4–1 record.

The Cowboys had to play in Minnesota in the first round, a tough assignment. The Vikings had the "Purple People Eaters" defense, which had allowed only 14 touchdowns all season. Their offense was not as strong—coach Bud Grant had rotated quarterbacks Gary Cuozzo, Norm Snead, and Bob Lee all season, with limited success—but the defense and home field advantage always made games in Minnesota a chore. The Cowboys had suffered their worst loss ever there 14 months earlier.

The day before the game, after a week of indecision, Grant announced that Lee would start at quarterback. Lee had thrown only two touchdown passes all season, but he was bigger than Cuozzo and more agile than Snead. "It seems like the thing to do," Grant said.

The game was scheduled for Christmas afternoon, and the Cowboys awoke that morning to their version of a present from Santa Claus: mild weather, with a temperature in the thirties and light winds. The Cowboys had feared another Ice Bowl, but many of them wore short sleeves.

The first half was unsettling; the Vikings' defense dominated the hot Cowboys' offense. The Cowboys led at halftime, 6–3. Early in the third quarter Lee threw long for Bob Grim, but Cliff Harris intercepted and returned the ball 30 yards to the Minnesota 13. On the next play Thomas found a hole off right guard—vacated by Alan Page, who took the bait on a "trap"—and scored the game's first touchdown.

The Cowboys broke the game open on their next possession. Staubach passed 30 yards to Alworth on third-and-15, hit Hill with a screen pass for 10, then scrambled out of the pocket and found Hayes in the end zone for a nine-yard touchdown pass. That gave the Cowboys a 20–3 lead. Grant pulled Lee, who had completed seven passes to the Vikings and three to the Cowboys. Cuozzo led the Vikings to a meaningless late touchdown. The final score was 20–12.

When reporters circled Staubach after the game, he said, "I was adequate, but the defense was outstanding. Go talk to them." The defense had forced five turnovers, a reminder that the Cowboys were more than just a prolific offense. Their defense was not as formidable as it had been down the stretch in '70, but it was still one of the game's best.

Playing on the road in the other semifinal, George Allen's Redskins led the 49ers at halftime and still trailed by just four points midway through the fourth quarter. But the 49ers held on to win, setting up a rematch in the NFC Championship Game: 49ers against Cowboys, Nolan against Landry, student against teacher. This time the game would be played in Dallas.

In the 12 months since their last game, the Cowboys had improved considerably. Thanks mostly to Staubach, they now had a potent offense to go with their strong defense. The 49ers had experienced no such sweeping changes. They had barely made the playoffs after losing four of their first 10 games. John Brodie was still their quarterback, and Gene Washington and Ted Kwalick were still his favorite receivers, but Brodie was 36 years old and increasingly erratic. The offense was dependent more and more on the running of fullback Ken Willard and a fleet rookie halfback named Vic Washington. The defensive line was able, but the rest of the defense was ordinary. The Cowboys were the better team.

Staubach was nervous in his first championship start: His passes sailed high early in the game and the offense failed to move. The 49ers' offense also struggled. The game was scoreless when the 49ers began a series at their 12 early in the second quarter. After a two-yard gain on the first down, Brodie faded to pass, faked a screen to the right, spun, and threw left for Willard coming out of the backfield. The ball flew right to George Andrie.

"I never saw Andrie," Brodie said after the game.

"I couldn't believe it," Andrie said. "I was just starting to move back to the inside when he threw me the ball."

Andrie intercepted the pass, headed for the end zone, and was tackled at the one. Calvin Hill scored the touchdown. The score held up as the defenses continued to dominate through the second and third quarters, with the only points coming on a field goal by the 49ers' Bruce Gossett midway through the third quarter. Brodie had driven the 49ers to the Dallas 21 before Cornell Green knocked away a third down pass.

The Cowboys had a four-point lead when their offense began a series on the Dallas 20 early in the fourth quarter. Two plays left Staubach in a third-and-seven hole. He faded to pass, found no receivers open, and started to scramble, but two 49er linemen cut him off. He turned around and drifted back to the five, perilously close to the end zone, then reversed directions again, scrambled across the field, and finally found Reeves open near the sideline for a 17-yard gain and a first down. It was a classic Staubach play:

unrehearsed and dramatic. "The five! Did I really go back that far?" Staubach said after the game. The crowd roared, and the offense began to move. Staubach converted two more third downs with passes to his tight ends, Billy Truax and Mike Ditka, then converted yet another third down to move the ball inside the 10. Thomas completed the 80-yard drive with a two-yard sprint around left end. The Cowboys had a 14–3 lead, more than enough with their defense.

The celebration in the locker room was subdued. "The Cowboys were so emotional after the game that you could hear a pin drop," wrote Bob St. John in the *Morning News*. They were pleased with the NFC championship, but it was not their goal. As Garrison said later, "We had only one goal that season: win the Super Bowl. It was time."

In the locker room after the 49er game, several out-of-town reporters asked Landry to explain what they called the Thomas "situation." What was it like, they asked, to have 39 players who spoke to each other and one who spoke to no one?

"I don't know if I can explain it," Landry said. "Duane is a unique individual. You just have to understand him. He acts as though he's not a part of the team, but he is. And I and the team have learned to understand that."

It sounded as if the Cowboys had the situation under control. They did not. Thomas missed practice on the Thursday before the team flew to New Orleans for the Super Bowl. There were rumors that he was not going to play in the game. "Tex called my house at 3:30 in the morning and said he had heard that Duane wasn't going to get on the bus and go to the game," Herb Adderley said. "Tex wondered if I knew where Duane was. Well, Duane was sleeping on my couch at that very moment. I was one of the few guys he would talk to."

Thomas returned to practice Friday, met with Landry for 40 minutes, and rejoined the team without incident. Once again, he had stared down the Cowboy establishment. He was with the team when it flew to New Orleans two days later.

The Cowboys' opponent in Super Bowl VI was the Miami Dolphins, a new team in the NFL's championship realm. They were young, attractive, and had captured imaginations across the country. Don Shula was their head coach; he had built them into a contender in three years. Their quarterback, Bob Griese, made few mistakes. The heart of their offense was the backfield, Larry Csonka and Jim Kiick, who called themselves "Butch Cassidy and the Sundance Kid" after the popular movie about two daring and lovable criminals. Griese's favorite receiver was Paul Warfield, the Cowboys' old playoff nemesis from Cleveland who had been traded to the Dolphins.

The Dolphins had won the AFC East with a 10–3–1 record, beaten the Chiefs in double overtime in the conference semifinals, then shut out the Colts in the AFC Championship Game, 21–0, before a roaring crowd at the Orange Bowl. They were a new, romantic team, much as the Cowboys had been against the Packers in '66. The Cowboys were the old pros now.

Not that they were uninteresting. Thomas put on a memorable show when reporters attempted to interview him at a group media session on Monday in New Orleans. He stretched out over a bench at the Saints' practice facility and gave reporters the same treatment he had given his teammates all season.

"Leave me alone; I don't want to talk to anyone," he said when reporters gathered around him.

"Why don't you want to talk?" one asked.

Thomas did not respond. Nor did he respond to three or four more questions. He just sat on the bench and glowered. The knot of reporters around him slowly shrank, until just three or four were left. Thomas stared off into space for 20 minutes, then suddenly spoke.

"What time is it?" he asked.

"Ten after 11," one of the reporters said.

Those were his last words. When the session was over, Thomas got up and left.

The Cowboys were supremely confident as the game neared—more confident than they had ever been before a championship game. The Dolphins were impressive but inexperienced, and the Cowboys, at last, were complete: They had offense, defense, experience, toughness, and a dynamic quarterback to lead them.

"Seldom could I predict how a team would do before a game, because you never know what will happen," Landry said years later, "but there was no doubt in my mind before [Super Bowl VI] that we were going to play great and win. That was one game where you could just tell beforehand. We had a team of veterans and they were just playing so well. They weren't making any mistakes."

Schramm said, "What they were, after all they had been through, was madder than hell. That was one mad team that went down there to play that Super Bowl. There was no way anyone was going to beat them."

The game-day weather was sunny and cool; sunlight glared harshly off the artificial turf at the Sugar Bowl, which was packed with 81,035 fans, including thousands from Dallas. The Cowboys were dressed in their familiar white uniforms, a positive sign for the fans. The Cowboys seldom played well in their blue uniforms.

The game's first break was a surprise: Csonka, who had not fumbled all season, muffed a handoff on the Dolphins' second series. The Cowboys recovered. "We were sticking Csonka pretty good early in the game," Adderley said. "They said he had never fumbled, but after we hit him a few times he said, 'Uh, oh.' "

Staubach and the offense took over at midfield and began to drive, utilizing mostly rushing plays. Landry had built his game plan around attacking Miami's fine middle linebacker, Nick Buoniconti. Noticing on film that Buoniconti had quick reactions and covered a lot of ground, Landry designed plays to take advantage of Buoniconti's mobility: Thomas and Garrison would start out running in one direction after the handoff, then cut back against the grain of the blocking as they hit the line. Buoniconti would react to the play's initial direction, then find Dave Manders and the guards waiting for him when he tried to cut back to get to the runner. "We killed him on his second reaction," John Niland said after the game. The result was a hole in the middle of the defense, a hole through which Thomas and Garrison ran all afternoon.

"I knew Nick wasn't going to hang back and play the cutbacks," Dolphins linebacker Bob Matheson said after the game. "He goes to the point of attack; that's the kind of ballplayer he is. He told me on the sidelines, 'There's no way I'm going to change my style for one game. We have other players out there who can stop that.' "

Not on this day. Gains by Thomas and Garrison carried the Cowboys' offense to the Miami four before Buoniconti and the defense made a stand and forced a short field goal by Mike Clark. The Cowboys had the lead, and the Dolphins' offense showed few signs it could wrest it away. Early in the second quarter, Griese faded to pass on a second down near mid-field.

"I made a quick escape [from the blocker]," Lilly said. "George [Andrie] and I had a stunt going and I think my guard thought he was supposed to block George."

Griese turned to avoid the onrushing Lilly, but there was Larry Cole, the left defensive end, who had made a similarly quick escape from his blocker. Griese, retreating as he ran, turned back in Lilly's direction, then back again toward Cole, finding no room to run.

"I saw Lilly on the left, so I stayed on the right," Cole said after the game. "It was like cutting out horses at the rodeo."

The crowd shrieked as Griese continued to retreat in a panic and finally was tackled by Lilly for a 29-yard loss.

"He just didn't have anywhere to go," Lilly said.

The Dolphins were staggered by the play. "Griese was never sure of himself after that," Lee Roy Jordan said after the game.

The Cowboys drove 76 yards in 11 plays to the game's first touchdown late in the second quarter, with Thomas and Garrison carrying the load. Staubach needled a seven-yard pass to Alworth in the corner of the end zone for the touchdown. The Dolphins responded with their only real drive of the day: Griese hit two passes and Garo Yepremian kicked a 31-yard field goal. The Cowboys had a 10–3 halftime lead that, despite their domination, felt less safe in the wake of the Dolphins' score.

Taking the second-half kickoff, the Cowboys' offense responded to the threat with a decisive scoring drive. With Thomas and Garrison cutting back against the grain for solid gains, the offense moved across midfield and deep into scoring territory. Thomas covered the last three yards with a pitchout around left end. The Cowboys had used up five minutes and taken a 17–3 lead.

"When they took the second-half kickoff and ripped us apart, that was the game," Shula said. "They just dominated us. Overpowered us. Tore us up."

The game moved swiftly; the Dolphins could not sustain drives and the Cowboys ate up chunks of the clock with each possession. They controlled the ball for 40 of the game's 60 minutes.

Early in the fourth quarter Griese aimed a pass toward Kiick at midfield. Chuck Howley was knocked down, but he rose in time to tip the ball and intercept it in the flat, with nothing but open space between him and the end zone. He took off running with a convoy of blockers, but he slipped and fell at the Miami nine. The offense came on to deliver a knockout punch. On third down, Staubach faked a handoff and lobbed a pass to Ditka for a touchdown. The Cowboys were up, 24–3.

After Griese fumbled to end a Miami drive, the Cowboys took the ball and drove to the Miami one, threatening to make the score embarrassingly one-sided, but Hill fumbled as he tried to leap over the goal line. The turnover was the Cowboys' first of the game and only their second of the playoffs. Their defense had forced 11 turnovers in the three playoff games.

As the final gun sounded, the players put Landry on their shoulders and carried him to midfield. Landry's broad smile was a surprising sight to fans accustomed to his impassive demeanor, but his delight was real and overdue.

"I don't think anyone who has won the Super Bowl could feel as good as we do," Lilly said in the locker room, chomping on a cigar.

"We knew we could win the big one, but you get scared when you get there so often and don't win," Howley said.

In the midst of the celebration, Thomas, who had rushed for 95 yards, finally let down his guard and spoke.

"Are you happy now?" a reporter asked.

"I never said I was sad," Thomas said.

"You don't look happy," the reporter said.

"Happiness is inside," he said.

Escorted by Jim Brown, the retired star running back who was now advising him, Thomas agreed to a national television interview with CBS announcer Tom Brookshier.

"Are you that fast? That quick?" Brookshier said.

"Evidently," Thomas said.

The locker room scene was joyful. The Cowboys had played 65 preseason games, 166 regular-season games, and 14 playoff games since their inception. They had traveled through an exhilarating terrain of peaks and valleys, stunning successes and abject failures. There had been many times when they thought they would never reach the place where they now stood: the summit of pro football. But as Bob St. John wrote in the *Morning News* the next day, the Cowboys were "free at last!"

They would play in three more Super Bowls in the '70s, losing twice to the Steelers and defeating the Broncos and quarterback Craig Morton in Super Bowl XII, but the victory over the Dolphins was the only Super Bowl triumph for Lilly, Hayes, Jordan, and most of the players who constituted the foundation of the team in the Cotton Bowl days. They would go down in history as a skillful, unusual team that did not grab all the glory within its grasp. "With a little luck, we could have played in eight or nine Super Bowls," Lilly said. "We had the team, the coach, everything. One little twist of fate in those Green Bay games could have changed so much."

Bob Ryan of NFL Films said, "It's all hypothetical, but once you win a championship game, you get that winning mind-set and it tends to lead to more wins. Winning that first game might have set the table for many more [championship] wins for the Cowboys."

Adderley said, "When I first got there in '70, they were mad. Those were some angry people in that locker room. Up on the bulletin there was a permanent sign, someone had etched it up there, that said, 'The Packers owe us blood, money, sweat, and tears.' They were really pissed off. Some of the guys are still upset today. Those two losses [to the Packers] were a bitter pill to swallow. But the Cowboys were a great team and they were dedicated enough to say, 'Well, we have the team, we have the coach, let's get back to winning championships.' They pulled it together. It all culminated against the Dolphins."

Years later, the players seemed grateful that they had won the one Super Bowl they did. Had they not risen to that occasion, they would have gone down in history as the forerunner of the Vikings, Bills, and Broncos, who lost 12 of the first 28 Super Bowls without winning one. The Cowboys escaped that identity by dominating a Miami team on the verge of greatness; the Dolphins went 32–2 with two Super Bowl victories in the next two seasons. The Cowboys got in their long-awaited triumph just in time.

"And we enjoyed that victory celebration for about a year," Lilly said. "We had been through so much together, and we really savored winning. It probably hurt us the next year that we were so relieved and excited to finally get over the top."

That they did win a Super Bowl enabled the Cotton Bowl Cowboys to color their years in rosier hues. Their endeavor was not fruitless. Their playoff losses to Green Bay and Cleveland were a hardship they overcame.

Their years in the Cotton Bowl were not a dead end, but a rousing, maddening period of evolution that culminated in Super Bowl VI. In the end, after a bitter struggle, they could call themselves champions.

Our family took a vacation to Miami Beach during the Christmas holidays that year. My father's mother spent the winter at a small condominium on Collins Boulevard. We stayed at a hotel next door, my parents in one room and my sister and I in an adjoining room. She was a college sophomore and not anxious to turn in early. While dancing in the club downstairs one evening she met the grandson of Leonard Tose, owner of the Philadelphia Eagles. I also had a social calendar to keep. The cutest girls from summer camp lived in Miami. I met up with them and several other friends. We hung around their houses and flirted.

On Christmas afternoon, my parents and I watched the Cowboys' first-round playoff game against the Vikings in our hotel room. The Cowboys led throughout the game, but their lead was tenuous until late in the third quarter, and my mother, a nervous watcher, often bolted to the adjoining room when things got tough. The late game that day was between the Dolphins and Chiefs in Kansas City, a classic that went into overtime. To my great dismay, we had to leave during overtime to eat dinner at a fancy restaurant; my grandmother and her cousin would not understand our pushing back dinner just because the game ran long.

The restaurant was empty; we were the only people in Miami not watching the Dolphins. The bus boys whispered updates to me and my father as they tended to our water glasses. They did not have to tell us when the Dolphins finally won in double overtime—there was an eruption of cheers outside the quiet restaurant.

"What was that?" my grandmother said.

"The Dolphins won," I said.

"They sure did," chimed in the waiter.

Twenty-five years later, my father and I still lament the dinner that forced us to miss the end of that game.

One of my sister's friends from Dallas flew in that night to join us on vacation. My father got caught in a huge traffic jam when he picked her up at the airport. Thousands of Dolphin fans had come to the airport to cheer the Dolphins' return from Kansas City. It took my father an hour to drive the last quarter-mile. Surrounded by whooping fans, he kept his loyalty to the Cowboys a secret.

The Dolphins were in the playoffs for the first time that year, in their sixth season since joining the AFL as an expansion team. They and their fans were experiencing that first rush to glory that the Cowboys and Dallas experienced in '66. Their fans were cocky. The father of one of my camp girlfriends had season tickets at the Orange Bowl.

"We're going to kick your butts in the Super Bowl!" he said.

"We'll see about that," I said.

Our vacation ended a few days later. We flew back to Dallas for a big football weekend: the Cotton Bowl on Saturday and the NFC Championship Game on Sunday. Penn State whipped Texas in the Cotton Bowl, but the Cowboys won the next day to set up the Super Bowl match with the Dolphins.

Two weeks later we watched the Super Bowl at home, in the den, with chili for lunch before kickoff. Uncle Milton came over to watch with us. I think we all knew before the game, as Landry himself did, that our frustrations probably were over. This Cowboy team was too powerful and determined to lose. Late in the game, with the Cowboys far ahead, I wanted to call my girlfriend's father in Miami and ask him when the Dolphins were going to start kicking the Cowboys' butts. "Let's be gracious winners," my father said.

We were so accustomed to disappointing endings that it was hard to know how to react to a Super Bowl victory. Much as the Cowboys themselves had felt little joy during the season, we felt slightly lost as the fourth quarter wound down. We counted down the seconds as though it were New Year's Eve, then threw pillows across the room when the clock ran out. My father popped open a bottle of champagne, and my mother called Pop, who was fuming over Hill's fumble late in the fourth quarter. I ran outside and gave a shout. When the echo died out, I could hear dozens of drivers honking their horns in the distance.

The Cowboys were all grown up. They had a Super Bowl victory, a palatial new home, and a national following. It was getting hard to remember their early days at the Cotton Bowl, when they were a losing team that competed with the Texans and drew sparse crowds. That already seemed ancient history.

I was not all grown up yet, but I was getting there. I had girlfriends—in the summertime, at least—and a basketball career to nurture. I was beginning to think about college. Later that year I took driver's ed at school. A ghoulish science teacher taught the class. On the first day he brought in a torn, bloody glove. "I just passed a terrible truck accident on my way here, and I found this in the street," he said dramatically. We believed him.

I celebrated my 16th birthday and went with my mother to get my driver's license, confident I would pass. I easily passed the written test, but I banged a fender against a post while parallel parking and the instructor flunked me. I was in tears, unspeakably embarrassed. "We don't have to tell anyone," my mother said as she drove us home. I certainly did not.

A week later I took the test again, handled the parallel parking, and passed. I stared with pride at my license as my mother drove us home. I was a legal driver now. It was late in the afternoon on a school day, and I went to my room to do my homework. Dinner was cooking in the kitchen. My mother knocked on the door after a few minutes.

"We need milk," she said. "Do you want to run and get it at the 7-Eleven?"

Did I ever. I took the keys to her wagon, wheeled out of the driveway, and headed down our street. There were no cars coming the other way, and no cars behind me. The street was empty. I was 16 years old and I had my freedom. The world beckoned. I would always love the Cowboys, but I was a boy turning into a man now, my attention increasingly diverted. I floored the gas pedal. The engine roared. The speedometer rose to 50 mph, then 70 mph, and then, thrillingly, to 90 mph. The wagon hurtled down the street, flying over bumps and potholes. I screamed at the top of my voice, an animal reaction, sheer joy and exultation. My own Cotton Bowl days had come and gone.

Index